Crisis IN *Black* AND *White*

CRISIS IN BLACK AND WHITE

Charles E. Silberman

RANDOM HOUSE NEW YORK

Third Printing

Library of Congress Catalog Card Number: 64–14843

Grateful acknowledgment is made to the following for permission to use material in this volume: *Amsterdam News,* the December 8, 1962, issue; *Brandt & Brandt* and the *Executors of the Estate of Stephen Vincent Benét,* from *John Brown's Body* by Stephen Vincent Benét, published by Holt, Rinehart and Winston, Inc., copyright, 1927, 1928, by Stephen Vincent Benét, copyright renewed, 1955, 1956, by Rosemary Carr Benét; *Fortune* and *Time Inc.,* for research materials collected for the article "The City and the Negro," by Charles E. Silberman, *Fortune,* March, 1963; *Harper's Magazine,* from "The Hillbillies Invade Chicago," by Alfred N. Votaw, from the February, 1958, issue, © copyright 1958, by Harper & Row, Publishers, Incorporated; *Harper & Row, Publishers, Incorporated,* from *An American Dilemma* by Gunnar Myrdal, and from "Heritage" in *Color* by Countee Cullen, copyright 1925, by Harper & Brothers, renewed 1953, by Ida M. Cullen; *Alfred A. Knopf, Inc.,* from *And Then We Heard the Thunder* by John Oliver Killens, and *Take Away the Darkness* by Witter Bynner; *Random House, Inc.,* from *Invisible Man* by Ralph Ellison, copyright 1947, 1948, 1952 by Ralph Ellison; *Washington Center for Metropolitan Studies,* for material from the mimeographed study, *In Search of a Future; World Publishing Co.,* from "The Man Who Went to Chicago," from *Eight Men* by Richard Wright.

MANUFACTURED IN THE UNITED STATES OF AMERICA BY
H. Wolff Book Manufacturing Co., New York

TO *Arlene*

to whose care, wisdom and patience every page bears witness,
this book is dedicated in love and gratitude.

CONTENTS

FOREWORD

A book like this is born in debt—the product of a union between journalism and scholarship. There are some, I know, who regard such a union as illicit; but living in both worlds, I have come to regard the union as invaluable. Scholarship has a dedication to the search for truth which the journalist needs; journalism has a passion for the relevant and the immediate which the scholar needs. The journalist is sometimes too impatient with the scholar's concern for substantiation; the scholar sometimes fails to remember what the journalist can never forget—namely that life can never wait until all the evidence is in, that important decisions must always be made on the basis of incomplete information. I have tried to combine the best attributes of the disciplines I have learned as a social scientist and as a journalist. There is a certain arrogance, I suppose, in any white man presuming to generalize, as I have done in the pages that follow, about how Negroes think and what they are likely to do; but the present situation demands that black and white understand each other. I have tried my best to achieve that understanding, and to help others to it. I have sought truth wherever it can be found—in novels and plays, newspapers and magazines, as well as in treatises in history, sociology, and psychology; and in conversation at every hour of the day or night. My debts therefore are almost too many to mention; as James Stephen once wrote, "Originality does not consist in saying what no one has ever said before, but in saying exactly what you think yourself." I have said what I think throughout; my hope is not that all will agree with me, but that all will find my meaning clear.

I owe a profound debt to my colleagues and editors at *Fortune* magazine, for the book is a direct outgrowth of an assignment I received nearly three years ago in the course of planning a series of articles on "The Public Business." We agreed that at least one article in the series should deal with the Problem of the City, and that the most pressing problem involved people rather than real estate; as an earlier *Fortune* series on "The Changing Metropolis" had pointed out, experience with public housing and urban renewal made it clear that poverty, and the social pathology associated with it, stemmed from something more fundamental than bad housing. The first working title for my article, therefore, was "Urban Squalor." As I studied and thought about the assignment, it appeared that there were several problems of urban poverty, but that the most pressing, as well as the most permanent, involved the difficulties recent migrants to the city have in adjusting to urban life; the working title was changed to "The New Immigrants." It did not take much more study to establish the fact that the difficulties the largest and most recent group of migrants were having stemmed less from their newness to the city than from their color. Indeed, the more I probed, the more apparent it became that just about *every* urban problem was bound up in some way with the problems of race and of racism. The result was "The City and the Negro," published in the March 1962 *Fortune*. I wish to thank Time Incorporated, publishers of *Fortune*, and in particular Brooke Alexander, Assistant to the Publisher of *Fortune*, for permission to quote from that article and from "The Businessman and the Negro" (*Fortune*, September 1963), as well as for permission to use material gathered in the course of preparing those articles.

My debt to Duncan Norton-Taylor, Managing Editor of *Fortune*, and Max Ways, Associate Managing Editor, is deeper and more difficult to express. The original article in *Fortune* would not have been possible without the encouragement and freedom they gave me to strike out in journalistically virgin territory; the favorable reception the article engendered, which stimulated the desire to expand it into a book, owes very much to their wise and subtle editing. I am grateful, also, for their invaluable criticisms of the first draft of this book. I am doubly indebted to Mr. Norton-Taylor and to Hedley Donovan, Editorial Director of Time Incorporated, for their graciousness in giving me the time, at considerable inconvenience to themselves, to research and write this book. I was able to utilize the time they provided because of generous support from the Public Affairs Division of the Ford Foundation, which gave a research grant to Columbia University on my behalf. I wish to thank Dr. Paul Ylvisaker, director of the Public Affairs Division, for his encouragement and in particular for his generosity in giving me complete freedom to bite the hand that fed me. I am indebted also to Dr. Clifford L. Lord, Dean of the School of General Studies of Columbia University, and Professor Harold Barger, chairman of the Department of Economics, for their interest and encouragement.

In the course of researching and writing this book, I traveled the length and breadth of the country and talked to more people than I can acknowledge. I am particularly indebted, however, to Saul D. Alinsky, who opened my eyes to a world of which I had been only dimly aware, and who shared his wisdom and insight and his passion for justice in innumerable meetings, phonecalls, and letters. I owe a great debt, also, to Mrs. Mary Burch for her friendship and for her judgment on a host of matters both big and small; to Dr. Hylan Lewis and Dr. Martin Deutsch, for sharing the fruits of their research and their encyclopedic knowledge, and for giving me the benefits of their criticisms of my first draft; to Evelio Grillo, a superb teacher and a good friend; to Henry Saltzman and Dr. Charles T. Leber, Jr., for answering countless questions and providing invaluable advice; to Margery L. Gross, a resourceful, indefatigable, and wise research assistant; to Judith Bardacke, who performed the prodigious feat of deciphering my handwriting and my erratic typing in addition to tracking down facts, books, magazines, and journals; and to two colleagues and friends: Lawrence A. Mayer, whose catholic taste in reading and energy in clipping brought innumerable facts, articles, and opinions to my attention, and Mary Grace, whose unerring taste and sense of style contributed greatly to whatever literary distinction this book may have.

I should like to express my thanks also, to a number of other people who shared their knowledge with me and who gave me access to their unpublished papers and files: Professor Morroe Berger, Professor Kenneth B. Clark, Professor Lawrence A. Cremin, David Danzig, Professor Dan W. Dodson, Leslie W. Dunbar, Professor G. Franklin Edwards, Professor Nathan Glazer, Mrs. Eunice Grier, Rabbi Abraham Joshua Heschel, Herbert Hill, Jacob Landers, Professor C. Eric Lincoln, Dr. John Henry Martin, Dr. Daniel Schreiber, and Professor Harry Sharp. I am indebted also to those Negro leaders who gave me time from their always hectic schedules: among them, Roy Wilkins and Dr. John A. Morsell of the NAACP; Whitney Young and Guichard Paris of the National Urban League; James Farmer of CORE; Rev. Martin Luther King and Rev. Ralph Abernathy of the Southern Christian Leadership Conference; Minister Malcolm X of the Muslim Mosque Inc., and Representative Adam Clayton Powell.

I wish to pay special tribute, moreover, to my beloved wife, Arlene Silberman, who put aside her own writing and teaching to act as research assistant, editorial adviser, conscience, and gadfly, and who taught me the meaning of courage and compassion; this book is dedicated to her and would not have been possible without her. I owe a very great debt, also, to David, Ricky, Jeff, and Steven, my four best reasons for hope, who endured eighteen months of paternal neglect without complaint. Nor could I conclude without acknowledging my deep indebtedness to my late father, Seppy I. Silberman, whose own life exemplified the Prophetic ideals of justice, honor, and reverence for God and for one's fellow man.

I hope that this book will serve at least as partial repayment of my intellectual and moral debts.

Freeport, N.Y.
March 1964

Crisis IN *Black* AND *White*

I

INTRODUCTION: THE STORMY PRESENT

> The dogmas of the quiet past are inadequate to the stormy present . . . Let us disenthrall ourselves.
>
> —ABRAHAM LINCOLN

This book is addressed to my fellow Americans, both black and white. It will, I hope, offend and anger both groups, for it is impossible to tell the truth about race relations in the United States without offending and angering men of both colors. The truth is too terrible, on both sides, and we are all too accustomed to the veil of half truths with which black men and white men cloak the subject. Neither white nor Negro Americans have been willing to face, or even to admit, the truth.

But the truth must be faced—now, while there is still time. It is never too soon for a nation to save itself; it can be too late. For a hundred years, white Americans have clung tenaciously to the illusion that if everyone would just sit still—if "agitators" would just stop agitating—time alone would solve the problem of race. It hasn't, and it never will. For time, as Rev. Martin Luther King points out, is neither good nor bad; it is neutral. What matters is how time is used. Time has been used badly in the United States—so badly that not much of it remains before race hatred completely poisons the air we breathe. America, as the Swedish social scientist Gunnar Myrdal warned twenty years ago, can no longer wait and see; she "must do something big, and do it soon."

But do what?—that's the rub. The prescription to "do something" appeals to the pragmatic bent of most Americans. But sheer busy-ness is not enough. Solving the problem of race is not only the most urgent piece of public business facing the United States today; it is also the most difficult. In approaching it, public officials and civic leaders might do well to ponder the traditional warning of mathematics teachers: don't worry so much about getting the right answer; what counts is setting up the right problem.

The prescription is easier to state than to fill, however. "American whites and blacks," the late Richard Wright wrote in 1945, "both possess deep-seated resistance against 'the Negro problem' being presented, even verbally, in all of its hideous fullness, in all of the totality of its meaning. The many and various commissions, councils, leagues, committees, and organizations of an interracial nature have constantly diluted the problem, blurred it, injected foggy moral or sentimental notions into it." The result is that a number of myths obscure the vision and misdirect the energies of those who are working toward improvement. For example, Northern white liberals frequently regard race as a peculiarly Southern problem that would be solved by desegregating Southern schools, buses, lunchrooms, and the like. Other liberals, particularly black liberals, see race as predominantly a white man's problem that would be solved easily if whites would just stop discriminating. A good many white Americans, on the other hand, insist that white prejudice and discrimination would disappear if Negroes would only "behave themselves"—*i.e.*, if they would just adopt white middle-class standards of behavior and white middle-class goals of economic success. Like all myths, each of these contains elements of the truth; but as partial truths, they obscure as much as they clarify, and they permit, may even encourage, Americans to avoid the painful facts and harsh decisions.

White Northerners have been able to persuade themselves that racism is a peculiarly Southern phenomenon in part, at least, because their contacts with Negroes have been infrequent and casual. Yet a hundred thirty years ago, that most astute observer of the American character, Alexis de Tocqueville, observed that in the Northern states, "slavery recedes, but the prejudice to which it has given birth is immovable." Indeed, Tocqueville reported that anti-Negro prejudice seemed stronger in the states that had abolished slavery than in those where it still existed, and that the free states "do what they can to render their territory disagreeable to the Negroes as a place of residence." An English Quaker, visiting Philadelphia in 1849, wrote that there was no city in the United States in which "hatred of the colored population prevails more than in the city of brotherly love." (Five race riots had occurred in the preceding seventeen years, in which Negro churches, meeting halls, and homes were burned to the ground.) As late as 1869, four years after the end of the Civil War and only one year before the ratification of the Fifteenth Amendment, the state of New York refused to grant Negroes the right to vote; four states in the free and open West actually barred Negroes from entering. Woodrow Wilson, elected President of the United States in 1912 on a platform pledging the "New Freedom" and guaranteeing "fair and just treatment" for all, made it clear as soon as he took office that "all" referred only to whites. Negro employees of the Treasury Department were assigned to separate rooms and forbidden to use the lunch tables and toilet facilities they had always shared with white employees. When a Negro delegation called on the President to remind him of his campaign promises, Wilson lost his temper, declaring that he would not be high-pressured. And, in 1919, one year after the close of the war which Americans fought to make the world safe for democracy, a Negro boy swam across an imaginary line separating blacks from whites at a Chicago beach, and thereby touched off a five-day race riot. Fifteen whites and twenty-three Negroes were killed, and a hundred seventy-eight whites and three hundred forty-two Negroes were injured during the fighting.

Thus the history of the Negro in the North is stained with prejudice. But the Union Army's victory in the Civil War gave Northerners a sense of moral superiority that has excused their own prejudice and dissolved their sense of responsibility. Just as the South convinced itself that it "knew" the Negro, and that the Negro was happy "in his place," so the North deluded itself with the notion that it had set the Negro free. Some Northerners still think that "their" victory excuses the de facto discrimination practiced in the North. In commenting editorially on the hundredth anniversary of the Emancipation Proclamation, for example, the Long Island newspaper *Newsday* warned Negroes to drop their militant demands and accept with gratitude whatever gifts of freedom were handed to them. The North, *Newsday* reminded Negroes with acerbity, "is acutely aware of its own shortcomings, but equally aware that its soldiers freed the slaves." (*Newsday* apparently is unaware that Negroes fought in the Union Army.)

The fact of the matter, as the abolitionist Wendell Phillips pointed out at the time, is that "The Emancipation Proclamation freed the slave but ignored the Negro." For a time after the Civil War, it appeared that the Federal Government might insist on a thorough reformation of Southern society to guarantee the freed men equality. But, in 1877, as part of a deal to elect Rutherford B. Hayes President, the Republicans agreed to the withdrawal of Federal troops, the dissolution of the Freedmen's Bureau, and a general acquiescence in the white South's demand that the Negro be restored to his proper "place." And so the North washed its hands of the whole question and proceeded to look away from a principal fact of life in the United States.

White Northerners can ignore the Negro no longer; his physical presence alone makes this impossible. Increasingly, Negroes are becoming residents of the Northern city rather than of the rural South. Indeed, the explosive increase in the Negro population of Northern cities is one of the most dramatic social changes in urban history. Between 1940 and 1960, the Negro population living outside the eleven states of the Old Confederacy increased two and a quarter times, from under four million people in 1940 to over nine million in 1960—roughly half the total Negro population in the United States. Most of this increase was concentrated in the central cities of the twelve largest United States metropolitan areas;* these now hold a quarter to a third of all American Negroes. In two cities, Washington, D.C., and Newark, New Jersey, Negroes constitute a majority of the population. In Detroit, Baltimore, Cleveland, and St. Louis, Negroes represent one-third or more of the population, and in a number of others *e.g.*, Chicago, Philadelphia, Cincinnati, Indianapolis, Oakland, they constitute well over one-fourth. Even at the height of European immigration to the United States, no ethnic group ever multiplied as rapidly, or made up as large a proportion of the big cities' population.

Thus "the Negro problem" is no longer hidden on the plantations of the Mississippi Delta nor in the sleepy towns of "the Old South," nor even in the bustling cities of "the new South." On the contrary, the most serious social problem confronting America today is to be found in the heart of the big cities that are the nation's ornaments: New York, Philadelphia, Washington, Chicago, Detroit, Milwaukee, San Francisco, Los Angeles—and in a score of smaller cities

* New York, Los Angeles, Chicago, Philadelphia, Detroit, San Francisco-Oakland, Boston, Pittsburgh, St. Louis, Washington, Cleveland, Baltimore.

like New Haven, Newark, Gary, San Diego. For there is not a city of any importance in the United States that does not now have a large and rapidly growing "Negro problem."

And so the North is finally beginning to face the reality of race. In the process, it is discovering animosities and prejudices that had been hidden in the recesses of the soul. For a brief period following the demonstrations in Birmingham in the spring of 1963—a very brief period—it appeared that the American conscience had been touched; a wave of sympathy for the Negro and of revulsion over white brutality seemed to course through the nation. But then the counterreaction set in, revealing a degree of anti-Negro prejudice and hatred that surprised even the most sophisticated observers. After interviewing whites from coast to coast, for example, the journalist Stewart Alsop and the public opinion expert Oliver Quayle reported in the *Saturday Evening Post* that "The white North is no more ready to accept genuine integration and real racial equality than the deep South." So strong and widespread was the prejudice they found that Alsop and Quayle concluded that for the moment, at least "there is simply no way to reconcile the aspirations of the new generation of Negroes for real integration and true equality with the resistance to those aspirations of the majority of whites." Pollster Louis Harris, who sent interviewers all over the country for *Newsweek,* reached much the same conclusion. He found that "Whites, North and South, do not want the Negro living next door"; that "Most whites fear and shun social contact with Negroes"; and that "the white image of the Negro is . . . an implausible and contradictory caricature, half Stepin Fetchit—lazy, unwashed, shiftless, unambitious, slow-moving—and half Sportin' Life—cunning, lewd, flashy, strong, fearless, immoral, and vicious." Writing two months before President Kennedy's assassination, Harris estimated that the racial issue had driven some 4.5 million white voters away from Mr. Kennedy.

It's not only the "great unwashed" who are affected by

the cancer of race hatred, moreover. Throughout the North, highly educated men who had always prided themselves on being free from prejudice—who saw themselves, in some cases, as fighters for Negro rights—are suddenly finding their commitment to brotherhood withering in the face of actual contact with the Negro of the Northern slum. As a white liberal put it in a Jules Feiffer cartoon, "civil rights used to be so much more tolerable before Negroes got into it." Some of these liberals—citizens of the world, who a few years ago, were attacking "petty nationalism" in the name of one world—are now patriots of a homogeneous neighborhood, ardently devoted to the principle of "the neighborhood school." (The closer Negroes come to the neighborhood, the more passionate the "patriots' " devotion.) Other liberals, ardent advocates of public education, find cogent reasons for sending their children to private schools. (Integration is for someone else's children, in some other neighborhood or town.) Or they enthusiastically support urban renewal projects which replace Negroes with trees (or college dormitories, or cultural centers, or co-operative apartment houses) in a marvelously impersonal way. Trade unionists or leaders of ethnic and religious groups, who only yesterday acquired power and position through appeals to group solidarity and bloc voting, are suddenly outraged by demands that Negroes be hired or appointed to trade union or public office because they are Negroes. (Men should be judged solely as individuals, not as members of groups, these group leaders insist.) White men who cannot wait until the light turns green to cross the street are becoming annoyed at Negro impatience over civil rights, and are warning Negroes that they are pushing too hard—for their own good, of course. Some liberals are even beginning to wonder whether there may not be, after all, something to the theory of racial inferiority.

What we are discovering, in short, is that the United States—all of it, North as well as South, West as well as East

—is a racist society in a sense and to a degree that we have refused so far to admit, much less face. Twenty years ago, Gunnar Myrdal concluded that "the American Negro problem is a problem in the heart of the American," and titled his monumental study of the Negro *An American Dilemma.** Myrdal was wrong. The tragedy of race relations in the United States is that there is no American Dilemma. White Americans are not torn and tortured by the conflict between their devotion to the American creed and their actual behavior. They are upset by the current state of race relations, to be sure. But what troubles them is not that justice is being denied but that their peace is being shattered and their business interrupted.

It will take more than an appeal to the American conscience, therefore, to solve "the Negro problem," though such an appeal is long overdue. Nothing less than a radical reconstruction of American society is required if the Negro is to be able to take his rightful place in American life. And the reconstruction must begin not just in Oxford, Mississippi, or Birmingham, Alabama, but in New York, Philadelphia, Chicago, and other great cities of the North as well. For when Negroes leave the South, they don't move to New York—they move to Harlem; they don't move to Chicago—they move to the South Side. Without question, Harlem is a great improvement over Birmingham—but not nearly so great as white men assume. Northern discrimination is less brutal and less personal than the Southern variety, and it lacks the overt sanction of law.† It hurts none the less. "What makes you think you are going to Heaven?" Langston Hughes asks his folk hero, Jesse B. Simple. "Because I have already been in Harlem," Simple replies.

The North must change for its own sake therefore. It

---

* Gunnar Myrdal, *An American Dilemma: The Negro Problem and Modern Democracy*. New York: Harper & Brothers, 1944.

† "De facto segregation," James Baldwin sardonically observes, "means that Negroes are segregated but nobody did it."

must change for the nation's sake as well, for the South will never change—and cannot be expected to change—until the North leads the way. At the moment, the North *is* leading, but in the wrong direction. It has shown the South that Negroes can be kept "in their place" without written laws. Southern cities are rapidly learning the de facto technique of the North. In the spring of 1963, for example, Albany, Georgia, removed all segregation ordinances from its city code in order to balk the Negro legal attack; the city remained as Jim Crow as ever.

It isn't enough for the white North or the white South to change, however; the black North and the black South must change as well. For "the Negro problem" is not just a white man's problem, as Myrdal thought; it is a black man's problem as well, because of what white prejudice and discrimination have done to the Negro's personality and self-esteem. In a recent *New Yorker* cartoon, one overstuffed tycoon grumbled to another, "Trouble is you start treating people like equals, they begin to believe it." The converse is also true: treat people as inferiors and they begin to believe *that*, too. White men began three and a half centuries ago to treat black men as inferiors, and they haven't stopped yet. A major part of "the Negro problem" in America lies in what these three hundred fifty years have done to the Negro's personality: the self-hatred, the sense of impotence and inferiority that destroys aspiration and keeps the Negro locked in a prison we have all made. Negroes are taught to despise themselves almost from the first moments of consciousness; even without any direct experience with discrimination, they learn in earliest childhood of the stigma attached to color in the United States: "If you're white, you're right," a Negro folk saying goes: "if you're brown stick around; if you're black, stay back." And they do stay back.

If whites were to stop all discriminatory practices tomorrow, this alone would not solve "the Negro problem." To be sure, an end to discrimination is a prerequisite to any solution. But too many Negroes are unable or unwilling to compete; segregation is an affliction, but for many it is a crutch as well.

The Negro will be unable to take his place in the main stream of American life until he stops despising himself and his fellows. The Negro will be unable to compete on equal terms until he has been able to purge from his mind all sense of white superiority and black inferiority—until he really believes, with all his being, that he is a free man, and acts accordingly. In this sense, therefore, only the Negro can solve the Negro problem. For freedom and equality, like power, cannot be given or handed down as a gift. They must be taken by people unwilling to settle for anything less.

This does not mean, however, that white Americans can simply toss the ball back to their Negro compatriots, as John Fischer of *Harper's* suggested a while ago. White Americans cannot duck their responsibility by placing the burden of change on Negroes themselves. On the contrary, the doctrine Fischer propounded represented but a slightly more sophisticated version of the old racist doctrine that Negroes "aren't ready" for equality. Writing from his chair as Editor-in-Chief of *Harper's,* Fischer called upon Negroes to redirect their energies from the field of civil rights to that of self-improvement. Since anti-Negro prejudice "is not altogether baseless," in Fischer's view, it cannot be eliminated by lecturing whites or by enacting new legislation. On the contrary, prejudice will disappear "only when a considerable majority of whites are convinced that they have nothing to fear from close, daily association with Negroes in jobs, schools, and neighborhoods." For that to happen, Fischer argued, Negro leaders will somehow have to arrange things so that "the average Negro is willing and able to carry the full responsibilities of good citizenship." But once this happy stage is reached, Fischer assured the Negroes of the United States, they will be "surprised to see how fast white prejudice begins to melt away."

Maybe; but there is little in the history of human bigotry—nothing, certainly, in the long history of anti-Semitism—to suggest that Fischer is right. Jews are as well-behaved as any other group; yet the calculated murder of six million Jews occurred not quite twenty years ago in the country in which Jews were proudest of their assimilation. And in our own country, Dr. Ralph Bunche, with whom Fischer presumably would not be afraid to associate, can be and has been denied hotel accommodations because of his race. What Fischer fails to see is that his own sense of superiority, his arrogant assumption that "the average Negro" has not yet earned the right to full citizenship, is responsible for the behavior he deplores! *For so long as Negroes feel excluded from American society, they are not going to feel bound by its constraints.* "I can hear you say, 'What a horrible, irresponsible bastard!' " the first person narrator of Ralph Ellison's *Invisible Man** declares. "And you're right. I leap to agree with you . . . But to whom can I be responsible, and why should I be, when you refuse to see me?"

To be sure, the behavior of a good many Negroes does help perpetuate white prejudice; too many Negroes make it too easy for too many whites to rationalize their discrimination with a "they're all alike" attitude. Thus, white prejudice evokes Negro lawlessless, irresponsibility, and dependency—and these traits in turn nurture white prejudice. This is the real "American dilemma," and Tocqueville pointed it out two decades before the Civil War. "To induce whites to abandon the opinion they have conceived of the moral and intellectual inferiority of their former slaves," he wrote, "the Negroes must change; but as long as this opinion persists, they cannot change."

And so we are all, black and white together, trapped in a vicious circle from which no one seems able to escape. But we must escape, and it is up to the whites to lead the way; the guilt and the responsibility are theirs. To insist that Ne-

* New York: Random House, Inc., 1952.

groes must change before whites abandon their discriminatory practices is to deny the very essence of the Judaeo-Christian tradition: its insistence on the infinite worth of every human being. "Inasmuch as ye have done it unto one of the least of these my brethren," Jesus declared, "ye have done it unto me." "Whoever destroys a single soul," the Talmud warns, "should be considered the same as one who has destroyed a whole world."

"Divine Providence," declared Pope John XXIII in opening the Ecumenical Council, "is leading us to a new order of human relations." That new order must be based on justice—and we must understand that justice is neither an abstraction, nor a sentiment, nor a relationship, but an *act*. When the Prophets of old spoke of justice, their injunction was not to *be* just but to *do* justice; it is the act that counts. There has been far too much talk, for far too long, about the need to change men's hearts, about the difficulty of legislating morality. The truth of the matter is that men's hearts follow their actions at least as often as their actions follow their hearts. An old Hasidic legend tells of a man who asks his rabbi what he should do, since he does not believe in God. "Act each day as though you believe in God," the rabbi tells him—recite all the prayers and perform all the rituals required of the believer—"and before long you will find that you *do* believe." White Americans would do well to follow the same advice. We cannot wait for time or education to erase the prejudice that is ingrained so deeply in our hearts and minds; we must act as though we really do believe in the brotherhood of man, as though we really do love our black neighbors as ourselves. The belief and the love will follow.

There is no other choice. Out of the smoke and fire on Mount Sinai came a warning which white Americans have ignored for too long: ". . . I the Lord thy God am an impassioned God, visiting the guilt of the father upon the children, upon the third and fourth generations of those who reject Me, but showing kindness to the thousandth generation of those who love Me and keep My commandments."* That warning represents not a spirit of vindictiveness but a basic law of human society: that while justice may be postponed, it cannot be denied. The longer justice is postponed, the greater the penalty, the more painful the inevitable confrontation. "I tremble for my country," Thomes Jefferson wrote, "when I reflect that God is just."

And that painful, inevitable confrontation is here and now. Ours is the fourth generation since the Civil War, and the sins of the last three generations (not to mention our own), are being visited upon us. We are just beginning to see how discrimination and indifference to discrimination have corrupted the souls of white men; in the general revulsion at pictures of white policemen unleashing dogs to keep Negroes from registering to vote, of vigilantes beating lunch-counter sit-ins while a crowd of white spectators grin and cheer, we are discovering the truth of Booker T. Washington's famous remark that the white man could not hold the Negro in the gutter without getting in there himself. White Americans are also discovering, to their surprise and horror, how deep is the store of anger and hatred three and a half centuries of humiliation have built up in the American Negro, and how quickly that anger can explode into violence. The real danger, however, is not violence but something deeper and far more corrosive: a sense of permanent alienation from American society. Unless the Negro position improves very quickly, Negroes of whatever class may come to regard their separation from Americen life as permanent, and so consider themselves outside the constraints and allegiances of American society. The Negro district of every large city could come to constitute an American Casbah, with its own values and controls and an implacable hatred of everything white that would poison American life.

It is not too much to say, therefore, that the plight of the Negro must become America's central concern, for he is the key to our mutual future. For one thing, the treatment of the Negro in America can affect this country's position in the world. What makes Red China loom so large a threat, for example—to the Russians as well as to us—is less its uncompromising totalitarianism than its evident desire to unite all the colored peoples of the world in holy war against the white race. It is in this context—not vague conversation about the importance of world public opinion—that what Africans and Asians think about the United States does matter. And what they think is clearly affected by Negro-white relations.

But the United States must solve "the Negro problem" out of more than political self-interest; it must accept the Negro as an equal and participating member of society because it is the only right thing, the only decent thing, to do. In the long run, the greatest threat to the United States is not political or military, but moral: the dehumanization of society that our awesome technology threatens, and that has been the central concern of theologians like Barth, Niebuhr, Buber, and Heschel, as well as of novelists and social critics.

The process is already too far advanced; man cannot deny the humanity of his fellow man without ultimately destroying his own. If we cannot learn now to reorder the relations between black and white—if we cannot allow the Negro to recover his lost identity by acknowledging his membership in America—we will never be able to handle the new problems of the age in which we find ourselves. In Camus' haunting phrase, "we are all condemned to live together." We must learn to live together in peace and in justice.

II

THE NEW MAJORITY

> And if a stranger sojourn with thee in thy land, ye shall not do him wrong. The stranger that sojourneth with thee shall be unto thee as one from among thee, and thou shalt love him as thyself; for ye were strangers in the land of Egypt: I am the Lord thy God.
>
> —LEVITICUS XIX, 33-34

It was only eight years after the founding of the Republic when a member of the House of Representatives took the floor to complain about the riff-raff flooding the big cities. Unrestricted immigration might have been satisfactory when the country was new and unsettled, he declared; but now that the United States had reached maturity and was fully populated, the nation's well-being required an end to immigration.

The congressman was not the first to voice these sentiments. Concern over the flood of foreign riff-raff had been growing throughout the eighteenth century; it was to remain a recurrent theme down to our own day. As early as 1718, "proper" Bostonians worried that "these confounded Irishmen will eat us all up"; and in 1729, a mob prevented the docking of several ships bringing immigrants from Belfast and Londonderry. Pennsylvanians were equally outraged by the flood of German immigrants into their territory: in the middle of the century, the great Benjamin Franklin delivered a number of attacks on "the Palatine Boors," *i.e.*, the Germans, migrating to Pennsylvania. Jefferson, too, opposed mass immigration, fearing that it would expose the new nation to the corrupting influence of a decadent Europe. And the first Congress heard a plea to bar admission of "the common class of vagrants, paupers, and other outcasts of Europe."

Thirty years later, things seemed to be going from bad to worse. "This inlet of pauperism threatens us with the most overwhelming consequences," the Managers of the Society for the Prevention of Pauperism in the City of New York reported in 1819. The immigrants, they added, "are frequently found destitute in our streets; they seek employment at our doors; they are found in our almshouses, and in our hospitals; they are found at the bar of our criminal tribunals, in our bridewell, our penitentiary, and our state prison. And we lament to say that they are too often led by want, by vice, and by habit to form a phalanx of plunder and depredation, rendering our city more liable to the increase of crimes, and our houses of correction more crowded with convicts and felons."

And the "inlet of pauperism" had barely begun! In the next decade, 152,000 immigrants entered the United States—half again as many as in the three preceding decades. Ten years later, the number of immigrants jumped to 599,000. And then the deluge began. Between 1850 and 1860, over 2.5 million immigrants entered the United States. By the 1880s the number exceeded five million; and in the first decade of this century, nearly nine million men, women, and children came to these shores. All told, some forty-two million immigrants have settled in the United States since 1820, the first year in which accurate records were kept.

The immigrants came for many reasons. Some came to seek political asylum, some because they had been forced off the land by famine or technological change, some because of religious persecution, some because the trip to America was a means of escaping jail or the debtors' prison. In the early years of the nation, some immigrants came because they were literally snatched off the streets of London and other towns to find themselves "slaveys"—indentured servants in the new land. But in every period, the immigrants came because the new nation, and especially its growing cities, needed their labor to build its streets and offices, lay its railroad tracks, service its homes and restaurants, and do all the dirty, menial jobs that the older residents disdained.

But the city did more than use its newcomers; it equipped them to take their places as fully participating members of United States society. Doing this—bringing people from society's backwaters into the main stream of American life—has always been the principal business, and the principal glory, of the American city. Cities have always had to create their own stable, cultivated citizenry from whatever raw material lay at hand. For the American city during the past hundred fifty years, the raw material was the stream of immigrants pouring in from Britain, Ireland, Germany, Norway, Italy, Russia, Poland, and a dozen other lands. Thus, most of the huge middle class that dominates American life today was manufactured in the big-city slums of yesteryear. Indeed, a great epoch of American history is now drawing to a close: the epoch of the ethnic groups. Increasingly the sons and grandsons and great-grandsons of immigrants find their identity through membership in one of the three main religions, as well as through ethnic affiliation. Election of a Catholic as President completed the transformation of the United States from a Protestant society with an Anglo-Saxon tradition to a pluralistic society with a Protestant tradition.

A new epoch is beginning, dominated instead by race. The immigrants still pour in—not from County Cork, or Bavaria, or Sicily, or Galicia, but from Jackson, Mississippi, and Memphis, Tennessee, and a host of towns and hamlets with names like Sunflower, Rolling Fork, and Dyersburg. No single European ethnic group ever increased as rapidly, or accounted for as large a proportion of the big cities' population as the current wave of newcomers. The new immigrants however, are distinguished from the older residents neither by religion nor by national origin; they are Protestant, for the most part, and can boast of an American ancestry much older than that of the established city dweller. Their sole distinguishing feature is color: the newcomers are black.

The new immigration is changing the character of the big cities as much as did the older immigration from Europe. It is also profoundly altering the nature of race relations in the United States. Only twenty years ago, Professor Myrdal reported "a sense of hopelessness in the Negro cause," stemming from the fact that Negroes "can never expect to grow into a democratic majority in politics or in any other sphere of American life." No longer; Negroes are beginning to see themselves as riding the wave of the future. They can begin to see the day when they will be in the majority in most large cities; already, they hold the political balance of power, although they have not yet learned how to take full advantage of the fact. Thus, the Negro vote catapulted an unknown, Jerome Cavanagh, into the mayoralty of Detroit in 1961, defeating a candidate backed by both businessmen and the United Automobile Workers. Negroes supplied 118,000 of the 139,000-vote plurality by which Chicago's Mayor Richard Daley won re-election in 1963.

The Negro migration to the city actually began about seventy-five years ago, when the Jim Crow system first began to take shape in the South and white men moved actively and brutally to force the Negro back into his pre-Reconstruction place. Contrary to the popular view that Southern folkways are immutable, the quarter-century following the Civil War had seen a considerable relaxation of the barriers between the races as the South accommodated itself to a new order. Negroes were accepted at the polls, in the courts and legislatures, in the police and militia, and on the trains and trolleys. Col. Thomas Wentworth Higginson of Boston, a noted abolitionist who had been one of John Brown's "Secret Six" before Harper's Ferry, went south in 1878, and reported in *The Atlantic Monthly* his pleasant surprise at how well Negroes were being treated, as compared with his native New England. "How can we ask more of the states formerly in rebellion," he wrote, "than that they should be abreast of New England in granting rights and privileges to the colored race?" In 1885, T. McCants Stewart, a Negro newspaperman from Boston, returned to the South for a visit and found traveling "more pleasant than in some parts of New England . . . I think the whites of the South," he reported, "are really less afraid to [have] contact with colored people than the whites of the North." Negroes were treated particularly well in Virginia. Thus in 1886 the Richmond *Dispatch* took what today would be considered a pro-Negro position:

> Our State Constitution requires all State officers in their oath of office to declare that they "recognize and accept the civil and political equality of all men." We repeat that nobody here objects to sitting in political conventions with negroes. Nobody here objects to serving on juries with negroes. No lawyer objects to practicing law in courts where negro lawyers practice . . . Colored men are allowed to introduce bills into the Virginia Legislature; and in both branches of this body negroes are allowed to sit, as they have a right to sit.

Racism was still widespread, of course, in all its ugliness. But it was held in check by a number of forces: Northern liberal opinion; the prestige and influence of Southern conservatives, with their tradition of *noblesse oblige* and their distaste for the venomous race hatred of the poor whites;* and the idealism of Southern radicals, who for a time dreamt

* "It is a great deal pleasanter to travel with respectable and well-behaved colored people than with unmannerly and ruffianly white men," a Charleston, South Carolina, paper observed, suggesting that "the common sense and proper arrangement . . . is to provide first-class cars for first-class passengers, white and colored."

of an alliance of all the propertyless against the propertied class. As a result of these competing pressures, Negroes were able to retain the suffrage they had won during Reconstruction. While Negroes were increasingly defrauded and coerced, they did continue to vote in large numbers, and Southern conservatives and radicals competed for their support. "The Southern whites accept them precisely as Northern men in cities accept the ignorant Irish vote," Colonel Higginson wrote, "not cheerfully, but with acquiescence to the inevitable; and when the strict color line is once broken, they are just as ready to conciliate the Negro as the Northern politician to flatter the Irishman. Any powerful body of voters may be cajoled today and intimidated tomorrow and hated always," the abolitionist added, "but it can never be left out of sight."

Beginning around 1890, however, the forces that had kept Southern racism and fanaticism in check rapidly weakened and became discredited. In the North, the desire for sectional reconciliation persuaded liberals to drop their interest in the Negro, who was the symbol of sectional strife; increasingly, liberals and former abolitionists began espousing the shibboleths of the Negro's innate inferiority in the pages of *The Atlantic Monthly, Harper's, The Nation,* and *The North American Review;* and this, in turn, encouraged the more virulent Southern racists. "Just as the Negro gained his emancipation and new rights through a falling out between white men," wrote historian C. Vann Woodward, "he now stood to lose his rights through the reconciliation of white men." * Not only did the Negro serve as a scapegoat to aid the reconciliation of Northern and Southern white men; he served the same purpose in aiding the reconciliation of estranged white classes in the South itself. The battles between the Southern conservatives and radicals had

* Professor Woodward's *The Strange Career of Jim Crow* (New York: Oxford University Press Galaxy Book, 1957) is a brilliant analysis of the origins of the Jim Crow system.

opened wounds that could be healed only by the nostrum of white supremacy.

The first and most fundamental step was the total disfranchisement of the Negro; disfranchisement served both as a symbol of "reform" and as a guarantee that no white faction would ever again seek power by rallying Negro votes against another group of whites. Because of the Federal Constitution, the Southern states had to rob Negroes of their vote through indirection: through the use of the poll tax, the white primary, the "grandfather clause," the "good character clause," the "understanding clause," and other techniques, some of which are still in use in states like Mississippi and Alabama. But while the methods were roundabout, the purpose was not. When the Mississippi Constitution was revised in 1890, for example, the purpose of revision was stated quite baldly: "The policy of crushing out the manhood of the Negro citizens is to be carried on to success." Addressing the Virginia Constitutional Convention eleven years later, the young Carter Glass, then a member of the Virginia State Senate, was no less blunt: "Discrimination? Why that is precisely what we propose; that, exactly, is what this convention was elected for—to discriminate to the very extremity of permissible action under the limitations of the Federal Constitution, with a view to the elimination of every Negro voter who can be gotten rid of, legally, without materially impairing the numerical strength of the white electorate." By the winter of 1902, the Convention had achieved its purpose. By 1910, the Negro was disfranchised in virtually every Southern state. In Louisiana, for example, the number of registered Negro voters dropped abruptly from 130,334 in 1896 to only 1,342 in 1904.

Disfranchisement was preceded and accompanied by an intensive campaign of race hatred, designed in good measure to allay the suspicions of the poor whites that they, too, were in danger of losing the vote. Although the regime of the carpetbaggers had been over for twenty years or more, all the old horror stories were revived and embroidered; the new generation of Southerners (and each succeeding one) was made to feel that it, too, had lived through the trauma of Reconstruction. Newspapers played up stories of Negro crime and "impertinence." The result was a savage outbreak of anti-Negro violence. In Atlanta, white mobs took over the city for four days, looting and lynching at will; in New Orleans, mobs rampaged for three days. And rigid segregation rapidly became the rule. Until 1900, Jim Crow laws had applied only to railroad travel in most Southern states; indeed, South Carolina did not require Jim Crow railroad cars before 1898, North Carolina before 1899, and Virginia before 1900. Until 1899, only three states required separate waiting rooms at railroad terminals. In the next six or eight years, however, Jim Crow laws mushroomed throughout the South, affecting trolleys, theaters, boarding houses, public toilets and water fountains, housing; in Atlanta Jim Crow extended even to the ultimate absurdity of providing separate Jim Crow Bibles for Negro witnesses to swear on in court, and, for a time, to requiring Jim Crow elevators in buildings.

In short, the South, whose leaders today deny the possibility as well as the desirability of rapid change, transformed the pattern of race relations almost overnight. Men's hearts changed as swiftly as their actions. As late as 1898, for example, the Charleston, South Carolina, *News and Courier,* the oldest newspaper in the South, ridiculed the whole idea of segregation of the races. "As we have got on fairly well for a third of a century, including a long period of reconstruction," the editor wrote, "we can probably get on as well hereafter without it, and certainly so extreme a measure [as Jim Crow railroad cars] should not be adopted and enforced without added and urgent cause." The editor went on to discuss the absurd consequences that would follow, once the principle of Jim Crow were accepted. "If there must be Jim Crow cars on the railroads, there should be Jim Crow cars on the street railways. Also on all passenger boats." Warming to his task, he continued: "If there are to be Jim

Crow cars, moreover, there should be Jim Crow waiting saloons at all stations, and Jim Crow eating houses . . . There should be Jim Crow sections of the jury box, and a separate Jim Crow dock and witness stand in every court —and a Jim Crow Bible for colored witnesses to kiss," and separate Jim Crow sections in government offices so that Negroes and whites would not have to mingle while paying their taxes. "In resorting to the tactics of *reductio ad absurdum,* Professor Woodward has commented, "the editor doubtless believed that he had dealt the Jim Crow principle a telling blow with his heavy irony." But the real irony was unintended: what the *News and Courier* editor regarded as an absurdity in 1898 very rapidly became a reality, down to and including the Jim Crow Bible. So rapidly did the change occur, in fact, that in 1906—only eight years later—the paper had swung completely around. Segregation was no longer ridiculous; it was merely inadequate. Only mass deportation could solve as grave a problem as the presence of Negroes in South Carolina. "There is no room for them here," the paper declared.

There *was* room in the North—and thus began the great migration. There had been a steady trickle of Negroes from the eleven states of the Old Confederacy since the end of the Civil War; emancipation had cut many Negroes loose from the land and started them wandering from place to place. In the last decade of the century, however, the number of Negroes leaving the Old Confederacy jumped to more than two hundred thousand from fewer than sixty thousand in the 1880-1890 period, and the number of migrants increased somewhat in the first decade of the twentieth century. The migrants included a great many of the preachers and politicians who had sat in Southern legislatures during Reconstruction and its aftermath, as well as less distinguished Negroes who had occupied minor political posts. But the majority were half-educated or illiterate country folk too restless or too proud to accept life on Southern terms.

It was World War One that broke the social and economic

fetters that had bound Negroes to the rural South almost as effectively as slavery itself, for the war created an enormous demand for previously untapped sources of labor. Business was booming as the United States supplied the Allies with weapons and matériel; but combat had cut off the flow of immigrants from Europe. With labor the scarce factor of production even before American entry into the war, Northern industries began sending labor agents into the rural South, recruiting Negroes just as they had recruited white workers in Ireland and Italy during the nineteenth century. The labor agents promised jobs and frequently offered free railroad tickets. Negroes began to move North in such numbers—emigration from the eleven states of the Old Confederacy jumped from 207,000 in 1900-1910 to 478,600 in 1910-1920—that white Southerners began to fear a shortage of labor in their own region and took measures to stop the Northern labor recruiters. In Macon, Georgia, an ordinance was passed requiring labor recruiters to pay a license fee of $25,000 and barring their admission unless recommended by ten local ministers, ten manufacturers, and twenty-five businessmen. In Montgomery, Alabama, fines and jail sentences were imposed on anyone found guilty of "enticing, persuading, or influencing labor" to leave the city, and throughout Mississippi, agents were arrested, ticket agents were intimidated to keep them from selling tickets to Negroes, and trains were actually stopped.

The Negroes kept leaving nevertheless. Besides the agents for Northern firms, Northern Negro newspapers also encouraged the migration editorially, as well as through advertisements offering employment. *The Chicago Defender*, in particular, exhorted Negroes to leave the oppression of the South for the freedom of the North. Copies of the *Defender* were passed from hand to hand, and from all over the South, Negroes wrote to its editor, Robert S. Abbott, asking for help and advice. "I would like Chicago or Philadelphia. But I don't Care where so long as I Go where a man is a man," wrote a would-be migrant from Houston, Texas. From the Black Belt of Mississippi came this letter, showing the hopes that moved the migrants:

Granville, Miss., May 16, 1917

Dear Sir:

This letter is a letter of information of which you will find stamp envelop for reply. I want to come north some time soon but I do not want to leve here looking for a job where I would be in dorse all winter. Now the work I am doing here is running a guage edger in a saw mill. I know all about the grading of lumber. I have been working in lumber about 25 or 27 years. My wedges here is $3.00 a day, 11 hours a day. I want to come north where I can educate my 3 little children, also my wife. Now if you cannot fit me up at what I am doing down here I can learn anything any one els can. also there is a great deal of good women cooks here would leave any time all they want is to know where to go and some way to go. please write me at once just how I can get my people where they can get something for their work. There are women here cookeing for $1.50 and $2.00 a week. I would like to live in Chicago or Ohio or Philadelphia. Tell Mr. Abbott that our pepel are tole that they can not get anything to do up there and they are being snatched off the trains here in Greenville and a rested but in spite of all this, they are leaving every day and every night 100 or more is expecting to leave this week. Let me here from you at once.

America's entry into World War One stimulated migration still more. As men were drafted, the labor shortage was intensified. And the draft brought thousands of Negro soldiers to Army bases in the North, opening a vision of a world beyond that of the small town in which, until then, their lives had been bound. The heavy traffic of Negroes moving North in turn persuaded others living along the main routes to join the trek. A migrant from Decatur, Alabama, reported that perhaps a third of the city's Negro population decided to leave after seeing all the migrants riding through. "And when the moving fever hit them," he said, "there was no changing their minds."

While Negroes were being pulled to the North by job opportunities, they were also being pushed off the land in the South. The full impact of the agrarian revolution was reaching the Southern cotton farmer, and the Negro was hit hardest of all. Farmers in the hot, dry climate of New Mexico and Arizona were producing a longer staple, better quality cotton than the farmers in the old Black Belt could produce, and so cotton production of Negro-operated farms east of the Mississippi began to decline. Mechanization of agriculture also hurt the Negro farmers, most of whom were sharecroppers and tenants. Finally, the ravages of the boll weevil, which plagued the Black Belt after 1910, intensified the Negro cotton farmer's already desperate plight. "The merchant got half the cotton, the boll weevil got the rest," went a Negro ballad. And as if the boll weevil weren't enough, a series of floods during the summer of 1915 added to the Negroes' woes.

The Negro was pushed off the land—but he could find no place in the cities of the South, for poor whites who were also being forced off the land pre-empted the jobs opening up in Southern industry. Indeed, not only were Negroes barred from jobs in the new textile mills and other industries springing up in the South, but they found their traditional occupations as well—as barbers and waiters, as carpenters, masons, and painters, as saw-mill operators—taken over by the desperate whites. And so the North, for all its faults, looked more and more like the promised land.

Once the forces of ignorance and inertia were overcome and a new pattern of behavior opened up, the movement northward rapidly gained momentum. The pull of demand continued after the end of the First World War, when the Immigration Exclusion Acts of the early twenties ended once and for all the immigration from Southern and Eastern Europe. And the agrarian revolution continued to push Negroes off the land, while discrimination barred them from jobs in Southern industry. Nearly 800,000 Negroes left the eleven states of the Old Confederacy during the 1920s, and almost 400,000 moved away during the Depression of the 1930s. Thus, the 1940 Census revealed that the Negro population outside the Old Confederacy had more than doubled in the preceding thirty years, increasing from 1.9 to 4 million. Within the Old Confederacy, by contrast, the Negro population had increased only 12 per cent. Yet these eleven states still contained over two-thirds of all Negro Americans.

World War Two really opened the floodgates. With ten million men in uniform and industry operating in full blast, labor again was a scarce and precious commodity. Negroes flocked to the assembly lines in Detroit, now turning out tanks and jeeps instead of autos; to the shipyards in Oakland, New York, and Camden; to the steel mills in Pittsburgh, Gary, and Chicago; to the aircraft plants in Los Angeles. After the war had ended, industry continued to boom; in the late forties and early fifties the auto companies sent labor agents fanning through the South to recruit Negroes for the busy assembly lines. In New York, Philadelphia, Chicago, and most other big cities, employment agencies still do a brisk business directing a steady flow of Negro women and girls to work as domestic servants in a newly affluent society.

Within the South itself, moreover, mechanization of agriculture has been forcing millions of people, black and white, off the land, even when there are no jobs in the cities. Thus, the number of farms in the United States declined by one-third during the fifties. As always, the Negro farmers were hardest-hit: the number of Negro farm operators dropped 41 per cent in the five years from 1954 to 1959, the latest year for which figures are available. Sharecropping—once the predominant method of Negro farming—has almost disappeared: the number of sharecroppers, black and white, dropped from 541,000 in 1940 (and 776,000 in 1930) to a mere 122,000 in 1959.

The result has been an enormous shift of population from

rural to urban areas: no fewer than 78 per cent of the counties of the United States suffered a net out-migration of population during the decade of the fifties. In the South itself, nearly four and a half million whites and two million Negroes moved from rural to urban places in the 1950s. The rural whites, for the most part, moved to Southern cities and towns, (though some 1.4 million left the South). Negroes on the other hand, left the South altogether: only 150,000 Negroes moved to Southern cities during the 1950s, since competition from white migrants, when added to traditional Southern discrimination, made it impossible for Negroes to find jobs in the Southern cities. In all, some 2.75 million Negroes left the South between 1940 and 1960.* Thus, the Negro population outside the Deep South has increased fivefold since 1910; it has nearly tripled just since 1940. Part of this expansion, of course, has come from natural increase rather than migration; but it is the migration of Negroes of child-bearing age that enabled the natural increase to occur outside the South. Within the South itself, migration has caused a substantial decline in the Negro population in rural areas; as a result, the population living in cities has jumped from 21 per cent in 1940 (and only 7 per cent in 1910) to 41 per cent in 1960.

Most of the Negroes moving to the North have crowded into the slums of the twelve largest cities, which in 1960 held 60 per cent of the Negroes living outside the Deep South. Between 1940 and 1960 the Negro population of New York increased nearly two and a half times to 1.1 million, or 14 per cent of the city's population. The Negro population of Chicago increased more than two and a half times to 890,000, or 24 per cent. In Philadelphia, between 1940 and 1960, the number of Negroes doubled to 529,000, or 26 per cent. The Negro population of Detroit has more than tripled to nearly a half-million, or 29 per cent of the city's popula-

* The statistics, of course, refer to *net* changes in population. A good many rural Southern Negroes moved to Southern cities, taking the place of Negroes who had moved to the North.

tion; and the Negro population of Los Angeles County has increased a phenomenal 600 per cent between 1940 and 1960, from 75,000 to 464,000. In recent years, moreover, Negro migration has fanned out to a host of smaller cities—Buffalo and Rochester, Toledo and Akron, Newark, New Haven, Fort Wayne, Milwaukee, Kansas City, Wichita.

The migration continues; Newark, which was 34.4 per cent Negro at the time of the 1960 Census, is now over 50 per cent Negro. But even if Negro migration were to stop completely (and it's bound to slow down), the Negro population of the large cities would continue to grow at a rapid rate, and Negroes would account for a steadily increasing proportion of the cities' population. For the Negro population is considerably younger than the white population of these cities; in addition, the Negro birth rate is considerably higher than the white. (In New Haven and Buffalo, for example, Negroes represent one person in eight out of the total population, but account for one birth in four.) Thus, Professor C. Horace Hamilton of the University of North Carolina, has predicted that Negro population outside the South will have doubled again by 1980, and that by the year 2,000, nearly three Negroes in four will be living in the North and West.

Were it not for the increase in their Negro population, the large cities would be losing residents at a rapid clip. For the stream of Negroes moving into the big cities has been paralleled by a stream of whites moving out to the suburbs. In the twenty-four metropolitan areas with a half-million or more residents, for example, the "central cities" lost 2,399,000 white residents between 1950 and 1960, a drop of 7.3 per cent.* They gained 2,641,000 new Negro residents in the same period, a rise of over 50 per cent; Negroes now account

* The twenty-four are New York, Los Angeles, Chicago, Philadelphia, Detroit, San Francisco-Oakland, Boston, Pittsburgh, St. Louis, Washington, D.C., Cleveland, Baltimore, Newark, Minneapolis-St. Paul, Buffalo, Houston, Milwaukee, Paterson-Clifton-Passaic, Seattle, Dallas, Cincinnati, Kansas City, San Diego, and Atlanta.

for over 20 per cent of the population of these cities. In the suburbs, by contrast, the white population grew by nearly 16 million, or 65 per cent; Negro population increased by 800,000, or better than 60 per cent, but remained a small proportion—under 5 per cent—of the total suburban population.

The dimensions of the suburban population explosion, incidentally, make it clear that the white exodus from the city has *not* been due primarily to the Negro influx, as sensitive Negroes (and a good many white liberals) frequently assert. On the contrary, the flight to the suburbs has been one of the dominant facts of city life for a century or more. Almost as soon as city dwellers become members of the middle class, they seem to long for a house and a patch of land, no matter how small. Hence the middle class has always been on the move, abandoning its homes near the center of town for sites farther out. The opening of an Illinois Central railway station at Fifty-fourth Street and Lake Park Avenue in 1856, and another at Forty-seventh Street, in 1859, led to the creation of the first suburbs south of Chicago's Loop; Hyde Park Village was incorporated in 1861, and by 1890, shortly before its annexation by the city of Chicago, boasted that its population of 85,000 made it the largest village in the world. In New York, as early as the 1870s, citizens were lamenting the exodus of men of "moderate income to the suburban towns," and complaining that the city was becoming the habitat only of the very rich and the very poor. (Manhattan reached its peak population in 1910 and has been losing residents ever since). To be sure, until the 1930s or 1940s, cities were able to recapture a large portion of their self-exiled residents by annexing the new suburbs to which the former urbanites had moved. But they depended for their growth on the steady stream of immigrants.

Like all previous immigrant groups, the Negroes have settled in the traditional "port of entry"—the oldest, least desirable section of the city, generally in or around the central business district. That is where the cheapest housing usually is to be found; more important, that is the only place the newcomers can find a place to live, since prejudice as well as income keeps them out of the "better" neighborhoods. (Immigrants, Negroes included, have always paid more for their housing, comparatively, than the established city dwellers. No urban industry is quite as profitable as slum manufacturing.) In Detroit, for example, the number of Negroes within an eight-mile radius of the central business district has increased eightfold since 1930, while the number of white residents has been halved.

As did each European immigrant group, moreover, the new Negro residents also figure disproportionately on the police blotters, the relief rolls, the truant officer's case load, the registers of rundown housing, the commitments for drug addiction, etc. In St. Louis, for example, Negroes represented 29 per cent of the population in 1959, but accounted for over 50 per cent of the crime. In Detroit, where Negroes make up about 30 per cent of the population, they comprise some 80 per cent of the people on relief. (One Negro in four in Chicago is receiving public assistance of some sort.)

To be sure, it is not Negroes alone who find the move painful. In New York, the Puerto Rican population has swelled from perhaps 100,000 in 1940 to over 700,000 in 1960; with this increase has come a host of social problems. And Cincinnati, Baltimore, St. Louis, Columbus, Detroit, and Chicago, among other cities, receive a steady stream of impoverished white hillbillies from the Southern Appalachian Mountains. These Appalachian whites—the oldest and purest Anglo-Saxon stock in the United States—have at least as much initial difficulty adjusting to the city as do the Negroes and Puerto Ricans. Consider this report, from *Harper's*,* on the hillbillies in Chicago:

---

* Albert N. Votaw, "The Hillbillies Invade Chicago," *Harper's*, February, 1958, pp. 65-66.

Settling in deteriorated neighborhoods where they can stick with their own kind, they live as much as they can the way they lived back home. Often removing window screens, they sit half-dressed where it is cooler, and dispose of garbage the quickest way. Their own dress is casual and their children's worse. Their housekeeping is easy to the point of disorder, and they congregate in the evening on front porches and steps . . .

Their children play freely anywhere, without supervision. Fences and hedges break down; lawns go back to dirt. On the crowded city streets, children are unsafe, and their parents seem oblivious. Even more, when it comes to sex training, their habits—with respect to such matters as incest and statutory rape—are clearly at variance with urban legal requirements, and parents fail to appreciate the interest authorities take in their sex life . . .

"Skid row dives, opium parlors, and assorted other dens of iniquity collectively are as safe as Sunday school picnics compared with the joints taken over by clans of fightin', feudin' Southern hillbillies and their shootin' cousins," said one ferocious exposé in the Chicago *Sunday Tribune*. "The Southern hillbilly migrants," the story continued, ". . . have the lowest standard of living and moral code (if any), the biggest capacity for liquor, and the most savage tactics when drunk, which is most of the time."

It is the explosive growth of their Negro populations, however, that constitute the large cities' principal problem and concern. The Puerto Rican and Appalachian whites affect only a limited number of cities, usually only in a limited way; but every city has a large and growing Negro population. In every city, white residents and civic leaders are concerned about the physical deterioration of neighborhoods inhabited by Negroes; about the rising adult crime and juvenile delinquency rates in Negro neighborhoods that spill over into the rest of the city, making the parks and sometimes even the streets unsafe; about the tensions unleashed by suits to force school desegregation, and the fiscal strain of building classrooms fast enough to hold the mushrooming enrollments in Negro areas, and the difficulty of hiring teachers to teach in these schools; about the burden of welfare payments and the horror they feel as they watch second- and third-generation relief recipients grow up without ever knowing, or even seeing, what it means to be self-supporting. And in every city, Negro residents are bitter about the high rents they have to pay for rundown and shamefully neglected tenements in segregated sections of the city; about the discrimination by businesses and trade unions alike that bars them from skilled crafts and white-collar jobs; about the overcrowding and lack of standards in the schools their children attend; about the snubs and hurts and humiliations—big and small, real and imagined—that are their daily lot; about the general indifference to their plight. There is no large city, in short, which does not have a large and potentially explosive Negro problem.

III

THE BEER CAN IN THE COTTON PATCH

To be a Negro in this country and to be relatively conscious is to be in a rage almost all the time.

—JAMES BALDWIN

1

Migration to the large city has always been painful, both to the migrants and to the people among whom they settled. A good many sociologists, city planners, and others concerned with urban problems have concluded, therefore, that the difficulties Negroes are having with the city, and the city with its Negro residents, represent simply one more chapter in the long saga of urban migration—a chapter which will end as happily as the preceding ones. The foremost proponent of this point of view is Professor Philip M. Hauser, Chairman of the Sociology Department of the University of Chicago, and Director of its Population Research and Training Center. According to Professor Hauser, "The problems which confront the Negro today, although perhaps differing in degree, are essentially the same kinds of problems which confronted our migrant groups in the past," and they will be solved in essentially the same way. Professor Hauser concedes that Negro migrants do not need "Americanization," as did their European predecessors, but he argues that they *do* need "acculturation" (some professors prefer the term "urbanization" or "accommodation"). This need for acculturation, in his view, forms the heart of the Negro problem of the large city. For Negroes have "been drawn from a primitive folk culture into a metropolitan way of life" in little more than a single generation—"as severe a problem of acculturation," Hauser argues, "as any group in history has ever faced." To solve "the Negro problem," he concludes, "the older residents must teach the newcomers what is expected of them in the city," thereby equipping them "to enter into the opportunities of the dominant culture." Unless the new Negro residents receive the proper instruction from their cultural superiors—so the theory runs—they are bound to make undesirable neighbors; for their "primitive folk culture" permits or even encourages behavior that clashes with the needs and standards of city life. "A Negro in the Mississippi Delta," Hauser suggests by way of illustration, "tosses his empty whisky bottle or beer can in a cotton patch, and what difference does it make? But on the asphalt pavements of a city it can make a difference, esthetically and with respect to safety. If physical violence is accepted in the south as a means of resolving conflict," Hauser continues, "nobody cares much; but in the urban community, such acts become felonies, with much more serious consequences." In one variant or another this theory that Negroes need "acculturation" underlies most of the public and private programs now being developed in Northern cities to ameliorate the Negro-urban problem. The Ford Foundation, for example, has committed a portion of its huge resources and influence to an attempt "to do in one generation for the urban newcomer what until now has taken three." The Foundation makes no distinction between the problems faced by Negroes and those faced by other contemporary migrants. The metropolis, Dr. Paul N. Ylvisaker, Director of the Foundation's Public Affairs Program, has told city planners and civic leaders, should be viewed "as a continuous system of attracting the newcomer (once the Scotch, the Irish, the Jews, the Italians, now the Negroes, the Puerto Ricans, the mountain whites, the Mexicans, and the American Indians) and of assimilating this newcomer to all that is up-to-date and sought after in the urban culture."

The "acculturation theory" can provide a useful perspective. Measured against the backdrop of history, the gangs and crime and squalor of today seem almost benign. Americans who have been shocked to read that women employees of the Supreme Court have been officially advised to secure a police escort before leaving the Court building at night should at the very least know that muggings and robberies in the capital antedate the recent Negro influx. In 1858, for example, when the Negro residents of the nation's capital still wore the fetters of slavery, a Senate committee investigated the city's rising crime rate. "Riot and bloodshed are of daily occurrence," the committee reported, "innocent and unoffending persons are shot, stabbed, and otherwise shamefully maltreated, and not infrequently the offender is not even arrested." And during the week-long Draft Riots in New York in 1863, when the Irish immigrants of Hell's Kitchen revolted against authority, federal troops had to be recalled from the front to restore order. Ninety-seven years later, the grandson of Irish immigrants was elected President of the United States. If the most backward, downtrodden, and discriminated-against European immigrant groups have now all moved up into the great American middle class —so the reasoning seems to go—then why not the Negroes, too?

Reasoning by analogy can be dangerously misleading, however; history does not usually repeat itself. Too many historians and sociologists—and far too many civic leaders —are using the "acculturation theory" as a license to look away from the uncomfortable fact of race and so to avoid the hard and painful decisions. Government officials can hardly be blamed for taking the easy way when academic authorities offer the bland reassurance that time and history will solve everything. To be sure, Hauser admits that the Negro's problem of adjustment may be more difficult than that of the European immigrants. But "forces are in motion," he assured the United States Civil Rights Commission, "that will enable the Negro to win his place as a full-fledged member of the American society." The motion Hauser is talking about is a lot slower than Negroes may be willing to accept, however. The process of acculturation, he told a Washington, D.C., audience in 1961, "requires time—time measured in human generations rather than years. I am displeased to report this," he dutifully added, "but it is the only honest thing to do."

Harvard's Professor Oscar Handlin offers much rosier lenses. "The experience of the past," he wrote at the end of *The Newcomers,** a study of Negro and Puerto Rican migration to New York City, "offers a solid foundation for the belief that the newest immigrants to a great metropolis will play as useful a role as any of their predecessors. They themselves need only show the will and energy, and their neighbors the tolerance, to make it possible." †

It will take a lot more than that. To suggest that good will alone will solve the urban Negro problem is fatuousness of the worst sort. Good will can never be relied upon to solve any hard problem, and the question of the Negro's place in America is the hardest problem this country has ever faced. It is equally fatuous to pretend that color is irrelevant, as so many adherents of the "acculturation theory" seem to do. The plain fact is that the Negro faces a problem different in

* Oscar Handlin, *The Newcomers,* Cambridge, Mass.: Harvard University Press, 1959.

† Professor Handlin's optimism reflects pedantry as well as naïveté. "It is often necessary in social science," he wrote in the opening sentence of *The Newcomers,* "to obscure reality in the interest of clarity of analysis." In real life, reality must be faced squarely, not obscured.

kind, and far more complex, than that faced by any of his European predecessors.

There are many differences. For one thing, the United States has far less need for unskilled labor today than it had when European immigrants were flooding our shores. It took no great transfer of skill for an Irish or Italian peasant to become a laborer on a construction gang. It takes an enormous transfer of skill, however, to enable a sharecropper from Mississippi to find a job as a computer programmer. And the gap is widening between Negro education and training, on the one hand, and the requirements of the labor market, on the other. Automation, new management techniques, and changes in consumer spending patterns are all reducing the demand for unskilled and semiskilled labor and increasing employment in professional, managerial, clerical, and sales jobs, many of which require considerable education and training. These white-collar occupations account for no less than 97 per cent of the total increase in employment that occurred between 1947 and 1963. The professionalization of the labor force accelerated during the mid-fifties, and will pick up momentum in the middle and late sixties. But Negroes are badly prepared for this change. Seven Negro men in ten now work in unskilled or semiskilled blue-collar jobs, compared to three out of ten white men; and more than half the Negro men over the age of twenty-five (*vs.* 21 per cent of white men) have had less than a grammar school education. Small wonder that in Northern industrial centers one out of every three Negro workers has suffered unemployment in the last several years, or that in some Negro neighborhoods, the unemployment rate may run as high as 40 per cent. To anyone walking through the Negro neighborhoods of any large city—and to the children who grow up in them—few sights are more familiar than the groups of idle Negro men congregating at street corners, or the lonely Negroes sitting on their front stoops all day long, sipping wine from bottles discreetly hidden in brown paper bags.

Negroes' lack of education and training and their concentration in unskilled occupations—conditions produced by past discrimination—do not entirely account for Negro poverty, however. Neither does the inadequate growth of the economy, which has caused high unemployment among unskilled whites as well as among Negroes. On the contrary, the Negro unemployment rate is higher than the white rate in *every* major occupational group. Among craftsmen and foremen, for example, Negro unemployment ran to 9.7 per cent in 1962, compared to 4.8 per cent for whites; among clerical workers, 7.1 per cent *vs.* 3.8 per cent; among unskilled laborers, 15.8 per cent *vs.* 11 per cent. While a great many Negroes cannot find jobs because they lack the necessary skills, all too many Negroes who do have the education and training are unable to put their skills to work.

It is a lot harder for Negroes today to bear their poverty and lack of status than it was for the European immigrants. If you have to be poor, John Kenneth Galbraith has quipped, at least have the good sense to be born during a time when *everybody* is poor. The European immigrants showed this good judgment; they arrived at a time when the great majority of the population was poor. The Negro migration, by contrast, is occurring in an affluent society. Hence the Negroes are an economic as well as a racial minority—the first minority poor the world has ever known. Two out of three Negro households earn less than $4,000 a year, and one Negro male in nine is out of work. This poverty and insecurity are particularly galling to the Negro, who sees the white society that surrounds him grow increasingly affluent while he remains mired in squalor. Contrary to popular impression, the Negroes' economic position has actually deteriorated over the last ten years, relative to that of whites. Negroes did make enormous advances during World War Two and the boom years that followed, for the shortage of labor drew them into factory and white-collar jobs that had always been barred to them. As a result, Negro income increased 80 per cent faster than white income, and the median income of Negro families jumped from only 37 per cent of white income in 1939 to 57 per cent in 1952. But this escalation halted with the general slowdown of the economy after the Korean war. As a result, the median income of Negro families dropped from its high of 57 per cent of white income in 1952 to 53 per cent in 1962.

The slum in which the Negro lives, moreover, has been bequeathed to him by the Italians and Poles, the Slovaks and Jews of yesteryear who have left for greener pastures. In contrasting his lot with theirs, the Negro is positive that "the man"—the white man—has stacked the cards against him.

Among the great mass of working-class Negroes, therefore, and among many of the middle class as well, apathy exists side by side with a growing, festering resentment of their lot. These Negroes are more and more convinced that they should have a better life; they are less and less convinced that they themselves can do anything about it.

2

Most important of all, however, the Hauser-Handlin-Ylvisaker approach, which sees the Negro problem as similar in kind to the problem faced by European immigrants in the past, or white migrants today, diverts attention from what is surely the central fact. The Negro is unlike any other immigrant group in one crucial regard: he is colored. And that makes all the difference. The Irish immigrants, to be sure, faced job discrimination as severe as the Negro faces today. A century ago, in fact, Negroes apparently were preferred over Irishmen. A want ad in the New York *Daily Sun* of May

11, 1853, for example, seeking a woman for general housework, specified "English, Scotch, Welsh, German or any country or color except Irish." But once the Irishman was "Americanized," his problem could be fairly easily resolved. He could lose his brogue and, if he so desired, change his name; and when his income permitted, he could move away from the slum and lose himself in the crowd. So, today, can the Appalachian whites and even most Puerto Ricans. But no Negro has ever made that much money in the United States; no matter how wealthy—or how educated, how "acculturated"—he may become, he cannot lose himself in the crowd. He remains a Negro. Sociologists and political scientists, for example, commonly refer to "Irish-Americans" or "Italian-Americans" or "Polish-Americans"—but to "American Negroes." The accent is always on "Negro."

The European ethnic groups, in short, could move into the main stream of American life without forcing beforehand any drastic rearrangements of attitudes or institutions. For the Negro to do so, however, will require the most radical changes in the whole structure of American society. The mere presence of a Negro in a white residential neighborhood unleashes fears and hatreds of the most elemental sort, and leads almost without exception to an exodus of the white residents. Residential segregation of Negroes has actually increased over the past several decades, despite the improvement in their economic position. This is in sharp contrast with the experience of European immigrant groups—or with the current experience of Puerto Rican immigrants. Traditionally, migrants have settled initially in ethnic ghettos in the slums of the central city and worked at the worst-paid and most menial occupations; but as they and their descendants move up the occupational ladder, they also move away from the ghetto to less and less segregated neighborhoods. Not so with the Negroes; the contrast between Negro experience and that of other immigrant groups is all the more striking in view of the fact that ethnic organizations generally have tried to *maintain* their ethnic colonies intact, whereas most major Negro organizations have been fighting for residential dispersal. And there seems to be little doubt that residential segregation in turn helps bar the Negro's assimilation into the economy and society at large.

The problem is double-barreled. On the one hand, "acculturation" is not enough; for all his culture or wealth, the educated Negro remains an alien in his own land.* But on the other hand, the process of acculturation doesn't seem to "take." Thus, Negroes have not been moving up the socio-economic ladder as rapidly as might have been expected; second- and third-generation Negro city dwellers achieve less in school than the second- and third-generation off-spring of immigrants; the crime rate in settled Negro areas is high and rising; and so on. Consider the following report:

> It cannot be denied that the main results of the development of the Philadelphia Negro since the war have on the whole disappointed his well-wishers. They do not pretend that he has not made great advance in certain lines, or even that in general he is not better off today than formerly . . . Yet there is a widespread feeling that more might reasonably have been expected in the line of social and moral development than apparently has been accomplished. Not only do they feel that there is a lack of positive result, but the relative advance compared with the period just before the war is slow, if not an actual retrogression; an abnormal and growing amount of crime and poverty can justly be charged to the Negro; he is not a large taxpayer, holds no conspicuous place in the business world or the world of letters, and even as a workingman seems to be losing ground.

The war in question was the Civil War, not World War Two; the writer was the great Negro sociologist, W. E. B. Du Bois,

* Statistically speaking, Negroes are now more urbanized than whites; that is, a slightly larger proportion of Negroes than of whites now live in urban areas.

in his classic study of *The Philadelphia Negro,* published in 1899.

Du Bois' observations remain uncomfortably pertinent. An increasing proportion of Negroes, moreover, are city-born and raised, but too many occupy the same relative position in society as did their parents and grandparents. In 1960, for example, 44 per cent of the Negro residents of Chicago were born in Illinois, and perhaps two-thirds of the older Negroes (those over forty-five) had lived in metropolitan areas for twenty years or more. Yet fully one-quarter of the Negro families in Chicago are receiving public welfare assistance; Negroes account for 25 per cent of the city's population, but over 80 per cent of the relief recipients. Negroes also account for a disproportionate amount of crime.

Much the same is true of Harlem, once the largest Negro community in the United States and still in a sense the intellectual and cultural center of American Negroes. Harlem receives a steady flow of migrants from the South (some seventy-five hundred came between 1955 and 1960), but it is predominantly a community of established city dwellers, with over two hundred fifty churches and some fifty-four social agencies in its service.* Only 4 per cent are recent migrants from the South—yet Harlem's juvenile delinquency rate is nearly two and one half times the city average, its venereal disease rate is nearly seven times as high. Considerably more than one-third of all Harlem births are illegitimate, a ratio nearly five times that of the city as a whole. Harlem's infant mortality rate—generally considered the best single measure of the state of a community's health—is nearly twice as high as that for New York City as a whole.

By any measure of social disorganization, in short, Harlem is a slum sunk in apathy and steeped in crime, narcotics addiction, poverty and disease. "Don't let this Harlem git you,"

* Harlem has approximately 200,000 residents, of whom about 125,000 are church-affiliated; an estimated 70,000 to 80,000 receive help from one or more of the social agencies.

a motherly Harlem matron advises the young hero of Ellison's *Invisible Man,* just recently arrived from the South. "I'm in New York, but New York ain't in me, understand what I mean? Don't get corrupted." But many do. And the worst corruption of all is not the crime but the apathy; not even the Black Muslims can attract any sizable membership in Harlem. The hopelessness seems to increase with the passage of time. "Yes, we've progressed," James Baldwin has quipped. "When I was a boy in Harlem, Negroes got drunk and cursed each other out. Now they become junkies and don't say anything."

They do not read anything, either—in part because they never learn to read fluently. In the New York City public schools, New York-born Negro youngsters read as poorly as in-migrant youngsters; by the sixth grade, both groups, on average, score at about the fourth-grade level, nearly two years below the national norm.* The fact that the city-born youngsters read no better than recent arrivals from the South is all the more striking in view of the fact that the former have somewhat higher IQs—in the sixth grade, an average of 90, compared to 85.8 for the in-migrants. Thus, the native-born children perform at a lower level relative to capacity than the newcomers. Residence in the Northern city seems to dull rather than to stimulate achievement.

If Negroes remain outside the main stream of city life, therefore—if they appear amoral, if their behavior clashes with city standards—the blame can be placed less and less on what Professor Hauser calls the "primitive folk culture" of the Negro South. A growing body of research—most notably, the studies of the Negro family in Washington, D.C., by Hylan Lewis and associates—suggests that urban Negroes in fact do share in middle-class values and aspira-

* White middle-class children in the New York metropolitan area tend to score about two years *above* the national average, so the Harlem youngster, be he native-born or in-migrant, is further below the city norm than the nationwide tests indicate.

tions. They, too, value financial success; they, too, want their children to be educated; they, too, are ashamed of illegitimacy, to cite a few examples. To be sure, lower-class Negroes do not always act accordingly; they do drop out of schools and they do have more illegitimate children than members of the middle class. But the reason, in many cases, is that their poverty—intellectual and cultural as well as financial—gets in the way. Some Negroes know what they want (according to middle-class standards) but do not know how to achieve these wants. Others know both, but their daily struggle for existence drains them of the energy they need to achieve their aspirations. These people, in Hylan Lewis' phrase, are "frustrated victims of middle-class values." Precisely because they have been acculturated into middle-class values, their inability to climb out of the lower-class slum persuades them that the cards are stacked against them, or reinforces their sense of worthlessness. In either case, the evidence of their lives suggests that there is no use in trying.

But the slum-dwelling Negro's behavior stems from something deeper-rooted, and harder to overcome, than poverty: his hatred of "the man," the white man, who seems determined to keep him in his place. Take Professor Hauser's tale of the Negro from Mississippi, who once threw his empty whisky bottle or beer can in the cotton patch and who, as Hauser puts it, now must be taught not to hurl it out his Chicago tenement window. There may well be some Negroes in Chicago who throw beer cans out of windows because they do not know any better; the great majority who do so, however, know perfectly well that their act is antisocial; that is precisely why they do it! They throw the beer can not through ignorance but through hate—because throwing it out the window is an act of defiance, a readily available means of social protest. There are other means of protest, of course: misbehaving in school, or dropping out of school altogether; not showing up for work on time, or not showing up at all (and lying about the reason); breaking school windows or ripping telephone receivers out of outdoor phone booths; or the oldest form of protest of all, apathy —a flat refusal to co-operate with the oppressor or to accept his moral code. "You can force a man to live in a prison," says Saul Alinsky of the Industrial Areas Foundation, "but you can't make him contribute to its upkeep."

Against what are the beer-can throwers or the drop-outs protesting? In a word, everything: the world about them, which dooms them to defeat and humiliation (or which they believe dooms them, which amounts to the same thing); and the weakness in themselves, which accepts humiliation, and so makes defeat inevitable. Something happens to the Negro in Harlem (or the South Side of Chicago, or North Philadelphia, or their equivalents in a dozen cities)—something which stifles the ambition and kills the spirit, and suffuses the whole personality with despair and emptiness. Like the immigrants of old, the Negro migrants, many of them, come in search of the promised land. But their aspirations are quickly trampled on. In one of the short stories in his *Eight Men,** the late Richard Wright described what moving to Chicago did to him:

> While working as a porter in Memphis I had often stood aghast as a friend of mine had offered himself to be kicked by the white men; but now, while working in Chicago, I was learning that perhaps even a kick was better than uncertainty . . . I had elected, in my fevered search for honorable adjustment to the American scene, not to submit and in doing so I had embraced the daily horror of anxiety, of tension, of eternal disquiet.
>
> To solve this tangle of balked emotion, I loaded the empty part of the ship of my personality with fantasies of ambition to keep it from toppling over into the sea of senselessness. Like any other American, I dreamed of going into business and making money; I dreamed of working for a

* Richard Wright, *Eight Men,* New York: World, 1960.

firm that would allow me to advance until I reached an important position . . . Yet I knew—with that part of my mind that the whites had given me—that none of my dreams were possible. Then I would hate myself for allowing my mind to dwell upon the unattainable. Thus the circle would complete itself.

Slowly I began to forge in the depths of my mind a mechanism than repressed all the dreams and desires that the Chicago streets, the newspapers, the movies were evoking in me. I was going through a second childhood; a new sense of the limit of the possible was being born in me. What could I dream of that had the barest possibility of coming true? I could think of nothing. And, slowly, it was upon exactly that nothingness that my mind began to dwell, that constant sense of wanting without having, of being hated without reason. A dim notion of what life meant to a Negro in America was coming to consciousness in me, not in terms of external events, lynchings, Jim Crowism and the endless brutalities, but in terms of crossed-up feeling, of emotional tension.

Despair and apathy, of course, are basic ingredients of any lower-class community, and a good many problems attributed to Negroes because of their race in fact are due to their class. But there is a special quality to the despair of the Negro slum that distinguishes it from any other. For the youngster growing up in Harlem or any other Negro slum, the gates of life clang shut at a terrifyingly early age. For one thing, the children become aware almost from infancy of the opprobrium Americans attach to color. They feel it in their parents' voices as they are warned to behave when they stray beyond the ghetto's wall. They become aware of it as they begin to watch television, or go to the movies, or read the mass-circulation magazines; beauty, success, and status all wear a white skin. They learn to feel ashamed of their color as they learn to talk, and thereby to absorb the invidiousness our very language attaches to color. White represents purity and goodness, black represents evil. The white lie is the permissible misstatement, the black lie the inexcusable falsehood; the black sheep is the one who goes astray (and when he goes astray, he receives a black mark on his record); defeat is black (the stock market crashed on "Black Thursday"), victory white. Even James Weldon Johnson's "Negro National Anthem" speaks of Negroes "treading our path through the blood of the slaughtered/ . . . Till now we stand at last/*Where the white gleam of our bright star is cast.*" [Emphasis added]

Language aside, Negro children learn soon enough—from their father's menial job, or lack of it, from his mixture of fear and deference and hate of "the man"—that the world is white and they are black. And the odds are small indeed that a Negro child can grow up without being abused or patronized, without being convinced by a hundred big and small humiliations, that he has no worth and no chance. "One did not have to be very bright," Baldwin has written of his childhood in Harlem, "to realize how little one could do to change one's situation; one did not have to be abnormally sensitive to be worn down to a cutting edge by the incessant and gratuitous humiliation and danger one encountered every working day, all day long." He continues:

> The humiliation did not apply merely to working days, or workers; I was thirteen and was crossing Fifth Avenue on my way to the Forty-second Street library, and the cop in the middle of the street muttered as I passed him, "Why don't you niggers stay uptown where you belong?" When I was ten, and didn't look, certainly, any older, two policemen amused themselves by frisking me, making comic (and terrifying) speculations concerning my ancestry and probable sexual prowess, and for good measure, leaving me flat on my back in one of Harlem's empty lots.*

And if the child should grow up somehow without confronting prejudice and discrimination directly, he meets it

* James Baldwin, *The Fire Next Time*, New York: Dial Press, 1963.

soon enough as an adult. He meets it whether he stays in the slum or moves to the top, for white men in authority do not always distinguish between Negroes who are "acculturated" and those who are not. The police are an ever-present threat; there is hardly a Negro community in the United States which does not regard the local police with suspicion, if not with hate. Consider the following report from the New York City *Amsterdam News* of December 8, 1962:

> Two young white cops were suspended from the New York City Police force last Wednesday after they were indicted and arrested on charges of brutal assault on a 30-year-old prominent Negro engineer in a West Side police station when he went in to complain about being unlawfully searched and assaulted by them earlier in the street . . .
>
> Victim of the police brutality was Marshal Whitehead, 30, of 116 W. 87 St., a prominent designing engineer with a Hempstead, L.I., firm.
>
> The brutality incident occurred last August 8 when Whitehead after returning home from a neighborhood softball game decided to run around the block and loosen up.
>
> As he was trotting in the area of 87th St. and Amsterdam Ave., the tactical police force car with four officers stopped, and several got out and slugged him and searched him, and then told him to get off the street.
>
> Whitehead, whose photo is to be on the cover of the forthcoming Emancipation issue of a popular magazine, wrote the police car number down and went home.
>
> Whitehead later went to the stationhouse to complain and was sent to a Detective Keogh, who after interviewing him, denied any knowledge of the police car number and tore up the slip containing the license number.
>
> As Whitehead was about to leave, he saw the four cops who had slugged him earlier, entering the stationhouse and identified [them].
>
> The cops reportedly said: "If you want something to complain about, then we'll give you something to complain about" and allegedly took him to the basement of the sta-

tionhouse, where Whitehead was brutally assaulted about the head and body, and later arrested for disorderly conduct and resisting arrest. [The charges were later dismissed.]

The occasional acts of police brutality, however, hurt less than the constant flow of petty indignities—indignities that seem to demonstrate, a dozen times a year, that no matter what a Negro does, no matter what he achieves, no matter what he is, the white world will never accept him. He can be Ralph Bunche, and still be refused a room in an Atlanta hotel while his secretary's reservation is immediately accepted. He can be a distinguished sociologist, yet in a restaurant two blocks from the White House be ushered to a table alongside the kitchen door while the front tables are all unoccupied. Experiencing hostility wherever they go, many Negroes begin to *expect* hostility wherever they go. They lose their ability to distinguish a real from a fancied injury; as James Baldwin has put it, "every American Negro risks having the gates of paranoia close on him," and he takes affront from anything and everything. Appearing in court to answer charges of assaulting a white musician, for example, the band-leader Charlie Mingus angrily turned on his own lawyer, who had described Mingus as "a great jazz musician." "Don't call me a *jazz* musician," he told the startled lawyer. "To me the word *jazz* means nigger, discrimination, second-class citizenship, the whole back-of-the-bus bit . . . I'm just a musician, man."

The worst indignity of all is being patronized by whites who "know how to handle Negroes." The housekeeper inspecting my wife's hospital room was obviously pleased with the way the Negro porter had cleaned the room. "You're a good boy, Jimmy," she told him by way of compliment; and Jimmy said "Thank you, Ma'am." Jimmy was forty-eight years old. Perhaps he had become so used to being treated like a boy that he took the insult as a compliment. Or perhaps he had merely learned, for his own well-being, to hide his anger behind a mask of servility. In any case, he knew that no supervisor would say, "You're a good boy, Jack," if the white orderly did a good job of mopping up after a patient. "There is a form of oppression which is more painful and more scathing than physical injury or economic privation," Rabbi Abraham Heschel told the first National Conference on Religion and Race. "It is public humiliation." Ancient Jewish law understood and underscored this fact. According to the Talmud, one should prefer to throw oneself alive into a burning furnace than to embarrass another person publicly. Indeed, the same Hebrew word denotes both murder and insult.

Negroes are given humiliation, insult, and embarrassment as a daily diet, and without regard to individual merit. They are convinced, as a result, that most whites never see them as individuals, that all Negroes look alike to whites; the theme of "facelessness" and "invisibility" runs through Negro literature. "No more fiendish punishment could be devised, were such a thing physically possible," the philosopher William James once wrote, "than that one should be turned loose in society and remain unnoticed by all the members thereof." The Negro is noticed, of course, for in rejecting him, white society must thereby notice him. But the Negro, too often, is noticed only to be rejected. "The dehumanized image of the Negro which white Americans carry in their minds, the anti-Negro epithets continuously on their lips," Richard Wright has written, "exclude the contemporary Negro as truly as though he were kept in a steel prison."

This sense of rejection by American society, a sense which dominates the lower-class Negro's life, tends to destroy his feeling of responsibility to law and authority; law and authority are always white and middle class and always seem designed to keep the lower-class Negro in his place. It also creates a good deal of class conflict and antagonism within the Negro community. Lower-class Negroes tend to resent

Negroes who have achieved economic success, especially if the success is in the white world, for they are convinced that whites have so stacked the cards against Negroes that none can rise through ability or merit. Hence, if another Negro has "made it" in the white world it must be because of favoritism, because he pandered to white prejudice or white vanities, and thereby betrayed his own race. (Since ability counts for naught in the white world, why else has he advanced while I'm held back?) This kind of intra-group hostility is fairly typical of disadvantaged groups—witness the "shanty Irish" resentment of the "lace-curtain Irish" a generation or two ago. And lower-class Negroes' resentment of "dickety" Negroes frequently exists side-by-side with a vicarious delight that "one of our boys has made it."

Most important of all, however, the Negro reacts to exclusion with anger and hate. Nor is it just the sullen, apathetic tenement dweller who hates "the man." On the contrary, it is hard to imagine how any Negro American, no matter how well born or placed, can escape a deep sense of anger and a burning hatred of things white. Some are better able to repress it than others, but few escape its demonic force. "To be a Negro in this country and to be relatively conscious," James Baldwin has written, "is to be in a rage almost all the time." With those Negroes who deny their hatred, the essayist-novelist J. Saunders Redding has written, "I have no quarrel . . . it is simply that I do not believe them." Some Negroes, he concedes, may be able to order their lives so as to avoid the experience of prejudice and discrimination—but to do so, in his view, requires an effort so great as to bring them to a psychopathic brink. "One's heart is sickened," he writes, "at the realization of the primal energy that goes into the sheer business of living as a Negro in the United States—in any one of the United States." It is impossible, in Redding's view, for a Negro to avoid a dual personality; inevitably, one part of him reacts to people and events as an individual, the other part reacts as a Negro.

The inevitability and the horror of this fact—the unending consciousness of color—were driven home to Redding by a traumatic experience he describes in his moving essay, "On Being Negro In America." The incident occurred during the thirties, when Redding was teaching at a Negro college in Louisville. His office window overlooked a white slum beginning at the edge of the campus. Standing at the office window one quiet winter Saturday, he saw a young woman lurching and staggering in his back yard, until she fell face down in the snow. He couldn't tell whether she was sick or drunk. "Pity rose in me," he relates, "but at the same time something else also—a gloating satisfaction that she was white. Sharply and concurrently felt, the two emotions were of equal strength, in perfect balance, and the corporeal I, fixed in a trance at the window, oscillated between them." The gloating won out. Redding decided not to go to her aid, but salved his conscience by calling the police to report "a drunken woman lying in the back yard of a house on Eighth Street." An hour later, the police came—and the next morning, Redding read on a back page of a newspaper that the woman had died of exposure following an epileptic seizure. "One can wash his hands," Redding concludes, "but the smudges and scars on the psyche are different."

Redding was troubled by the conflict between his instincts as a Negro and his instincts as a human being, and scarred by his decision to follow the former. A good many Negroes would have felt no such qualms of conscience afterward, nor would they have felt beforehand the tug of war Redding describes, between his desire to help the woman and his glee that a white person was in trouble. On Sunday, June 3, 1962, when news was flashed around the United States that a chartered airplane bound from Paris to Atlanta had crashed, killing 130 of the 132 aboard, Malcolm X, then the number two man in the Black Muslim movement, now leader of his own black nationalist group, was delivering a sermon to fifteen hundred Muslims in Los Angeles. He immediately shared the good news with his audience:

> I would like to announce a very beautiful thing that has happened . . . Somebody came and told me that [God] had answered our prayers in France. He dropped an airplane out of the sky with over 120 white people in it because the Muslims believe in an eye for an eye and a tooth for a tooth. But thanks to God, or Jehovah or Allah, we will continue to pray and we hope that every day another plane falls out of the sky . . . We call on our God—He gets rid of 120 of them at one whop.

Whites have generally been shocked by the animal-like hatred Muslim leaders have expressed on this and other occasions. They should be upset; but they shouldn't be surprised. There's no reason to assume that black men are more immune to the cancer of hate than white men, and we have seen more than enough examples of white hatred and brutality in recent years: in mobs rioting in Oxford, Mississippi, to block James Meredith's admission to the University, and in the obscene insults flung at him by his fellow students—the flower of Mississippi gentry—throughout his stay there; in the famous pictures of three Birmingham policemen forcing a single Negro woman to the ground, and pinning her there with their knees; in crowds in Chicago hurling rocks to try to stop a Negro from moving into a previously all-white neighborhood. And Malcolm X's pleasure at the plane crash was no more vengeful than the glee expressed by Eugene "Bull" Connor, then-Commissioner of Public Safety of Birmingham, Alabama, when he learned that Rev. Fred T. Shuttlesworth, Alabama Negro leader, had been injured by a spray of water from police hoses. Connor was sorry that he hadn't been present to see the event—he'd been waiting all week to see Shuttlesworth hurt, he said—and he expressed regret that Shuttlesworth was carried away in an ambulance instead of a hearse. The Black Muslims' hatred, in short, is the mirror image of white hatred.

To be sure, the Muslims have been able to enroll no more than 100,000, and perhaps as few as 50,000, Negroes as active members. But they have captured the sympathy of an enormous segment of Northern urban Negroes, who are unwilling to embrace the Muslim's strict discipline and religious tenets but who are delighted to hear the anger they feel being expressed so clearly. "I don't know how many followers he's got," a Harlem cabdriver told *Life* photographer Gordon Parks, who had just left Malcolm X, "but he has sure got a hell of a lot of well wishers." The cabbie was one of the latter. "Those Muslims or Moslems, 'ever what you call 'em, make more sense to me than the NAACP and Urban League and all the rest of them put together," he told Parks. "They're down on the good earth with the brother. They're for their own people and that Malcolm ain't afraid to tell Mr. Charlie, the FBI or the cops or nobody where to get off. You don't see him pussyfootin' 'round the whites like he's scared of them." Asked whether the Muslims hated all white men, the cabbie replied succinctly that "if they don't, they should, 'cause [the whites] sure don't waste no love on us. I used to live in Mobile and I lived in Memphis and I've lived in New York for fifteen years," the driver finished, "and I've come to one conclusion. No matter where the white man is, he's the same—the only thing he respects is force. And the only things gonna change him is some lead in the belly."

Nor are the relatively uneducated the only ones to respond to the Muslim's siren song of hate. On the contrary, the Muslims have struck a responsive chord in the most sophisticated Negro circles—among men and women in the forefront of the drive for integration, as well as in those who have held themselves aloof from any contact with "the problem." "Malcolm says things you or I would not say," a former president of the New York NAACP chapter confesses in admiration. "When he says those things, when he talks about the white man, even those of us who are repelled by his philosophy secretly cheer a little outside ourselves, because Malcolm X really does tell 'em, and we know he frightens the white man. We clap."

▼

3

To be a Negro in the United States, therefore, is to be angry—if not all the time, then most of the time. More than that, to be a Negro is to suspect, and even to hate, white men. ("Maybe freedom lies in hating," Ralph Ellison speculates in *Invisible Man.*) The anger and the hatred are facts—uncomfortable facts, but facts nonetheless. They must be taken into account in any effort to improve Negro-white relations; they must be taken into account in any program to help disadvantaged Negro youngsters or adults climb out of the slum; they must be taken into account in any program to help Negro adults. For the anger and hate are there; unless they find some constructive outlet, they inevitably poison and corrode the spirit. Unless they are recognized and dealt with, they doom to failure the best-intentioned attempts at speeding "acculturation," for Negroes regard doing the things that "acculturation" implies as "going along with Mr. Charlie's program."

Well-intentioned whites are surprised by the depth of Negro anger and frequently talk as if it were something new; they read James Baldwin with a shock of discovery, not knowing that Richard Wright was saying the same things twenty-five and thirty years ago. Negro anger is not new; it has always been there. What *is* new is simply the Negro's willingness to express it, and his ability to command white attention when he does. For three and a half centuries, Negroes were taught to hide their true feelings. Under slavery, an expression of anger carried the risk of severe beating, of being sold away from family and friends, even of death. Knowing and fearing the consequences, the slave commonly suppressed any expression of rage or aggression; the surest way of avoiding the consequence was to replace anger with submission and humility.* Nor did Emancipation change matters significantly in this regard. As recently as two decades ago, the Negro still took great pains not to provoke the white. Writing after America's entry into World War Two, Gunnar Myrdal reported that "it is the custom in the South to permit whites to resort to violence and threats of violence against the life, personal security, property, and freedom of movement of Negroes." (There are a good many areas in Mississippi and Alabama where the custom still holds.) Any white man, Myrdal went on to say, can strike or beat a Negro, steal or destroy his property, cheat him, and in some communities even take his life without fear of reprisal; how a white man handles "his niggers" is his business, and anyway, the Negro must have deserved whatever punishment was meted out. Even Negro leaders, Myrdal reported, were forced to be accommodating in their approach. "It is a political axiom," Myrdal wrote, "that Negroes can never, in any period, hope to attain more in the short-term power bargain than the most benevolent white groups are prepared to give them."

For their own protection, therefore, Negroes, no matter how rich or how poor, had to avoid any form of provocation. But the anger and hate were there (increased by Negroes' hatred of their own submissiveness) and had to find some outlet. They found expression by being directed against other Negroes—thus, in a sense, against themselves. Until very recently, a very large proportion of Negro crime involved violence against other Negroes. This outlet was encouraged by the Southern tradition of ignoring Negro criminality as long as white lives or property were not involved; crime and violence *within* the Negro community were tolerated with a "Nigras will be Nigras" attitude.

* The impact of slavery on the personality of the American Negro is explored at length in the next chapter.

Increasingly, however, Negroes are losing their fear of "the man"; increasingly, they are directing their anger against its real object. The turning point was World War Two. A war fought in the name of the Four Freedoms, but managed so as to preserve segregation, was bound to increase the American Negro's already ample store of hate. When the war began, Secretary of the Navy Knox stated that Negroes were acceptable aboard ship only as messmen, *i.e.*, as officers' servants; Admiral Nimitz defended the Navy's discrimination as "in the interests of harmony and efficiency." An Army spokesman informed a group of Negro newspapermen in 1941 that "The Army did not create the [race] problem . . . The Army is not a sociological laboratory; to be effective it must be organized and trained according to principles which will assure success." (Apparently treating Negroes as men would not have assured success.) As the war progressed, the most blatant discrimination was abolished; Negroes were accepted as combat soldiers and sailors, but almost always in segregated units. And the majority of Negro servicemen were assigned to menial or construction labor rather than to combat. Negroes were usually barred from the USO on the nights white soldiers were there—unless separate recreation facilities were provided for white and colored servicemen; a Negro who entered a USO or service club on his post might be arrested and court-martialed. The Red Cross, universal symbol of help and healing, "helped" by operating segregated entertainment centers and "healed" by segregating blood from white and colored donors. Negro soldiers even suffered the ultimate humiliation of seeing Nazi prisoners of war treated with more respect than they received. The prisoners were allowed to eat with white soldiers and civilians in railroad dining cars or in station restaurants while the Negro soldiers —assigned to guard the Nazis en route to Southern POW camps—were barred. Witter Bynner dramatized one such incident in his poem "Defeat":

On a train in Texas German prisoners eat
With white American soldiers, seat by seat,
While black American soldiers sit apart,
The white men eating meat, the black men heart.
Now, with that other war a century done,
Not the live North but the dead South has won,
Not yet a riven nation comes awake.
Whom are we fighting this time, for God's sake?
Mark well the token of the separate seat.
It is again ourselves whom we defeat.*

World War Two also destroyed whatever illusion American Negroes may have had remaining about white sincerity, about white Americans' willingness to grant them equality. "White folks talking about the Four Freedoms," Negroes cynically observed, "and we ain't got none." Being drafted only increased the Negro's cynicism and discontent. "You ain't even a second-class citizen any more," a character in John Oliver Killens' bitter novel about World War Two, *And Then We Heard The Thunder*,† observes; "You're a second-class soldier."

Killens' book is a weak novel but a powerful sociological tract. Killens' hero, Solly Saunders, an ambitious and handsome young idealist, had been graduated from New York's City College. The model of the completely acculturated Negro, he had entered the Army as an anti-fascist, believing in the "Double V"—victory over the enemy abroad and the enemy at home. In the beginning, the enemy at home is the idea of racism; at the end, the enemy is the white man—*any* white man—as Saunders discovers that to whites his acculturation is irrelevant; he is still just a Negro. He reacts with hate. "You hate me because I'm white, and I don't blame you," Saunders' white mistress complains after he rudely rejects her protestation of love, "but it isn't fair—it

* Witter Bynner, "Defeat," in *Take Away the Darkness*, New York: Alfred A. Knopf, Inc., 1947.
† John Oliver Killens, *And Then We Heard the Thunder*, New York: Alfred A. Knopf, Inc., 1963.

just isn't fair." "Fairness is a thing no white man has a right to ask of colored," Saunders tells her. "I mean, look—who's been unfair to whom? Who's been unfair to my mother and her mother and my father and his father and who'll be unfair to my son and his children? 'Fairness' is a word that should choke in the white man's throat. I'm not asking any white man to be fair with Solly Saunders, baby. I live with no such false illusions."

World War Two not only shattered Negroes' illusions about white sincerity, it destroyed their fear of white authority as well. In the beginning, Killens' soldiers are angry but docile. "Charlie's got a plantation and you all his slaves, and ain't a damn thing you can do about it," one man cautions the rest. "You sure can't rise up against him and make a revolution." But in the end the soldiers do make a revolution, and quite a revolution it is! Stationed in Australia after a long tour of combat in the South Pacific, the Negro soldiers are angered when they find themselves received as men by the Australians, but still treated as *niggers* by their white superiors. When one of the company is arrested by military police for visiting a local pub at which they are welcomed, but which the Army had declared off limits, the company goes to his rescue. A bloody battle ensues when a company of southern whites is turned loose to subdue the black rebels. Killens' hero, Solly Saunders, gets word of the revolt at the apartment of his Australian mistress. "All my life, everything that ever happened to me, has brought me to this very moment," he tells her as he gets dressed to join the fray. But the full meaning of the battle is not revealed to Saunders until he reaches the scene and finds his buddies all dead. Then comes the moment of truth, the realization that his color takes precedence over everything else, that in trying to play the game according to the white man's rules—in trying to please white officers to gain a commission for himself, in trying to act out his role as an "acculturated" Negro—he had been betraying his soul.

> And now he knew what he hoped he never would forget again. All his escape hatches from being Negro were more illusion than reality and did not give him dignity. All of his individual solutions and personal assets. Looks, Personality, Education, Success, Acceptance, Security, the whole damn shooting match, was one great grand illusion, without dignity . . . If he signed a separate treaty with Cap'n Charlie, would it guarantee him safe conduct through the great white civilized jungle where the war was raging, always raging? Would his son also get safe passage? Anywhere any time any place? He had searched in all the wrong places.

Killens' account is fictional only in the specific details; it is based on a racial explosion that occurred in Brisbane, Australia, in 1943. Nor was this the only Negro revolt during World War Two, by any means. Thousands of spontaneous and individual rebellions went unrecorded and unnoticed, except perhaps by War Department statisticians surprised at the unusally heavy casualties suffered by white officers who led Negro soldiers into battle. (Pentagon statisticians, analyzing the casualties after the fact, had no way of determining by whose bullets the officers had died.) Other revolts were too formal to be ignored, though news of them was suppressed rather systematically, and the details frequently kept out of Army records. Deaths resulting from race riots were ascribed to "motor vehicle accident" or some such category when they occurred within the United States, to combat when they occurred abroad. War Department files dealing with Negro discontent and with racial conflict were classified to prevent their use or dissemination. Within the United States, race riots occurred at the Mobile Naval Yard and at Fort Bragg, Fort Dix, Camp Davis, Camp Lee, and Camp Robinson; abroad, there were riots at Wiltshire, England, in October of 1943, and at the Guam Naval Base on December 24 and 25, 1945.* At Mabry Field, Florida, and

* More recently—on the night of September 6, 1963—a Southern white Air Force man was killed during a riot between white Air

Port Chicago, California, Negro servicemen refused to perform work they felt had been assigned them solely because of their color. At Freeman Field, Indiana, a hundred Negro officers of the 477th Bomber Group were arrested and placed in the stockade when they entered a "For White Only" officers club; they were cleared after being held for some time, but were transferred to a Southern post as punishment.

Acts of defiance aside, the war drastically altered the relations between Negroes and whites. By 1945, a million Negroes were in uniform. Men who had been decorated for "outstanding courage and resourcefulness" at Bastogne, who had built the Lido Road in Southeast Asia or manned the "Red Ball Express" in France or landed in the first invasion wave at Okinawa were not likely to be quite as afraid of white authority as their fathers. What Negroes discovered during the war (and what they have been rediscovering ever since) was their power to intimidate—not by violence, but by their very presence. Writing about the First World War, W. E. B. Du Bois spoke of "the deep resentment mixed with the pale ghost of fear which Negro soldiers call up in the white South." What was true of World War One was even truer of World War Two. And as Negroes began to sense this, their own attitude changed: one need not fear—and certainly not respect—the man who fears you.

Thus, Negroes in civilian life, as well as those in uniform, lost their fear of speaking up and acting out. When the country began its defense preparation after war broke out in Europe, Negroes were systemically denied employment; in contrast to the situation at the beginning of World War

---

Force men and Negroes belonging to an Army Quartermaster company stationed at the United States Air Force base at Evreux, sixty miles outside Paris. The riot was touched off by an argument over Alabama Governor George Wallace's defiance of the late President Kennedy over desegregation of the Alabama public schools.

One, there was still a large pool of unemployed whites from which to draw. Early in 1941, therefore, A. Philip Randolph, President of the Brotherhood of Sleeping Car Porters, advanced the idea of assembling fifty to a hundred thousand Negroes to march on Washington to demand employment of Negroes in defense industries. Governmental alarm matched Negro enthusiasm; the officials understood only too well the embarrassment that would be caused the United States if the march were to come off. Randolph could not be dissuaded until President Roosevelt issued his famous Executive Order 8802, prohibiting discrimination in defense industries and establishing a Fair Employment Practices Committee. The Executive Order was relatively unimportant in itself, since it lacked any real enforcement provisions. But its issuance was enormously significant: it represented the first time since Reconstruction that the Federal Government had intervened on behalf of Negro rights; and it demonstrated that Negro militancy could pay off. The seeds of the protest movements of the 1950s and 1960s were sown by the March on Washington. As the war progressed, Negroes were drawn into better-paying and higher status jobs in the cities of the North and West. Thus, the Negro population of Los Angeles County doubled during the course of the war.

And now, as might be expected, the closer Negroes come to full equality, the angrier they become over the disparities that remain. Their anger is expressed in a variety of ways. Testifying before a congressional committee studying the integration of Washington, D.C., public schools, a pitifully naïve white principal told how a "Negro girl will stand in the aisle and dare a white girl to pass her . . . Or walking down the halls and stepping on their heels. Little things that show an antagonism for which I can see no reason." Sometimes the hostility takes a more direct and dangerous form, exploding in a paroxysm of violence, as in the 1962 Thanksgiving Day race riot in Washington, following the defeat of an all-Negro public-high-school football team by a predominately white parochial-school team. Here is one reporter's description:

> Inside the stadium, the shouting mob had fought its way into the St. John's seats and forced retreating white spectators to jam up the exit ramps. Racing up an aisle to reach the petrified whites, a colored woman, approximately 45 years old, slapped a white teen-age girl, added her hateful reason: "You're white."
>
> Pushing, shoving and purse snatching characterized the stampede to clear the stadium, which suffered little damage. Trampled under foot were combs, lipsticks and rosary beads that had fallen out of ripped open purses. Spectators were called "you white bastard," or "you white sonofabitch," or "white mother f———r."
>
> On the broad, uncluttered streets, parking lots, and plazas outside the stadium, the riot broke out in full fury . . . "It was nothing short of pure terror," said one frightened father as he observed some of the harm inflicted. A sample of the terror:
>
> • Because he wanted to sit with some of his friends for the second half of the game, 15-year-old Lawrence Linson, a St. John's freshman, made arrangements to meet his family at the car after the game. As he was waiting by the car, young Linson was pummelled by ten Negroes. He suffered a compound fractured jaw and lost three teeth from the simultaneous blows.
>
> • Michael Belmore, 15-year-old student at Montgomery Northwood High School, was in a party of six teenagers who stopped their car at a traffic light at 17th Street. A gang of fourteen Negroes approached the car and the leader said to Belmore, "Gimme a cigarette." Answering that he did not smoke, Belmore was promptly hit in the mouth. He required six stitches in his upper lip.
>
> • A fourteen-year-old white boy was chased for a quarter of a mile by a band of twenty-five Negroes. Hemmed in by the approaching mob, the youth's only recourse was to run,

fully clothed into the Anacostia River. The hoodlums stood on the bank, jeered at him, then left.

• Three religious brothers who are substitute teachers at St. John's were beaten by six Negroes. Trying to protect the girl cheerleaders . . . the brothers were punched and shoved to the ground.

The riots in Birmingham in the spring of 1963, moreover, showed how quickly anger can erupt into violence—and how much Negroes have lost their fear of whites. The rioters were the unemployed and the poor and the uneducated —those who had always suppressed their hatred to protect their own skulls. They had had no part in the non-violent demonstrations led by Martin Luther King and his followers, and the ministers wanted no part of them. But for two weeks they had watched the police dogs and the police hoses at work, and their hatred built up; they had watched the disciplined young ministers of King's organization defy the police, and they had seen shiny-faced school children marching off to jail, and their courage built up. The spark was ignited when the Gaston Motel and the home of Dr. King's brother were bombed. And when the Birmingham cops ran for cover under a barrage of rocks and bottles, instead of opening fire in return, the Negro revolt entered an entirely new stage. The echoes were wide and far. In Chicago, a few days later, two Negroes assaulted the Mayor's eighteen-year-old nephew, shouting "This is for Birmingham." It was for Birmingham, all right—but it was for three hundred fifty years of history before Birmingham as well.

IV

THE PROBLEM OF IDENTIFICATION

The worst crime the white man has committed has been to teach us to hate ourselves.

—MALCOLM X

Men are what they have had to be.

—WILL DURANT,
The Story of Civilization

1

Hatred of "the man" may explain why Professor Hauser's migrant from the Mississippi Delta hurls the beer can out the window of his Chicago slum. It does not explain why Negroes whose families have been living in the city for three or four generations are still mired in the slum—uneducated, unskilled, and unaspiring. The relative lack of Negro progress must be explained and understood if it is to be reversed. Seventy years ago, for example, both Booker T. Washington, the great apostle of accommodation, and W. E. B. Du Bois, the great militant, were urging Negroes to go into business in order to develop the wealth and power they needed to change their position in American society. Their exhortations were in vain; if anything, Negro business is relatively less important now than at the turn of the century. Only about a hundred thousand Negroes in the United States, for example, operate their own businesses or hold managerial positions; beauty parlors, barber shops, undertaking, and cosmetic manufacturing are the only kinds of Negro businesses which provide signficant numbers of jobs for other Negroes or produce substantial revenue. Negro insurance companies, banks, and publishing companies are important symbolically as evidences of Negro achievement, but they account for very little wealth or employment.

The usual explanation—discrimination—is not sufficient. Why, for example, do Negroes not own the small grocery stores they patronize, as the Puerto Ricans in New York have always done?* Nor do lack of distinctive ethnic tastes or character—another popular explanation—explain enough. There is nothing in Chinese culture, certainly, to account for the number of Chinese laundrymen. In proportion to their numbers, Chinese-Americans derive forty-five times as much income from Chinese-owned businesses as Negroes do from Negro-owned businesses.

There are other mysteries, too, in the lack of Negro advance. The 1950 Census, for example, revealed that there were only 1,450 Negro lawyers in the entire country, and but 1,800 Negro dentists. More puzzling, there were only 4,026 Negro doctors in all of the nation—only six hundred more than there had been in 1910, when most Negroes lived in the rural South. To be sure, Negroes faced obstacles no white student could even imagine to becoming a doctor: difficulties in gaining admission to medical school, in finding a hospital willing to provide an internship, in securing hospital affiliation and establishing a practice. But these

* A quarter-century ago, the Negro writer Claude McKay observed that virtually all the local trade done in the Puerto Rican section of Harlem was "done by Puerto Ricans and other members of the Spanish-speaking community. Yet they started moving into Harlem in considerable numbers only about 1925, twenty years after the Negroes had established themselves there."

obstacles had been far, far greater in 1910, when there had been 3,400 Negro doctors. What can explain the fact that the number of Negro doctors was almost static for forty years —forty years, moreover, during which the Great Migration to the Northern cities was going on? *

More important, perhaps, attempts to open new occupations and new industries to Negro employment frequently founder because no Negroes come forward to apply. In the spring of 1963, for example, the U. S. Department of Labor persuaded a number of trade unions in Washington, D.C., to open their apprenticeship programs to Negroes on a merit basis. After a good deal of negotiation and screening, the Department arranged for seventeen youngsters to take the necessary tests; only eight showed up. In New York, during the summer of 1963, Negro activists used a wide variety of techniques to force the building-trades unions to permit employment of Negro workers: at various times, various Negro groups staged sit-ins in the offices of the Mayor and the Governor and at the construction sites of a number of public buildings. In response, the city opened twenty offices in Negro neighborhoods and launched a large-scale campaign to register all Negroes who were interested in obtaining skilled jobs. After four weeks and a great deal of fanfare, no more than twenty-one hundred Negroes had applied.

None of this is to suggest that white prejudice and discrimination are not basic to "the Negro problem," or that an end to discrimination is not prerequisite to any solution. But the fact remains that the Negro advance depends on changes within the Negro community as well as within the white community. If all discrimination were to end immediately, that alone would not materially improve the Negro's position. The unpleasant fact is that too many Negroes are unable—and unwilling—to compete in an integrated society. As the United States commission on Civil Rights con-

* The number of Negro doctors has doubled since 1950, a useful index of current changes. These changes will be discussed below.

cluded sadly in 1961, a principal reason for continued Negro poverty is "the lack of motivation on the part of many Negroes to improve their educational and occupational status."

In short, apathy appears to be the crux of the Negro's "Negro problem." But apathy is itself just a cover for a more basic problem: self-hatred. "The Negro," says Elijah Muhammad, titular head of the Black Muslims, "wants to be everything but himself. He wants to be a white man. He processes his hair. Acts like a white man. He wants to integrate with the white man, but he cannot integrate with himself or his own kind. The Negro wants to lose his identity because he does not know his own identity."

To be sure, Negroes are not alone in facing a problem of identity; the rapidity of social and technological change makes identity a problem for many people in contemporary society. Psychiatrists find that an increasing proportion of neuroses stem from a diffuse anxiety, an uncertainty about the answers to the questions, "Who am I?" and "What am I doing?" But Negro Americans have *always* had a problem of identity more serious than that faced by any white. James Baldwin has written movingly of the enormous toll extracted by the effort to discover his own identity, which required first that he escape from the traditional stereotype of the Negro in America. His father, Baldwin tells us, had "had a terrible life; he was defeated long before he died because, at the bottom of his heart, he really believed what white people said about him." Young Jimmy tried terribly hard not to believe "what the white people said," and so he struggled to avoid anything that might smack of the old stereotype—refusing to eat watermelon or to listen to Negro jazz. It was only when he began living the life of an American expatriate in Paris that Baldwin began to resolve the question of his own identity.

As long as he lived in the United States, he writes, "there was not, no matter where one turned, any acceptable image of oneself, no proof of one's existence. One had the choice, either of 'acting just like a nigger' or of *not* acting just like a nigger—and only those who have tried it know how impossible it is to tell the difference."

What makes the problem of Negro identity so complex and tortuous for both white and black is the fact that the "nigger" of whom Baldwin complains is not purely a figment of the white imagination. On the contrary, he was, and to a considerable degree still is, a reality—the end-product of the American system of slavery. To say this is not to accept the Southern view of inherent Negro inferiority, nor is it to insist that all Negroes are alike; obviously they are not. It is, rather, to insist that the problem of Negro personality and behavior be faced squarely and honestly.

The problem has not been faced squarely until now; it must be faced if white prejudice and Negro apathy are to be conquered. The apologists first for Negro slavery, then for segregation, have based their case on the assertion of inherent Negro inferiority. As proof, they have pointed to the persistence of certain alleged traits of character and behavior: Negroes are docile but irresponsible, loyal but lazy, humble but given to lying and stealing—in short, carefree, happy-go-lucky, amoral, dependent children, albeit children with a powerful sexual drive and a lot of rhythm.* Until very recently, this was the image of the Negro almost invariably projected by theater, films, and radio: witness the popularity of Stepin Fetchit and Amos and Andy. The image is still widespread; according to a poll taken by Louis Harris in the summer of 1963 for *Newsweek*, 85 per cent of American whites believed that Negroes laugh a lot, 75 per cent that Negroes tend to have less ambition than whites, 69 per cent that Negroes have looser morals, 61 per cent that Negroes keep untidy homes, 50 per cent that Negroes have less

* The new breed of intellectual racists try to prove Negro inferiority largely by reference to the wide gap between scores registered by Negroes and by whites on IQ and standardized achievement tests. Their arguments are analyzed in chapter IX.

native intelligence. (In the South, of course, the proportions were very much higher on all counts: *e.g.*, 73 per cent believed that Negroes have less native intelligence.)

The opponents of slavery and of segregation have permitted the racists to dictate the terms of the debate. For the past century and a half, liberals and men of good will have argued that no specific Negro traits exist—and that in any case, these traits would disappear automatically as soon as slavery were abolished or segregation ended. "Negroes," the historian Kenneth M. Stampp has put it, "are, after all, only white men with black skins, nothing more, nothing less."

But Negroes are not white men with black skins; to argue that they are is to pretend that we are all engaged in a masquerade. The difference in skin color is a fact, as are the differences in bone structure and configuration, amount and texture of hair, and so on. The question is not whether differences exist but what they mean; to refuse to acknowledge the reality of racial differences is to betray a fear that differences somehow connote inferiority. The fact of the matter is that geneticists, biologists, anthropologists, *et al* do not as yet know enough about race to draw *any* conclusions about the significance of racial differences. As the late Professor Ernest A. Hooton, the Harvard anthropologist, said, "Science can make no valid assertion that this or that race is either superior or inferior to another. [But] it is equally unable to put forward the claim that all races are equal biologically or in cultural capacity." The distinguished British scientist and philosopher J. B. S. Haldane was even blunter in a speech he delivered in 1963 at the International Congress of Genetics: "Perhaps the most important thing which human geneticists can do for society at the moment," he suggested, "is to emphasize how little they yet know . . . It is vastly easier to proclaim the equality or inequality of different races," he went on to say, "than to state not merely that we are ignorant but that insofar as the races may be adapted to different environments, the question may be unanswerable." Professor Sherwood L. Washburn of the University of California, a former president of the American Anthropological Association, has put it, "The issue is not whether there may, or may not, be some differences (between races), but whether there are differences of an order so great that they must be considered in the operation of democratic society." To this latter question, as Professor Washburn adds, the answer is unequivocally no.

Liberals have countered the racist argument, moreover, by calling it a stereotype, as if labeling the argument disposed of it. It does not: on the contrary, the stereotype is at least partly a description of reality. That is to say, Negroes *do* display less ambition than whites; as we have seen, apathy (with the self-hatred that produces it) is the worst disease of the Negro slum. Negroes *do* have "looser morals": there is no belying the promiscuity of the Negro slum-dweller or the high and apparently growing rate of illegitimacy. The Negro crime rate is substantially higher than the white. Negroes do "care less for family"; the rate of separation is six times greater among Negro families than among the white. Negroes score lower on IQ tests than whites of comparable socio-economic status, and Negro children do poorer work in school.

To acknowledge these unpleasant facts, however, does not imply that they are inherent characteristics or that they reflect intrinsic Negro inferiority. On the contrary, every one of them can be explained by the facts of Negro history in the United States. In denying the existence of these traits, white and black liberals merely betray their uneasy suspicion that perhaps the racists are right after all. They obviously are afraid that to admit the existence of unflattering traits of character or performance would be to admit that Negroes are inferior. No such conclusion is warranted; our own age offers proof enough of the ease with which human character and personality can be shaped and reshaped. Professor Stanley M. Elkins of the University of Chicago, author of the most brilliant and probing study of slavery in the United States,* has pointed out the parallels between the way the Nazi concentration camps changed the personalities of the prisoners who survived and the way in which slavery in the American South altered the personalities of Negroes brought from Africa and shaped the character of Negroes born here. There are risks in any such comparison, of course. But as Elkins puts it, "The only mass experience that Western people have had within recorded history comparable in any way with Negro slavery was undergone in the nether world of Nazism. The concentration camp was not only a perverted slave system; it was also—what is less obvious but even more to the point—a perverted patriarchy." Its product, consequently, was surprisingly like nineteenth-century Southern descriptions of the slave: "The Negro . . . in his true nature is always a boy, let him be ever so old, . . . He is . . . dependent upon the white race; dependent for guidance and direction even to the procurement of his most indispensable necessaries. Apart from this protection he has the helplessness of a child. . . ."

The most striking aspect of the concentration camp inmates' behavior, Elkins writes after surveying the extensive literature on the subject, "was its *childlike* quality." Many inmates—among them mature, independent, highly educated adults—were transformed into fawning, servile, dependent children. Infantile behavior took a variety of forms: "The inmates' sexual impotence brought about a disappearance of sexuality in their talk; instead, excretory functions occupied them endlessly. They lost many of the customary inhibitions as to soiling their beds and their persons. Their humor was shot with silliness and they giggled like children when one of them would expel wind." Dishonesty was endemic; prisoners became chronic and pathological liars; like adolescents, they would fight each other bitterly one

* Stanley M. Elkins, *Slavery: A Problem in American Institutional and Intellectual Life*, Chicago: University of Chicago Press, 1959.

moment and become close friends in the next; "dishonesty, mendacity, egotistic actions, . . . theft" were commonplace. This childlike behavior, moreover, was in part a reflection of an even more fundamental change, in which some prisoners identified with their SS guards and accepted the Gestapo's value system. They imitated the guards in many ways—sewing their uniforms to look more like those of the SS, imitating their mannerisms, absorbing their German nationalism and anti-Semitism (even some Jewish prisoners became anti-Semitic), outdoing the SS guards in brutality when placed in supervisory positions over their fellow-prisoners. "To all these men," Elkins observes, "reduced to complete and childish dependence upon their masters, the SS had actually become a father-symbol," for they were every bit as dependent upon the SS guards as infants upon their parents: the prisoners were kept in a state of chronic hunger and a guard could, at his pleasure, bestow or withhold food; the prisoner had to ask permission for every single thing—even to go to the latrine—and permission would not always be granted. The prisoner, in short, was reminded hour after hour that the SS guard had power of life or death over him. The result, curiously, was to lead the prisoner to identify with the guard instead of hating him. "In a system as tightly closed as the plantation or the concentration camp," Elkins explains, "the slave's or prisoner's position of absolute dependency virtually compels him to see the authority-figure as somehow really 'good.' Indeed, all the evil in his life may flow from this man—but then so also must everything of any value. Here is the seat of the only 'Good' he knows, and to maintain his psychic balance he must persuade himself that the good is in some way dominant." Thus social workers dealing with maltreated children frequently have the experience of having the child beg to remain with the brutal parent.

Transforming the concentration camp inmates into servile children, it should be recalled, was accomplished in a matter of months or at most years. The American Negro has been subject to a system designed to destroy ambition, prevent independence, and erode intelligence for the past three and a half centuries. Hence, nothing could be more foolish or more damaging to the Negro cause, than to refuse to face the harsh reality of what three hundred fifty years of white oppression have done to Negro personality and behavior. Uncomfortable as we all may find the truth, the truth is that the "nigger" with which Baldwin is obsessed, the "Sambo" of Southern folklore, was a reality and to a considerable extent still is. Not for all Negroes, certainly, and not in all places—but for enough Negroes, in enough places, over a long enough time, that the Negro cannot move into the main stream of American life unless he is able to destroy the image in his own mind and in the mind of the white. That image stems directly from slavery. A hundred years after its abolition, Negroes are still bound by its effects on their minds and spirits.

So are white Americans—even those whose fathers or grandfathers arrived long after slavery had ended. European immigrants acquired the racist attitudes of the native-born even before they acquired citizenship. Slavery was "the congenital defect" with which this nation was born; the depth and persistence of racist attitudes among white Americans go back to slavery, whose shadow is still very much with us. Understanding the peculiarity of slavery in the United States thus is the key to understanding both the white man's and the black man's Negro problem.

▼

2

The fact that Negroes were slaves is important in itself, for it means that few Negroes ever came to the United States voluntarily, that every Negro bears in his color the stigma of slavery. Tocqueville appreciated the significance of this fact a hundred and twenty-five years ago: "There is a natural prejudice that prompts men to despise whoever has been their inferior long after he has become their equal." In the ancient world, he added, men could move from slavery to freedom without great difficulty because former slaves could not be distinguished from those who had always been free. The Negro, by contrast, "transmits the eternal mark of his ignominy to all his descendants; and although the law may abolish slavery, God alone can obliterate the traces of its existence."

By itself, however, the fact of slavery does not begin to explain "the crushing sense of nobodiness" with which Negroes are afflicted. People of Slavic descent have no trouble holding their heads aloft, although "Slav" originally meant "slave." And the Jews, far from trying to erase the memory of slavery, have made it central to their religion: every Jew is enjoined to recall the fact that "we were slaves to Pharaoh in Egypt." The pronoun "we" is used because each individual is to imagine that he himself, not just his ancestors, had been enslaved.

Understandably enough, Negroes have been unable to recall their experience of slavery in the same light. After all, the Jews, under Moses' leadership, freed themselves, and they went from Egypt to Mount Sinai; slavery was followed almost immediately by a moment of spiritual glory. The Negroes, on the other hand, did not free themselves; they were freed by others, as a by-product of a political dispute between two groups of whites. Negroes were not even permitted to fight on the Union side until fairly late in the Civil War. And Emancipation was not followed by Exodus.

The fact is that Negro slavery in the United States and in the other British colonies was completely unlike slavery in any other part of the globe or any other period of history. Tocqueville saw this clearly in 1837: "The only means by which the ancients maintained slavery were fetters and death; the Americans of the South of the Union have discovered more intellectual securities for the duration of their power. They have employed their despostism and their violence against the human mind." The ancients, Tocqueville pointed out, took care to prevent the slave from breaking his chains. The Southerners, by contrast, have adapted "*measures to deprive him even of his desire for freedom.*" [Emphasis added]

Tocqueville went to the heart of the matter: deprive the Negro of his desire for freedom is precisely what the Southerner did, and still does to a considerable extent. Liberal historians have gone to great lengths to discover examples of Negro courage, Negro rebelliousness, Negro hatred for slavery—that is to say, all the attributes one would expect to find in those who are "merely white men wearing black skins." But the ghost of "Sambo" cannot be exorcised that easily. Professor Stampp, for example, who has written a major critique of the Southern view of slavery, is forced to concede: "To be sure, there were plenty of opportunists among the Negroes who played the role assigned to them, acted the clown, and curried the favor of their masters in order to win the maximum rewards within the system." And when the much-heralded slave revolts are examined closely, they turn out to be rather insignificant. Of the two hundred fifty "revolts" which the historian Herbert Aptheker has uncovered, for example, only three are really worthy of the term "revolt." The two best organized—those led by Vesey and Gabriel—were suppressed quite easily, and the most dramatic, the Nat Turner rebellion, was little more than aimless butchery. The remaining "revolts," even under Aptheker's sympathetic description, are clearly insignificant —little more than outbreaks of local vandalism. More to the point, the rebellions were suppressed easily, in part because they involved only a handful of slaves, and in good measure because fellow-slaves almost invariably informed on the rebels. In any case, the rebellions in no way ameliorated the slaves' condition; on the contrary, the revolts were generally followed by harsh repression. The only way a slave could change his situation was by escape—a form of withdrawal—or by cajolery and flattery of his master.

We need not labor the point. What is essential is neither to rewrite history as some liberals have done nor to pretend that the by-products of a slave system are nonexistent. Instead, Negro and white need to use that history for an understanding of the current "inferiorities" that *do* exist, and to search for new identities.

The submissiveness of the slaves is all the more striking in terms of the cultures from which most of them came. Modern historical and anthropological scholarship have made it clear that the traditional view of Africa as a place of savagery and barbarism is almost pure myth. (For a more detailed discussion of African culture, see chapter VII.) "Fifty years ago," Professor Elkins has written, "if the American Negro was congratulated for anything, it was for his remarkable advancement from a state of primitive ignorance. Now, however, looking back upon the energy, vitality, and complex organization of West African tribal life, we are tempted to reverse the question altogether and to wonder how it was ever possible that all this native resourcefulness and vitality could have been brought to such a point of utter stultification in America."

Some of the slaves, for example—no one knows how many—were Moslems, from the highly cultivated Negro Moslem empires of the western Sudan. Accounts of a number of these Moslem slaves were collected and preserved by three amateur ethnologists of the nineteenth century, Theodore Dwight, William Brown Hodgson, and James Hamilton Couper.* The most distinguished, by far, was Dwight, a great-grandson of Jonathan Edwards, nephew of

* For more details, *see* Morroe Berger, "The Black Muslims," *Horizon*, January, 1964.

one president of Yale and cousin of another, who served as recording secretary of the American Ethnological Society. In the *Methodist Quartery Review* of January, 1864, Dwight attacked the notion of Negro inferiority, insisting upon the high level of both Moslem and pagan Negro civilization in Africa, and telling the stories of a number of Moslem slaves he had met. "Among the victims of the slave trade among us," he wrote, "have been men of learning and pure and exalted characters, who have been treated like beasts of the field by those who claimed a purer religion." Perhaps the most interesting story that has survived concerns one Job, son of Solomon, who was born around 1701 in the Kingdom of Futa near the Gambia River. Around 1730, Job was sent to the coast to trade with the English but was captured by other Africans and sold into slavery. Ending up on a Maryland tobacco plantation, he escaped and was jailed. When his story became known, abolitionists arranged for his freedom and passage to England; en route, he wrote out, from memory, three copies of the Koran. In England, he met members of the royal family and became friendly with Sir Hans Sloane, president of the Royal Society, for whom he translated a number of Arabic inscriptions. After he returned to Futa in 1735 or 1736, he corresponded with his English friends, telling them of his problems of adjustment after five or six years in England and America.

Most of the slaves, to be sure, were considerably less educated and cultivated, coming from pre-literate pagan societies, especially those inhabiting the strip of land along the old Ivory Coast, Gold Coast, and Slave Coast.* These societies, while preliterate, were far from primitive; in terms of their ability to mobilize resources and utilize power, they were on a par with the European states of the Middle Ages. Indeed, they were powerful enough to prevent the Europeans from penetrating beyond the coast until the late nineteenth

* This territory is now the states of Nigeria, Dahomey, Togo, Ghana, and the Ivory Coast.

century; it took the English, for example, nearly a hundred years of warfare to subjugate the Ashanti. If anything like a typical West African tribesman can be said to have existed, it is clear that he was neither meek nor submissive nor childlike. He was, on the contrary, an essentially heroic, warlike individual with a deep sense of family responsibility, living by an elaborate and formalized set of rules, practicing a highly developed religion, and influenced by clearly defined esthetic principles.

What happened to transform the heroic African into the submissive slave?

For one thing, the process of enslavement subjected the African to a series of traumas that tended to sever him from his culture and institutions and destroy his sense of identity. First, there was the physical torment of the long march to the sea from the point of capture: tied together by their necks, the slaves walked barefoot for weeks through the steaming jungles; those who wearied were abandoned to died a slow death by starvation. (The British abolitionist Thomas Fowell Buxton wrote of having seen hundreds of skeletons lining one of the caravan routes.) Arriving at a coastal trading port, the slaves were subject to the further shock of being exhibited naked to the European slave traders. The slaves who were brought were branded like cattle and, like cattle, herded on shipboard; those considered unfit or undesirable were abandoned to starve to death.

Then began the greatest trauma of all: the dread Middle Passage, a trip so brutal that only an age which has been debased by the existence of the Nazi crematoria could believe it really happened. Here is one description:

> . . . The height, sometimes, between decks, was only eighteen inches; so that the unfortunate human beings could not turn around, or even on their sides, the elevation being less than the breadth of their shoulders; and here they are usually chained to the decks by the neck and legs.

> In such a place the sense of misery and suffocation is so great that the Negroes . . . are driven to frenzy. They [the slave traders] had on one occasion taken a slave vessel in the river Bonny: the slaves were stowed in the narrow space between decks, and chained together. They heard a horrid din and tumult among them, and could not imagine from what cause it proceeded. They opened the hatches and turned them up on deck. [The Negroes] were manacled together, in twos and threes. Their horror may be well conceived, when they found a number of [Negroes] in different stages of suffocation; many of them were foaming at the mouth, and in the last agonies—many were dead. The tumult they had heard was the frenzy of those suffocating wretches in the last stage of fury and desperation, struggling to extricate themselves. When they were all dragged up, nineteen were irrecoverably dead. Many destroyed one another, in the hopes of procuring room to breathe; men strangled those next to them, and women drove nails into each other's brains. Many unfortunate creatures, on other occasions, took the first opportunity of leaping overboard, and getting rid, in this way, of an intolerable life.*

It is estimated that approximately one-third of the Africans taken prisoner died en route to the coast and at the embarkation station, and that another third died during the Middle Passage and the "seasoning" that followed. Most slaves were landed first in the West Indies, where they were "seasoned" or broken in to their new roles as slaves; only afterward were they transshipped to the United States.

Concentration camp prisoners went through an analogous series of shocks. The first was the shock of "procurement": Gestapo policy was to make arrests at night, to heighten the element of shock, terror, and unreality. A day or two later came the second shock, transportation to the camp, which "involved a planned series of brutalities inflicted by guards making repeated rounds through the

---

* Rev. R. Walsh, *Notes of Brazil,* 1831.

train"; prisoners transported in cattle cars were sealed in, under conditions much like those of the Middle Passage. When they arrived at the camp, there were sham ceremonies designed to reassure the prisoners—so that the next round of terrors would have even greater impact. Those not marked for early extermination would go through "registration," filled with indignities, including inspection while naked. (Descriptions of this process in the concentration camps is remarkably similar to descriptions of the inspection of slaves in the eighteenth century.) In the concentration camp, registration ended with perhaps the most devastating weapon of all: being marked with a number—which symbolized the prisoners' loss of his name, hence of his identity. "Because he . . . had become a number," the psychologist Elie Cohen has written, "the prisoner belonged to the huge army of the nameless who peopled the concentration camp." Without question, the African slave's loss of his own name —slaves were given new names by the traders or by their new masters—was even more devastating, for in pre-literate society, a man's name is considered an essential part of his personality. Surely it is significant that the Black Muslims insist on discarding their "slave names" and taking new names instead.

Traumatic as all these experiences were, however, they go only part of the way toward explaining the impact of slavery on the American Negro. The Africans who were transported to South America went through the same experiences as those who landed in the United States, yet slavery had totally different effects in the two continents, as Elkins has shown, following Professor Frank Tannenbaum's pioneering essay.* Very much more of African culture survived in South America; the survivals are so distinct

---

* Frank Tannenbaum, *Slave and Citizen: The Negro in the Americas*, New York: Alfred A. Knopf, Inc., 1946. Reprinted in Vintage paperback.

that they can be identified by tribe, whereas American anthropologists are still arguing over whether *any* African survivals can be identified among the Negroes of the United States. More important, slavery carried little taint of inferiority in the Spanish and Portuguese colonies; it was regarded, rather, as a misfortune that could have happened to anyone. As a result, the South American system of slavery contained a fluidity that made it relatively easy for a slave to move to freedom; color did not represent a disability that would block the slave's incorporation into the larger society, as it did in the United States. Thus, an English visitor to Brazil in the mid-nineteenth century reported that he had "passed black ladies in silks and jewelry, with male slaves in livery behind them. Today one rode past in her carriage, accompanied by a liveried footman and a coachman. Several have white husbands. The first doctor of the city is a colored man; so is the President of the Province." As early as the eighteenth century, in fact, there were Negro priests and even Negro bishops in Brazil; in the seventeenth century, the Negroes had established a reputation for courage and military ability.

It may seem paradoxical that slavery was so much more tolerable in the colonies of the feudal and despotic Spanish and Portuguese empires than in the democratic United States. Yet it was precisely the persistence of feudalism in Spain and Portugal and its absence in the United States (and in the other British colonies) that explains the difference. Although slavery had long since died out everywhere else in western Europe, the institution had survived in the Iberian peninsula down to the fifteenth century, in part because of the continuing wars with the Moors. There was, indeed, a tradition of slavery and of slave law going back to the Justinian Code and to earlier times. The Romans (as did most other ancients) saw slavery as a normal condition of man—the result of accident and misfortune, rather than of human nature. In this view, slavery affected only the body of the slave—that is, only his labor; his mind and soul remained free. As the Roman author Seneca wrote, "A slave can be just, brave, magnanimous." Spiritually, the slave was his master's equal; intellectually, he could be his superior.

When Negro slavery began in Spain and Portugal in about the mid-fifteenth century, therefore—a century and a half before it was introduced into North America—the slaves found not just a tradition of slavery but an incredibly elaborate body of law and custom designed to protect the slave's status as a human being. This body of law was transferred to the colonies in the New World. Thus, South American law gave the slaves the right to acquire and hold property and to buy their own freedom at a fixed price, generally the price paid at the time of purchase. A codification in 1789 gave urban slaves two hours a day to use in "occupations for their own advantage"; rural slaves were permitted to sell the produce of their own gardens, and save the proceeds toward purchasing their freedom. As Professor Tannenbaum has put it, "for all practical purposes slavery here had become a contractural arrangement that could be wiped out by a fixed purchase price"—a contract, moreover, in which a master owned a man's labor, not the man himself.

Nor was this all. In this feudal society, the Catholic Church asserted its vested interest in the souls of the slaves. Since marriage is a sacrament, slaves had to be married in the church; once married, the slaves could not be separated. Slaveowners, moreover, were required to give their slaves religious instruction. Since the Crown as well as the Church had an interest in all its subjects, an elaborate body of law protected the slaves against mistreatment by their owners. To enforce this law, each colony had an official protector of the slave, known variously as the syndic, procurator, or attorney general. Priests who made regular rounds of the estates were required to submit reports from the slaves regarding mistreatment, and these reports were investigated systematically. Fines levied for mistreatment of slaves were divided three ways: one-third to the informer, one-third to the judge, and one-third to the Crown.

The result, was an "open system" that permitted a relatively smooth transition from slavery to freedom. Because Spanish and Portuguese law saw slavery as a misfortune that could happen to anyone, and because it insisted that the slave had a soul and mind and personality of his own, the opprobrium Americans attached to color never developed. It would be wrong to suggest that South American slavery was benign; it was frequently quite brutal. But the cruelties and brutalities were against the law and were punishable if discovered. More important, South American whites never seriously maintained that a Negro slave was *incapable* of being free. On the contrary, freed slaves enjoyed the same legal rights as the white man and on the whole the same social status. And in fact freed slaves did participate actively and fully in the life of their new countries. The literature of South American slavery therefore shows no trace of the "Sambo" of United States tradition. "Sambo" never took root in South American soil.

He flourished in the United States, however, for on this continent slavery developed in such a way as to convince the whites that Negroes were inherently inferior and incapable of freedom. Equally important, the system of slavery was administered so as to make the Negroes behave as if they *were* inferiors—to distort their personalities and suppress their mentalities in such a way as to make them in fact incapable of utilizing the "freedom" that finally became theirs after two and a half centuries of enslavement.

Slavery took its peculiar and brutal form in the United States (and in all the other English colonies) *precisely because there was no precedent either in tradition or in common law.* Catholic Portugal and Spain had seen slavery as a natural condition of man; in these feudal societies, freedom was conditional for every man, and there was a whole series of gradations of status from slavery to freedom. Protestant England and America, however, saw slavery as completely unnatural; serfdom had been abolished some time before, and slavery had been unknown since Roman times. Introducing slavery into a society of free men thus posed a real dilemma; how justify slavery in a society based, as John Locke had argued, on a contract among free men? The dilemma was resolved very neatly through an appeal to the Africans' alleged inferiority. If the Negroes were inherently inferior, if they lacked the capacity to be free men, then slavery could be justified and indeed defended as a service to the slaves themselves, as well as to the masters.* And the rules and practices that developed out of this rationale in turn created a system that made the slaves into dependent, servile, infantile creatures who indeed seemed incapable of exercising freedom. Thus the circle was completed.

The absence of feudal institutions and customs had still another effect in the American colonies: there were no institutions able or willing to interpose their interests in the slave's well-being against the property interests of the slaveowner. There was no Catholic Church to assert its proprietary interest in the souls of the slaves; the various Protestant denominations had trouble enough exercising any influence over the white planters. Nor was there a feudal monarchy interposing itself between slave and master; the English crown was interested mainly in tobacco revenues and left government to the colonists as long as the revenues continued to flow. And so the economic interests of the planters and other slave-owners went unchallenged. Professor Elkins points out that slavery in the United States—

---

* "I get my sailing orders from the Lord."
He touched the Bible. "And it's down there, Mister,
Down there in black and white—the sons of Ham—
Bondservants—the sweat of their brows." His voice trailed off
Into texts. "I tell you, Mister," he said fiercely,
"The pay's good pay, but it's the Lord's work, too.
We're spreading the Lord's seed—spreading his seed—"

(From Stephen Vincent Benét, *John Brown's Body*, New York: Holt, Rinehart & Winston, 1960.)

like the Nazi concentration camps—was a "closed system" in which "all lines of authority descended from the master and in which alternative social bases that might have supported alternative standards were systematically suppressed."

In this newly developing capitalist society, therefore, the laws of slavery became an absolute and total condition in which the proprietor owned the slave's mind and soul as well as his body and labor. Because there was no precedent for slavery, the jurists of the new colonies had to find precedents where they could—in the laws governing chattel property. A horse, a cow, a house, have no rights vis-à-vis the owners. Thus it was with this new type of property. "A slave is in absolute bondage; he has no civil right," maintained the law. And so a slave could not own property except at his master's pleasure.

More important, the slave could not enter into a contract for any purpose, since "neither his word nor his bond has any standing in law." Hence a slave could not marry; slaves could live together, but their relationship had no legal status. "The relation between slaves," a North Carolina judge wrote, "is essentially different from that of man and wife joined in lawful wedlock . . . [for] with slaves it may be dissolved at the pleasure of either party, or by the sale of one or both, depending on the caprice or necessity of the owners." Slave law not only refused to recognize marriage, it reversed the common-law tradition that children derive their status from their father, maintaining that "the father of a slave is unknown to our law." To have held otherwise would have raised the embarassing question of what to do with the children born of a white father and a slave mother; the old common law would thus have created a large class of free mulattos.* Thus not only was a slave father legally unknown, but he was legally stripped of the last semblance of masculinity as well—his right to his marriage bed. As one

* In actual practice, planters frequently freed the children born of their illicit relations with their slaves. Hence the free Negroes tended to be of lighter color than those who remained in slavery.

legal authority observed, "a slave has never maintained an action against the violator of his bed. A slave is not admonished for incontinence, or punished for fornication or adultery; never prosecuted for bigamy. . . ." Slave marriage, such as it was, was defined as "only that concubinage with which . . . their condition is compatible."

From this it followed quite logically that there could be no question of the slaveowner's right to separate husband from wife and children from parents. Individual slaveowners, in their mercy, may have refrained from such separations; but the practice was legal and common. Consider this advertisement from a New Orleans newspaper (*ca.* 1830):

> NEGROES FOR SALE——A negro woman, 24 years of age, and her two children, one eight and the other three years old. Said negroes will be sold SEPARATELY or together, as desired. The woman is a good seamstress. She will be sold low for cash, or EXCHANGED FOR GROCERIES. For terms, apply to Mathew Bliss & Co.

Even without these laws, a stable family life would have been extremely difficult, for in most Southern states male slaves greatly outnumbered females until the 1840s—the plantations, after all, were industrial enterprises requiring male labor. For a large proportion of the male slaves, therefore, there was no opportunity for permanent association with a woman, even under the limitations of slave law. Thus, a visitor to Louisiana reported in 1802 that "Those who cannot obtain women (for there is a great disproportion between the numbers of the two sexes) traverse the woods in search of adventure." In general, therefore, what sexual contact there was between slaves was bound to be casual and temporary.

The shortage of slave women, moreover—together with the interferences imposed upon the slave trade in the late eighteenth and early nineteenth centuries—led to the ultimate perversion: the breeding of slaves like cattle. In 1796, for example, a slaveowner advertised fifty slaves for sale:

> . . . they are not Negroes selected out of a larger gang for the purpose of a slave, but are prime, their present Owner, with great trouble and expense, selected them out of many for several years past. They were purchased for stock and breeding Negroes, and to any Planter who particularly wanted them for that purpose, they are a very choice and desirable gang.

A Charleston paper advertised for sale a twenty-year-old slave girl who "is very prolific in her generating qualities, and affords a rare opportunity for any person who wished to raise a family of strong, healthy servants for . . . his own use." And Thomas R. Dew, president of the College of William and Mary boasted in the 1830s that "Virginia is in fact a negro raising state for other states; she produces enough for her own supply, and six thousand for sale . . . Virginians can raise them cheaper than they can buy; in fact, it is one of their greatest sources of profit."

If slaves, as chattel, could be separated from parents or children and bred like cattle, then it also followed that the law would give them no protection against mistreatment by their masters. For one thing, slaves were universally prohibited from testifying in court except against each other. For another, punishing a slaveowner for mistreating his own property seemed a logical absurdity; self-interest would clearly prevent a master from injuring his slave unless necessary to correct the latter's misbehavior.

It would be hard to conceive a system better designed to create the submissive, infantile, incontinent, undisciplined, dull, dependent "Sambo" of Southern legend. The results seem to justify the system: no one looking at the slaves could doubt their inferiority; to argue otherwise was to deny the evidence of one's senses.

Having erected the system of slavery on the assumption of Negro inferiority, and then having produced the behavior that seemed to justify the assumption, it was inevitable that America would refuse to admit free Negroes to full membership in their society. Slavery became associated with race, and race with inferiority; the two concepts merged. And so black meant inferior; inferior meant black. Thus, even when a black man became free, white America offered him neither equality nor citizenship in any meaningful sense of the word. Free Negroes lived in a limbo somewhere between slavery and freedom. In 1857, Chief Justice Taney declared the belief of the Supreme Court that "a Negro has no rights which a white man need respect." In the Court's interpretation of the Constitution, the words "people of the United States" did not include Negroes. Understandably enough in the light of this view, free Negroes were denied the vote in most Northern states as well as in the South; New Jersey and Ohio rejected equal suffrage in 1867, and New York rejected it as late as 1869. In many states, free Negroes were denied trial by jury. Upon arrival in the nation's capital, every Negro over the age of twelve had to post bond, as if he were out on bail, and had to report within five days of his arrival. Negroes could not appear on the streets after 10 P.M. without special permit; a permit was also required for any public gathering, while private meetings were expressly forbidden. The burden of proof was on free Negroes to prove their freedom; in the absence of proof, they could be jailed, and even if they subsequently demonstrated their free status, they could be sold into slavery if they were unable to pay for their keep while in jail. As mentioned before, four states in the West literally barred Negroes from physical entry; in Oregon, free Negroes could enter, but they could not own real property, could not sign contracts or engage in law suits. Even the Great Emancipator himself, before he became president, expressed his unalterable opposition to political or social equality between the races. Thus, in a speech he gave in 1858 he said:

> I will say then that I am not, nor ever have been in favor of bringing about in any way the social and political equal-

ity of the white and black races—that I am not nor ever have been in favor of making voters or jurors of Negroes, nor of qualifying them to hold office, nor to intermarry with white people; and I will say in addition to this that there is a physical difference between the white and black races which I believe will forbid the two races living together on terms of social and political equality. And inasmuch as they cannot so live, while they do remain together, there must be the position of superior and inferior and I as much as any other man am in favor of having the superior position assigned to the white race.

▼

3

The Emancipation Proclamation, to repeat Wendell Phillips' epigram, freed the slave but ignored the Negro. It was almost inevitable that this be so. Lincoln had reached the decision to free the slaves with some reluctance, and he rather hoped that once freed, they would solve the problem by returning to Africa. In any case, the exigencies of war left little time to prepare any program to help the newly-freed slaves move into the main stream of American life. The abolitionists, moreover, were no help at all, for they failed to understand the dimensions of the problem. The Southerners had justified slavery in terms of Negro inferiority. The abolitionists accepted the Southerners' terms and simply reversed the argument, drawing upon the then-current notions of human perfectibility. According to William Jay, for example, emancipation would immediately "stimulate [the Negroes'] morals, quicken their intelligence, and convert a dangerous, idle and vicious population into wholesome citizens." The transformation from slavery to freedom, in his view, could be made "instantaneously, and with scarcely any perceptible interruption of the ordinary pursuits of life." With such a view there clearly was no need to develop any program to assist the slaves in making the difficult transition from total dependence to freedom and independence.

More to the point, the abolitionists were incapable of proposing any program, for they saw slavery as a moral abstraction, not as a social problem. Hence the most vocal abolitionist of all, William Lloyd Garrison, proclaimed the problem "solved" once the Emancipation Proclamation had been issued. Solved, because the problem was the immorality of slavery, not the condition of the slaves. Thus, Garrison quickly lost interest—at the same time that he expressed his belief that the freedmen were not yet ready for "political rights and realities."

In fact, the Negroes were totally unprepared; never was a people less prepared for freedom. Slavery had emasculated the Negro males, had made them shiftless and irresponsible and promiscuous by preventing them from ever assuming responsibility, negating their role as husband and father, and making them totally dependent on the will of another. There was no stable family structure to offer support to men or women or children in this strange new world. With no history of stable family ties, no knowledge even of what stability might mean, huge numbers of Negro men took to the roads as soon as freedom was proclaimed; the right to move about was seen as the crucial test of freedom.* Thus there developed a pattern of drifting from place to place and job to job and woman to woman that has persisted (in lesser degree, of course) to the present day. Here is a portion of the life story of one "Black Ulysses," as told to Professor E. Franklin Frazier in the thirties:

* "After the coming of freedom," Booker T. Washington wrote in his autobiography, *Up From Slavery*, "there were two points upon which practically all people on our place were agreed, and I find that this was generally true throughout the South: that they must change their names, and that they must leave the plantation for at least a few days or weeks in order that they might really feel sure that they were free."

> . . . Nine months ago when I left home I went to Atlanta, Georgia. I left home [Chattanooga] on a Friday afternoon and hoboed a freight train and stayed there a week and one day. From Atlanta I went to Savannah, Georgia, stayed there one day and from there to Shreveport, Louisiana, for two days, then to Baton Rouge for four days. Then I went to New Orleans for two days and then on to Chicago. I never stayed three days in Chicago. I stayed in the jungles . . . then I went to Louisville, Kentucky . . . In Louisville I just stayed here one day and came back down the L. & N. to Guthrie, Kentucky and from there back over to Milan, Tennessee and from there back to Jackson, Tennessee, and from there over here.

This man, Frazier reports, "began his sex experiences when fourteen as the result of the example and instructions of older boys. At the present time his sexual life is entirely of a casual nature. When he arrives in a city, he approaches women on the street or gets information on accessible women from men of his type . . . They take him to their lodgings, where he remains until his hunger as well as his sexual desires are satisfied, and then he takes to the road again. Occasionally, he sends a card to a woman to whom he takes a special liking, but usually he forgets them." *

If the newly-freed slaves had no emotional anchorage, neither did they have any economic base from which to create a self-respecting role for themselves. Some, to be sure, were skilled craftsmen and others continued as domestic servants. The majority were plantation laborers, with nothing to offer but their muscles. Perhaps Lincoln, had he lived, might have been able to see the need for redistribution of the land; forty acres and a mule might have created an independent Negro peasantry. But freeing the slaves was as daring an attack on the rights of property as that generation of Americans was willing to undertake. And so the system of

* E. Franklin Frazier, *The Negro Family in the United States,* Chicago: University of Chicago Press, 1939.

sharecropping replaced slavery, substituting debt peonage for legal bondage and keeping the Negroes impoverished and uneducated.

And servile and dependent—always servile and dependent! On this the Southern whites were insistent. For it, they were willing to pay a heavy price. For the constant expression of humility and servility and dependency by Negroes, that is to say, Southern whites were willing to put up with inefficiency and indolence. Negro workers came to be paid as much for their servility and for their adeptness at flattering the master as for their ability. Indeed, the belief in Negro inferiority meant that the Negro worker had fewer definite obligations as well as fewer definite rights. As George Washington Cable wrote in 1888, the Southern ruling class "tolerates, with unsurpassed supineness and unconsciousness, a more indolent, inefficient, slovenly, unclear, untrustworthy, ill-mannered, noisy, disrespectful, disputatious, and yet servile domestic and public menial service than is tolerated by any other enlightened people." Cable may have been exaggerating, but his point was essentially correct: so long as a Negro remembered his place and acted obsequiously enough, the white man was ready to excuse—indeed, to expect—laziness, indolence, inefficiency, and a certain amount of petty thievery. For all this, after all, was in the Negro's nature. Equally important, as Professor John Dollard has pointed out, "the relatively indulgent behavior permitted to Negroes in lieu of the struggle to achieve higher social status" has served as an invaluable device for maintaining the rigid caste structure of Southern society." * The one sure way for the Negro to lose favor—in rural areas, to place himself in jeopardy—was to show signs of ambition: that is, to seek to rise above his "place." And if by any chance he did manage to secure an education and to better himself economically, he was well-advised to conceal the fact and simulate dependence.

* John Dollard, *Caste and Class in a Southern Town,* Garden City, N.Y.: Doubleday Anchor Books, 1949, ch. XVII.

Negroes learned to play the game accordingly: they became masters at turning obsequiousness and flattery into weapons of defense or offense. "Playing the fool," if done adroitly enough, could make the white man appear the fool, could lead him to accept inferior performance. And flattery, if handled properly, could sometimes turn the head of even the hardest white, and lead him to further his flatterer's objectives. ". . . The Negro uses his intimate knowledge of the white man to further his own advancement," Robert R. Moton, who succeeded Booker T. Washington as head of Tuskegee Institute, wrote in 1929. "Much of what is regarded as racially characteristic of the Negro is nothing more than his artful and adroit accommodation of his manners and methods to what he knows to be the weakness and foibles of his white neighbors. Knowing what is expected of him, and knowing too what he himself wants, the Negro craftily uses his knowledge to anticipate opposition and to eliminate friction in securing his desires."

Indeed, Negroes take enormous pride in the fact that while whites boast that they "know" the Negro, it is in reality the Negro who knows the whites. Whites rarely know what Negroes are thinking, for the latter have learned to hide their true feelings behind a mask of submissiveness, or pleasure, or impassivity, or humility.

The "Uncle Remus" stories provide a perfect case in point, as Bernard Wolfe has pointed out.* The setting for these stories is invariable: the little white boy, son of "Miss Sally" and "Mars John," comes into the old Negro's cabin back of the "big house"; Uncle Remus' face "breaks up into little eddies of smiles," and he takes the admiring child on his knees and caresses him. The relationship appears to be one of pure tenderness: Uncle Remus gives with a "kindly beam" and a "most infectious chuckle"; the little boy receives with awe and delight. "But if one looks more closely," Wolfe points out, "within the magnanimous caress is an incredibly malevolent

* Bernard Wolfe, "Uncle Remus and the Malevolent Rabbit," *Commentary,* July, 1949, pp. 31-44.

blow." In the first and most famous collection of Uncle Remus stories, for example, Brer Rabbit trounces the Fox nineteen times out of twenty encounters. Brer Rabbit also wins out over the wolf, the bear, and on one occasion the entire animal kingdom. In all, there are twenty-eight victories of the Weak over the Strong; ultimately all the Strong die violent deaths at the hands of the Weak. "Admittedly, folk symbols are seldom systematic, clean-cut, or specific," Wolfe concludes, but Brer Rabbit seems to be "a symbol—about as sharp as Southern sanctions would allow—of the Negro slave's festering hatred of the white man." That hatred couldn't be expressed directly or overtly: "A Negro slave who yielded his mind fully to his race hatreds in an absolutely white dominated situation must go mad," Wolfe suggests. "The functions of such folk symbols as Brer Rabbit is precisely to prevent inner explosions by siphoning off these hatreds before they can completely possess consciousness. Folk tales, like so much of folk culture, are part of an elaborate psychic drainage system—they make it possible for Uncle Tom to retain his façade of grinning Tomism and even, to some degree, to believe in it himself."

The most humble "Uncle Tom," in short, in reality can be a man who hates the whites and persuades them, however unconsciously, to serve him. Nowhere is the cynicism underlying Southern Negro humility revealed more sharply than in Ralph Ellison's portrait of a Negro college president—modeled perhaps after the late Dr. Moton of Tuskegee—in *Invisible Man*. The protagonist, a naïve student at the college, had been assigned to drive a distinguished white trustee around the area. At the trustee's request, the student had shown him the old slave's quarters, and then had taken him to a Negro bar, where the trustee is injured during a brawl. The student brings him back to his rooms at the college, and then calls for Dr. Bledsoe, the president.

> "Boy, are you a fool?" Dr. Bledsoe asked the student.
> "Didn't you know better than to take a trustee out there?"

"He asked me to, sir."

We were going down the walk now, through the spring air, and he stopped to look at me with exasperation, as though I'd suddenly told him black was white.

"Damn what *he* wants," he said, climbing in the front seat beside me, "Haven't you the sense God gave a dog? We take these white folks where we want them to go, we show them what we want them to see. Don't you know that? I thought you had some sense."

Reaching Rabb Hall, I stopped the car, with bewilderment . . . Just inside the building, I got another shock. As we approached a mirror Dr. Bledsoe stopped and composed his angry face like a sculptor, making it a bland mask, leaving only the sparkling of his eyes to betray the emotion that I had seen only a moment before . . .

Later on, in the privacy of his office, Dr. Bledsoe upbraids the young student still more for having taken the trustee to see the old slave cabins:

". . . Haven't we bowed and scraped and begged and lied enough decent homes and drives for you to show him? Did you think that white man had to come a thousand miles—all the way from New York and Boston and Philadelphia just for you to show him a slum? Don't just stand there, say something!"

"But I was only driving him, sir. I only stopped there after he ordered me to . . ."

"Ordered you?" he said. "He *ordered* you. Dammit, white folk are always giving orders, it's a habit with them. Why didn't you make an excuse? Couldn't you say they had sickness—smallpox—or picked another cabin? Why that Trueblood shack. My God, boy! You're black and living in the South—did you forget how to lie?"

"Lie, sir? Lie to him, lie to a trustee sir? Me?"

He shook his head with a kind of anguish. "And me thinking I'd picked a boy with brain," he said. "Didn't you know you were endangering the school?"

"But I was only trying to please him . . ."

"*Please* him? And here you are a junior in college! Why,

the dumbest black bastard in the cotton patch knows that the only way to please a white man is to tell him a lie! . . ."

And when the young man threatens to expose Bledsoe's duplicity after he has been expelled by him, Bledsoe only laughs at him:

> "Tell anyone you like," he said. "I don't care . . . Because I don't owe anyone a thing, son. Who, Negroes? Negroes don't control this school or much of anything else—haven't you learned even that? No, sir, they don't control this school, nor white folk either. True they *support* it, but *I* control it. I's big and black and I say 'Yes, suh' as loudly as any burr-head when it's convenient, but I'm still the king down here. I don't care how much it appears otherwise. Power doesn't have to show off. Power is confident, self-assuring, self-starting and self-stopping, self-warming and self-justifying. When you have it, you know it. Let the Negroes snicker and the crackers laugh! Those are the facts, son. The only ones I even pretend to please are *big* white folk, and even those I control more than they control me . . . You're nobody, son. You don't exist—can't you see that. The white folk tell everybody what to think—except men like me. I tell *them;* that's my life, telling white folk how to think about the things I know about. Shocks you, doesn't it? Well, that's the way it is . . . I don't even insist that it was worth it, but now I'm here, and I mean to stay—after you win the game, you take the prize and you keep it, protect it; there's nothing else to do."

But the game is never worth—can never be worth—the prize. The psychic costs are too heavy. "Play the game, but don't believe in it," Ellison's young hero is advised when he is expelled from college. But how not believe in it when you have to scrape and bow and defer and smile and humble yourself every day of your life? No matter how great the Negro's ability or his achievement, the Southern social system was bound to insinuate itself into his mind and soul and make him wonder if perhaps the whites were not right after all. Here is W. E. B. Du Bois writing in 1903, in *The Souls of Black Folk:*

> Behind the thought lurks the afterthought: suppose if all the world is right and we are less than men? Suppose this mad impulse [*i.e.*, the demand for freedom and equality] is all wrong, some mock mirage from the untrue . . . a shriek in the night for the freedom of men who themselves are not yet sure of their right to demand it?

As Myrdal wrote in the 1940s, "a psychological milieu more effective in stifling spontaneous ambition is hardly thinkable."

It was not only ambition that was stifled, however, but ego—consciousness of self—as well. For the Negro had to learn to suppress any knowledge or assertion of self in order to hold his job, or his life. He had to become schizophrenic in order to survive. "The steady impact of the plantation system upon our lives," Richard Wright put it, "created new types of behavior and new patterns of psychological reaction, welding us together into a separate unity with common characteristics of our own." He continued:

> We strove each day to maintain that kind of external behavior that would best allay the fear and hate of the Lords of the Land, and over a period of years this dual conduct became second nature to us and we found in it a degree of immunity from daily oppression. Even when a white man asked us an innocent question, some unconscious part of us would listen closely, not only to the obvious words but also to the intonations of voice that indicated what kind of answer he wanted; and automatically, we would determine whether an affirmative or negative reply was expected, and we would answer, not in terms of objective truth, but in terms of what the white man wanted to hear.
>
> If a white man stopped a black on a southern road and

> asked: "Say there, boy: It's one o'clock, is it, boy?" the black man would answer: "Yessuh."
>
> And if the white man asked, "Say, it's not one o'clock, is it boy?" the black man would answer, "Nawsuh."
>
> And if the white man asked: "It's ten miles to Memphis, isn't it, boy?" the black man would answer: "Yessuh."
>
> And if the white man asked: "It isn't ten miles to Memphis, is it boy?" the black man would answer: "Nawsuh."
>
> Always we said what we thought the whites wanted us to say.*

What this does to the mind and soul can hardly be imagined. "In the main we are different from other folks," Wright wrote, "in that, when an impulse moves us, when we are caught in the throes of inspiration, when we are moved to better our lot, we do not ask ourselves: 'Can we do it?' but 'Will they let us do it?' Before we black folks can move, we must first look into the white man's mind to see what is there, to see what he is thinking. . . ." The result is to repress the will, destroy ambition, to limit the choices so as to make action virtually impossible. "If you act at all," Wright concludes, "it is either to flee or to kill; you are either a victim or a rebel. And almost all were victims."

The Negroes of the North were better off, of course—but not enough better off to enable them to shuck off the heritage of slavery. Before Emancipation, as we have seen, the free Negroes lived in a kind of limbo somewhere between the slaves and the whites.

Yet before the Civil War there *was* hope, there was aspiration, based on the dream that some day slavery would end and all black men would be admitted to full membership in American society. Partly as a result of this hope, Negroes showed a remarkable zeal for self-improvement. In Washington, D.C., for example, of the fifty-two schools established for Negro children between 1807 and 1861, forty were

* Richard Wright, *Twelve Million Black Voices*, New York: The Viking Press, 1941.

founded and run by Negroes themselves. As the historian Constance McLaughlin Green has written, "hard-working Negro families who observed the law meticulously made astonishing material progress and won new respect from upper-class whites." The New York City and County Suffrage Committee of Colored Citizens had twenty branches within the city itself, and more throughout the state. Almost every city and a good many villages had literary societies, dedicated to "the stimulation of reading and the spreading of useful knowledge by providing libraries and reading rooms." The historian Benjamin Quarles reports the existence of at least forty-five such societies in the North. In Baltimore, for example, there was the Young Men's Mental Improvement Society for the Discussion of Moral and Philosophical Questions of All Kinds; Pittsburgh Negroes had their Young Men's Literary and Moral Reform Society; and the hundred twenty Negro families in Greenville, Indiana, boasted of having "a very good Literary Debating Society."

To the free Negroes of the North, moreover, the Civil War seemed like the dawn of a new day. For example, George T. Downing, a prosperous caterer, compared the Negro's lot in 1861 with that of a quarter-century before. Then, he observed,

> a colored man had to take the gutter side of the pave, and dared not show his face in a concert, lecture, or library-room; schools, colleges and literary associations closed their doors against him . . .

But now, Downing reported,

> Colleges and lectures are alike open to all on equal terms, as are also the lecture, the concert and the library-room; . . . see him participating at the bar, in the workshop, in the studio, occupying professorships, and then say, if you can, there is not hope for the future.

Thomas Hamilton, publisher of the *Anglo-African,* a literary monthly magazine, agreed that "No one thing is beyond the aim of the colored man in this country," and used his editorial columns to urge Negroes to raise their sights. The hopes continued for a decade or two after the end of the Civil War, as Negroes were elected and appointed to public office, enfranchised, accepted as members of white churches, and for the first time given the protection of the law. The motto of the Class of 1886 at Tuskegee Institute was "There Is Always Room At The Top."

But Negroes discovered very rapidly that in the North as well as in the South, the room at the top was for whites only. Indeed, it rapidly began to appear that there was room for Negroes only at the bottom. After the Compromise of 1877 ended Reconstruction, the North returned fairly rapidly to the pattern of segregation and discrimination on which Tocqueville had commented, thereby persuading Negroes that aspiration was futile and self-improvement useless.

In the large cities, competition from the European immigrants pushed Negroes out of jobs that had always been theirs. In Philadelphia, for example, an analysis prepared in 1881 blamed the difficulties experienced by the city's Negroes on the Irish newcomers: "Southern cities were built by colored mechanical labor. In this city twenty years before the late war, it was no unusual thing to find a majority of colored mechanics engaged in all the leading trades . . . But Irish migration was destined to strike a blow at the colored mechanic, from which it will take years for him to recover." Besides competing with Negroes for jobs, the Irish picked up the general prejudice against a black skin a good deal faster than they lost their brogue, and they used all their influence and a good deal of brute force to make sure that the Negroes occupied a status below theirs; the Negro, as James Baldwin has observed, tells you where the bottom is.

The same process was repeated with the arrival of each

new immigrant group. And if it was not the immigrants from Europe, it was the Negro migrants from the South who complicated matters. For a quarter-century after the Civil War, the Negro population of New York City had been remarkably stable, and the black citizens gradually improved their status; Negroes, for example, dominated the catering business. In the next twenty years, however—between 1890 and 1910—the Negro population of the city quadrupled, as the Great Migration from the South got underway. When Negroes became visible, New York began adopting extralegally the same Jim Crow customs that were being legislated all through the South. After a quarter-century of relatively free admission, Negroes began to be barred from restaurants, theaters, hotels, and stores. The YMCA built a Negro branch, and then proceeded to bar Negroes from all its other branches.

Nor was New York unique. In Washington, D.C., the Negro position also deteriorated rapidly, and without any great influx either of foreigners or of poor Negroes. "For Negroes," Constance McLaughlin Green has said, "the satisfactions of life in the capital diminished steadily after 1878. Between white and colored people such tolerant friendliness as had survived the seventies slowly disappeared. White citizens forgot that Negro leaders had formerly commanded respect and, by their behavior, had encouraged belief in the possibility of building an intelligent bi-racial community. In 1888 the Washington *Elite List* carried the names of five or six Negroes; by 1892 they had been dropped. The white press, increasingly critical of Negroes' 'shiftlessness' and the high rate of crime among them, gradually reduced other news about colored people to an occasional facetious comment on a colored social gathering. Exasperation or disgust blotted out compassion for the great mass of blacks, while white peoples' interest in the careers of gifted Negroes became so condescending as to be insulting . . . By the mid-nineties a reader of the white newspapers might have supposed Washington had no colored community, let alone three separate Negro communities. White people, in short, in the course of the twenty-odd years resolved the problem of race relations by tacitly denying its existence." *

While the Washington newspapers dealt with the Negroes by ignoring their existence, owners of theaters, restaurants, hotels, and so on, dealt with them by excluding them from their premises. Public accommodation bills that had been passed in 1869 and 1870 were simply ignored. In most instances Negroes were too frightened to sue; when they did, the courts made a mockery of the law: a suit against the owner of the Opera House for preventing a Negro from occupying an orchestra seat for which he had paid, netted the plaintiff damages of one cent. After the turn of the century, the Jim Crow system gained force very rapidly. In 1908, Negro members of the Women's Christian Temperance Society were asked to withdraw and form a separate unit. The Congregational Church, which had welcomed Negro members in the 1870s, gave an ovation to a congressman from Maine who declared that Negroes should never have been enfranchised en masse, but given the vote one by one as they proved themselves ready. The Episcopal bishop went much further: Negroes should not have been given equal suffrage at all, since they were "morally and intellectually a weaker race." And when the World Sunday School Convention met in Washington in 1910, the local committee on arrangements refused to seat local Negro delegates although they were members of the World Association and had participated in earlier conventions.

Negroes were excluded from the city's economic life as systematically as they were from its social life. Trade unions began excluding Negro craftsmen and artisans. More important, Negroes were gradually squeezed out of the gov-

* Constance McLaughlin Green, *Washington: Capital City, 1879-1950*, Princeton, N.J.: Princeton University Press, 1963.

ernment jobs they had acquired after the Civil War. In 1891, nearly 2,400 of the 23,000 federal employees in Washington were Negro. Promotion became rarer and rarer; the Civil Service Commission rules allowed department and division chiefs to choose any of the three top candidates qualified for a job, and Negroes were rarely chosen. Thus, by 1908, the number of Negro employees had dwindled to only 1,450, all but 300 of them messengers or common laborers. The climax came in 1912, when Woodrow Wilson, Virginian by birth, acceded to the Presidency, and dismissed all but two of the Negroes appointed by Taft.

What happened in Washington and New York was repeated in one way or another in virtually every city of the North. With the abolitionists long since gone, and consciences salved by the Civil War and Emancipation, Northern public opinion took a racist turn: the fact that the mass of poor Negroes had not become cultivated gentlemen in two or three decades since Emancipation seemed to justify all the old notions about inherent Negro inferiority. Thus, the Supreme Court turned its back on Reconstruction in 1896, when it established the "separate but equal" doctrine in the case of *Plessy v. Ferguson*, upholding a Louisiana law requiring separate railway facilities for Negro and white passengers. Mr. Justice Brown declared in giving the Court's opinion:

> The object of the [Fourteenth] amendment was undoubtedly to enforce the absolute equality of the two races before the law but in the nature of things, it could not have been intended to abolish distinctions based upon color, or to enforce social, as distinguished from political equality, or a commingling of the two races upon terms unsatisfactory to either . . . *If one race be inferior to the other socially, the Constitution of the United States cannot put them on the same plane.* [Emphasis added]

Surveying the position of the Northern Negroes just after the turn of the century, the social worker and reformer Mary

White Ovington concluded that the Negro was permitted to be no more than "half a man."

The new racism took on added strength as the United States joined the European powers in assuming the white man's burden around the globe. Racist doctrine was accompanied by racist activity. A number of towns in Ohio and Indiana barred Negroes from residence, and major race riots broke out in Greenwood, South Carolina, and Wilmington, North Carolina, in 1898; in Statesboro, Georgia, and Springfield, Ohio, in 1904; in Atlanta, Georgia, Greensburg, Indiana, and Brownsville, Texas, in 1906; and in Springfield, Illinois—Abraham Lincoln's home town—in 1908. In the Springfield riots, as Mary White Ovington described it, "a mob containing many of the town's 'best citizens' raged for two days, killed and wounded scores of Negroes, and drove thousands from the city." Surveying the scene in 1908, the historian Charles Francis Adams concluded that the "melting pot" theory of assimilation of all races had broken down because of the Negro, who was "a foreign substance" that could "neither be assimilated nor thrown out." And in 1910, the critic and opponent of the "booboisie," H. L. Mencken, wrote that "The educated Negro of today is a failure, not because he meets insuperable difficulties in life, but because he is a Negro. His brain is not fitted for the higher forms of mental effort; his ideals, no matter how laboriously he is trained and sheltered, remain those of a clown. He is, in brief, a low-caste man, to the manner born, and he will remain inert and inefficient until fifty generations of him have lived in civilization. And even then, the superior white race will be fifty generations ahead of him."

▼

4

Such a history has left the Negro with a problem that cuts far deeper than whether or not to eat watermelon or listen to Negro jazz. In contrast to European immigrants, who brought rich cultures and long histories with them, the Negro has been completely stripped of his past and severed from any culture save that of the United States. In Du Bois' phrase, "there is nothing so indigenous, so completely 'made in America' as we." Yet America has steadfastly refused to accept its own product. Hence every Negro must grapple with the universal "who am I?" in a way no white man can ever know. For always the Negro must come up against the knowledge of the white world's distaste for him, and so always there remains a lingering doubt.

Moreover, the problem of Negro personality is not merely, as the psychiatrists Abram Kardiner and Lionel Ovesey have put it,* that the Negro's "self-esteem suffers because he is constantly receiving an unpleasant image of himself from the behavior of others to him." It is that the Negro begins to wonder if he really exists at all. Mistreatment and overt prejudice hurt, to be sure; the social ostracism that seems to deny the Negroes' existence hurts far more. The problem of "facelessness," as James Baldwin puts it, is the main preoccupation of Negro literature, each writer using his own metaphor to describe it. Du Bois,† for example, felt it as a sense of never being heard:

---

* *See* Abram Kardiner and Lionel Ovesey, *The Mark of Oppression,* Cleveland, Ohio: World Publishing Co., 1962.

† W. E. B. Du Bois, *Dusk of Dawn,* New York: Harcourt Brace & Co., 1940, pp. 130-131. Quoted in Myrdal, *op. cit.,* p. 680.

> It is as though one, looking out from a dark cave in a side of an impending mountain, sees the world passing and speaks to it; speaks courteously and persuasively, showing them how these entombed souls are kindred in their natural movements, expression and development; and how their loosening from prison would be a matter not simply of courtesy, sympathy, and help to them, but aid to all the world. One talks on evenly and logically in this way but notices that the passing throng does not even turn its head, or if it does, glances curiously and walks on. It gradually penetrates the minds of the prisoners that the people passing do not hear; that some thick sheet of invisible but horribly tangible plate glass is between them and the world. They get excited; they talk louder; they gesticulate. Some of the passing world stop in curiosity; these gesticulations seem to be pointless; they laugh and pass on. They still either do not hear at all, or hear but dimly, and even what they hear, they do not understand. Then the people within may become hysterical. They may scream and hurl themselves against the barriers, hardly realizing in their bewilderment that they are screaming in a vacuum unheard and that their antics may actually seem funny to those outside looking in. . . .

Ralph Ellison, uses a different metaphor—invisibility—to describe the same phenomenon. "I am an invisible man," he states in the opening paragraph of his novel:

> No, I am not a spook like those who haunted Edgar Allan Poe; nor am I one of your Hollywood-movie ectoplasms. I am a man of substance, of flesh and bone, fiber and liquids—and I might even be said to possess a mind. I am invisible, understand, simply because people refuse to see me. Like the bodiless heads you sometimes see in circus sideshows, it is as though I have been surrounded by mirrors of hard, distorting glass. When they approach me they see only my surroundings, themselves, or figments of their imagination—indeed, everything and anything except me.
>
> Nor is my invisibility exactly a matter of bio-chemical ac-

cident to my epidermis. That invisibility to which I refer occurs because of a peculiar disposition of the eyes of those with whom I come into contact. A matter of the construction of their *inner* eyes, those eyes with which they look through their physical eyes upon reality . . . It is sometimes advantageous to be unseen, although it is most often wearing on the nerves. Then, too, you're constantly being bumped against by those of poor vision. Or again, you often doubt if you really exist. You wonder whether you aren't simply a phantom in other people's minds. Say, a figure in a nightmare which the sleeper tries with all his strength to destroy. It's when you feel like this that, out of resentment, you begin to bump people back. And, let me confess, you feel that way most of the time. *You ache with the need to convince yourself that you do exist in the real world, that you're a part of all the sound and anguish, and you strike out with your fists, you curse and you swear to make them recognize you. And, alas, it's seldom successful.* [Emphasis added]

To James Baldwin, on the other hand, the problem is that "nobody knows my name."

It is not just the white man who does not know the Negro's name, however; the Negro does not know either. In the literal sense, the Negro American has never been able to decide what to call himself. The Black Muslims, for example, violently object to use of the term "Negro," which they feel connotes slavery; the Muslims insist on the term "black" or "black men," though in actual conversation even so controlled a Muslim leader as Malcolm X occasionally forgets himself and unconsciously uses the forbidden term. (A predecessor group rejected "black" as well, requiring adherents to call themselves "Asiatics," "Moors," or "Moorish Americans.") But the Muslims compound the problem of identity in another way by requiring their followers to drop their family names (derived from white former slaveowners) and use instead a first name followed by "X"—the most literal symbol of non-being, as Professor Harold Isaacs observed.* Other black nationalist groups also reject the term Negro, preferring "Afro-American" or simply "African."

Black Americans have objected to the term "Negro" off and on for a century and a half; on a number of occasions, disagreement over proper terminology has erupted into heated debate. Some object to the term because the slave traders used "Negro" as synonymous with slave; but the slave traders used the term "black" in the same way. A dictionary published in 1721 blended the terms in this way, and a century later, in a commonly cited decision, a South Carolina court held that the word "Negro" meant "slave." The term "Negro" is objectionable to other blacks because it blends so easily into *nigger* or the slurring Southern pronunciation, *Nigra,* which many find even more objectionable. The term *Negress* is most objectionable of all, purportedly because it is closely associated not only with the slave auction but with animals as well (tigress, lioness).

There is more to it than that, however. The debate over the group name has been bound up with the most fundamental questions not only of identity but of role, of the relations between blacks and whites, of the relations of people of varying shades of darkness within the black community itself: the ways in which black Americans have related (or have tried to relate) to their African origins and to contemporary Africa; and most important of all, the debate has been bound up with the ways in which black Americans have tried to find a place in the white society which has so consistently and completely excluded them. By the time of the first census in 1790, there were 59,000 free Negroes; the free blacks began to try to distinguish themselves from the slaves by calling themselves African. Thus, the institutions founded

* Professor Isaacs' book, *The New World of Negro Americans* (New York: John Day Co., 1963), is a brilliant and probing analysis of the way the rise of the African states is affecting the problem of Negro identity.

in the early years of the Republic use that adjective: the African Baptist Church (founded in 1779), the first African Lodge of Masons (1787), the African Methodist Episcopal Church (1796); the first schools established for the children of these former slaves were called "Free African Schools."

By 1830, however, "African" had fallen into disrepute among the free Negroes, probably because a concerted movement had developed among whites to persuade them to return to Africa. Since the former slaves wanted no part of any such return—they wanted instead to be admitted to full citizenship in the United States—they abandoned the label "African." By this time, moreover, a sizable group of freedmen had developed in the South. A large proportion of these people had received their freedom because they were the products of miscegenation; the freedmen were of lighter color than the slaves, and proud of it. Thus, the free Negro community of Charleston formed a "Brown Fellowship Society" which barred black men. After Emancipation, whites continued to refer to the former slaves as Negroes, and the movement to adopt the name "Afro-American" never gained much currency. The debate grew heated at the turn of the century when Booker T. Washington expressed a preference for the term "Negro." His opponents attributed this to his general submissiveness, but the debate became totally confused when W. E. B. Du Bois, the leading militant, also espoused "Negro" as well as "black"; what mattered, Du Bois insisted, was not what you were called but who you were and what your position was in society. The Garvey movement of the post-World War One era—the first significant black nationalist organization—used the term "Negro" in its title (The United Negro Improvement Association), though Garvey preferred the term "black" as an expression of racial solidarity. In the next few decades, "Negro" stuck; agitation centered over the question of spelling "Negro" with a capital "N." (The *New York Times* capitulated on March 15, 1930, with an editorial announcing its decision to use N.) And there the matter stands.

In the last analysis, the confusion and controversy over name is bound up with the most fundamental question of identity: the flight from blackness, the hatred of self, the yearning to be white. As pointed out in chapter III, the symbolism which associates black with evil, corruption, death, and despair, and white with purity, goodness, and hope is deeply rooted in human consciousness. Moreover, the symbolism is not limited to western culture; as Professor Isaacs has pointed out, it is highly visible in other cultures and predates any contact with Western Europe. In the highly stylized Chinese theater, for example, the hero's makeup is always white, the villain's always black; the same is true in the depiction of good and evil in the traditional theater of southern Asia, and in the coloring of the puppets used in the most popular traditional art of Java. The symbolism can even be found in a number of African tribes. Isaacs cites a striking example in the performances of Les Ballets Africaines, a dance troupe from the highly nationalistic state of Guinea, which toured the United States in 1959: the troupe performed a traditional, ritualistic dance depicting the theme of the duel between good and evil. Both dancers, of course, were black. But the good spirit was dressed in a white tunic and white headdress with white plume; the evil demon was identically dressed—but in black.

The symbolism which elevates white and debases black inevitably affects the consciousness of every person, white or black. As Isaacs has said, "This arrangement of things [is] communicated to all in our culture by all its modes and means, passed by osmosis through all the membranes of class, caste and colour of relationships, caressingly and painlessly injected into our children by their school texts and, even more, their story-books." It may not be true, as Lt. Joe Cable sang in *South Pacific*, that "you have to be taught to hate and fear"; our culture is so steeped in symbolism associating black with evil that it may be truer to say that "you have to be taught *not* to hate or fear."

Certainly the Negro child has to be taught not to hate himself; everything in his environment conspires to destroy any sense of his own worth. By first grade, if not sooner, Negro children feel negative about themselves. In its work with Negro and white slum children, for example, the Institute for Developmental Studies at New York Medical College gives youngsters a test in which they are asked to complete a number of sentences. One of them reads: "When I look at other boys and girls, and then look at myself, I feel ————————." Thirty per cent of the white children complete the sentence with some unfavorable judgment about how they compare to other children ("I feel ashamed," "I feel sad," etc.). But fully eighty per cent of the Negro children draw an unfavorable judgment about themselves. (The difference is not due to poverty or social class; the Negro and white youngsters come from the same social and economic background.) This self-deprecation continues and expands as the child matures.

The Negro's self-esteem suffers not only from the hurts of discrimination but also from his sense of powerlessness and impotence, his conviction that whites control everything—control everything moreover, in a manner calculated to keep him in his place. In one of the most poignant scenes in Richard Wright's *Native Son,* Bigger Thomas and his friend Gus are watching a plane skywriting.

> "You can hardly see it," Gus said.
>
> "Looks like a little bird," Bigger breathed with childlike wonder.
>
> "Them white boys sure can fly," Gus said.
>
> "Yeah," Bigger said wistfully. "They get a chance to do everything . . ."
>
> "How high you reckon he is?" Bigger asked.
>
> "I don't know. Maybe a hundred miles; maybe a thousand."

"I could fly one of them things if I had the chance," Bigger mumbled reflectively, as though talking to himself.

Gus pulled down the corners of his lips, stepped out from the wall, squared his shoulders, doffed his cap bowed low and spoke with mock confidence.

"Yessuh."

"You go to hell," Bigger said, smiling.

"Yessuh," Gus said agin.

"I *could* fly a plane if I had a chance," Bigger said.

"If you wasn't black and if you had some money and if they'd let you go to that aviation school, you *could* fly a plane," Gus said.

For a moment, Bigger contemplated all the "ifs" that Gus had mentioned. Then both boys broke into hard laughter, looking at each other through squinted eyes. When their laughter subsided, Bigger said in a voice that was half-question and half-statement:

"It's funny how white folks treat us, ain't it?"

"It better be funny," Gus said.

"Maybe they right in not wanting us to fly," Bigger said. " 'Cause if I took a plane up, I'd take a couple of bombs along and drop 'em sure as hell. . . ." *

The sense of powerlessness is particularly destructive to Negro men, for masculinity is closely tied to power in our society. To survive the blows to his ego and potency, the Negro must erect a number of defenses. The most common is withdrawal. Low self-esteem quite naturally produces a fear of failure in any new or unfamiliar situation: school, job, marriage. But if you do not involve yourself in the task in the first place, you can excuse your failure very easily: you failed because you did not try, not because you were incompetent; if you had really cared, you could have succeeded.

This tendency to withdraw affects not just the Negro's capacity to compete but his ability to relate to other people. Negro men have much greater difficulty than white men

---

* Richard Wright, *Native Son*, New York: Harper & Row, Publishers, Inc., 1957.

playing the usual male role. Partly because of prejudice, partly because of their own lack of education and training, they have difficulty finding work that will enable them to support their families. The result, inevitably, is a feeling of shame and failure. But the man's ego is too frail to withstand any further blows; to avoid hating himself still more, he turns his hatred against his family, or simply cuts off any feelings for them at all. Bigger Thomas is a classic example:

> Vera went behind the curtain and Bigger heard her trying to comfort his mother. He shut their voices out of his mind. He hated his family because he knew that they were suffering and that he was powerless to help them. He knew that the moment he allowed himself to feel to its fullness how they lived, the shame and misery of their lives, he would be swept out of himself with fear and despair. So he held toward them an attitude of iron reserve; he lived with them, but behind a wall, a curtain. And toward himself he was even more exacting. He knew that the moment he allowed what his life meant to enter fully into his consciousness, he would either kill himself or someone else. So he denied himself and acted tough.

This denial extends to Bigger's friends as well as his family. Thus, Bigger starts a fight with Gus, his closest friend, because he is afraid to go through with the robbery of a white storekeeper that the boys had planned.

> Like a man staring regretfully but hopelessly at the stump of a cutoff arm or leg, he knew that the fear of robbing a white man had had hold of him when he started that fight with Gus; but he knew it in a way that kept it from coming to his mind in the form of a hard and sharp idea. His confused emotions had made him feel instinctively that it would be better to fight Gus and spoil the plan of the robbery than to confront a white man with a gun. But he kept this knowledge of his fear thrust firmly down in him; his courage to live depended on how successfully his fear was

> hidden from his consciousness. He had fought Gus because Gus was late; that was the reason his emotions accepted and he did not try to justify himself in his own eyes, or in the eyes of the gang. He did not think enough of them to feel that he had to; he did not consider himself as being responsible to them for what he did, even though they had been involved as deeply as he in the planned robbery. He felt that same way toward everybody. As long as he could remember, he had never been responsible to anyone. The moment a situation became so that it exacted something of him, he rebelled. That was the way he lived; he passed his days trying to defeat or gratify powerful impulses in a world he feared.

Male impotence and withdrawal, moreover, both stem from and contribute to a strong matriarchal tradition. Under slavery, such family life as existed centered inevitably around the woman. A variety of economic and social factors since Emancipation have kept the woman in the dominant role. Because her husband cannot support the family, the Negro wife goes to work; she has an easier time finding a job than her husband, since domestic work is almost always available. But the reversal of roles almost invariably poisons the marital relationship, a theme which John A. Williams sensitively explored in his novel, *Sissie.** Sissie's unemployed husband Ralph insists that she prepare dinner for him, no matter how tired she is:

> "I don't give a goddamn how hard you been out workin—when you get your backside in here, remember you're my wife, and you're supposed to cook my damned dinner and don't ever forget it."
>
> Sissie's perpetual reply was, "Sure I'm your wife, but I'm not the man in the house; you're the man, but you don't act like it. Somebody's got to be the man here and make some money to bring in here, and it sure ain't you!"

* John A. Williams, *Sissie,* New York: Farrar, Strauss, & Cudahy, 1963.

> Ralph would stalk out, slamming the door.
>
> Sissie, left in the vacuum of silence which was broken only by the questions put to her by her son, would ask herself, Why couldn't he find work? Why was it that all the men paced the streets mornings, heads bent, steps slow? At what point had she become the man and he less the man than he had seemed to be? . . . She wanted him to be a man but knew he couldn't; vaguely she perceived that the fault was not his, yet she couldn't find out whose fault it was. . . .

The result, all too frequently, is more than just psychic withdrawal. Unable to play the usual male role, the husband all too often tries to demonstrate his potency through a display of sexual prowess. But the effort fails as it must, and so he begins to wander and ultimately leaves for good. Her husband's desertion, meanwhile, helps confirm what the wife had suspected all along—that men are just no good; her father had deserted *her* mother, and so she had learned in childhood to distrust men—a fact that had interfered with her ability to help her own husband. Her hatred of men reflects itself in the way she brings up her own children: the sons can fend for themselves but her daughters must be prepared so that they will not have to go through what she has gone through. (Considerably more Negro girls than boys go to college, for example; among whites, the reverse is true.) And so the matriarchy perpetuates itself.

So does self-hatred. Self-hatred is manifested in a number of ways. The most obvious is the use of hair straighteners, skin bleaches, and the like in the desperate but futile attempt to come close to the white ideal. ("NADINOLA brightens your opportunities for romance just as swiftly and surely as it brightens and lightens your skin"; "Hair straightened the famous PERMA-STRATE way looks and manages just as if it were *naturally* straight . . . for three months or more!") Pursuit of the white ideal in this way not only is a symptom of self-hate; it is a path that leads, inevitably, to further self-hatred and to perpetual frustration—as Kardiner and Ovesey wrote in *The Mark of Oppression,* "a slow but cumulative and fatal psychological poison." Fatal, because the Negro can never become white.

Self-hatred is evident also in the caste of color that still infects the Negro community, though to a lesser extent than before. "Anyone who has been part of a family of mixed bloods in the United States or the West Indies," the novelist Pauli Murray has written, "has lived intimately with the unremitting search for whiteness. To deny that it is part of one's heritage would be like saying one had no parents." Indeed, Miss Murray describes her childhood as a never-ending obsession with color:

> The world revolved on color and variations in color. It pervaded the air I breathed. I learned it in hundreds of ways. I picked it up from grown folks around me. I heard it in the house, on the playground, in the streets, everywhere.
>
> Always the same tune, played like a broken record, robbing one of personal identity . . . It was color, color, color all the time . . . Two shades lighter! Two shades darker! Dead white! Coal black! High yaller! Mariny! Good hair! Bad hair! Stringy hair! Nappy hair! Thin lips! Thick lips! Red lips! . . .

Among the lower classes, moreover, self-hatred is expressed also in apathy (See chapter III): there is no use trying anything, joining anything, doing anything, because you are just no damned good—"Been down so long that down don't bother me," runs an old Negro blues song. Among the middle and upper classes, who have come close to white society and thus resent all the more their inability to *become* white, self-hatred frequently leads to a flight from reality, or at the very least, to an attempt to escape any association with the Negro lower class. The pressure is all the greater because housing segregation makes it so difficult for middle- and upper-income Negroes to escape physically, the way upwardly-mobile European ethnics were able to do. Hence the Negro who has "made it" feels a dreadful compulsion to escape psychologically—to avoid any association with his less cultivated brethren, to show by his manner of living that he is not one of *them.*

The black bourgeoisie's distaste for the Negro lower class is returned in kind. Lower-class Negroes tend to resent the "dickety" upper class, particularly those members who have achieved success in the white world.

A terrible vacuum of leadership results. For one thing, as soon as a Negro leader gains acceptance from the white community—as soon as he is able to move with ease among whites, and raise money from them—he loses his rapport with the lower-class Negroes, who resent his "going white" and accuse him of becoming "a white man's Nigger." Thus the spectacle, in the summer of 1963, of Martin Luther King being pelted with eggs in Harlem as he arrived to address a church rally.* If "the masses refuse to follow their leaders, moreover, the leaders generally refuse to lead." Writing about the Negro upper and middle class in 1899, Du Bois pointed out that

> . . . in general its members are curiously hampered by the fact that, being shut off from the world about them, they are the aristocracy of their own people, with all the responsibilities of an aristocracy, and yet they, on the one hand, are not prepared for this role, and their own masses are not used to looking to them for leadership. As a class, they feel strongly the centrifugal forces of class repulsion. . . . They do not relish being mistaken for servants; they shrink from the free and easy worship of most of the Negro churches, and they shrink from all such display and publicity as will expose them to the veiled insult and deprecia-

* Dr. King is, pre-eminently, the leader of the middle-class and would-be-middle-class Negroes. A good many—though certainly not all—lower-class Negroes resent Dr. King and his philosophy of non-violence.

> tion which the masses suffer. Consequently this class, which ought to lead, refuses to head any race movement on the plea that they draw the very color line against which they protest.

Du Bois' observations still obtain. When a Negro educator and civic leader in one of the large eastern cities formed a social work agency for adolescents a few years ago, she had difficulty persuading her friends to assist her in providing guidance to Negro youngsters; indeed, many friends stopped visiting the woman and her husband for fear of contact with the slum children who, in the early years, met in their home. Even now, when the program has demonstrated its ability to motivate Negro children to go to college, the director has great difficulty recruiting volunteers from the Negro community; she frequently has to pay "volunteers" to guarantee their appearance on the days promised. Following the riots in Birmingham during the summer of 1963, Rev. Wyatt T. Walker, executive director of the Southern Christian Leadership Council, expressed great bitterness over white reporters' failure to distinguish between the rioters and the people who had staged the non-violent demonstrations downtown. "All Negroes are the same to you," he told a group of reporters. "Those rioters the other night were hoodlums, winos from over on Fourth Avenue. *None of them were our people*, but you can't see the difference. They were all just Negroes to you." [Emphasis added]

V

CIVIL RIGHTS AND SELF-IMPROVEMENT

> Man has to live with the body and soul which have fallen to him by chance. And the first thing he has to do is decide what he is going to do.
>
> —ORTEGA Y GASSET

1

So much for the diagnosis of "the Negro problem." What is the solution?

Not the panacea of "acculturation," certainly, dear as that concept is to academic sociologists and historians and to the foundation "philanthropoids." The differences between the Negro migration and the earlier European immigration, it should now be clear, are differences of kind, not just degree. Hence "acculturation" is not enough. It doesn't come to grips with Negro hatred of "the man" and of himself; and it leaves white prejudice completely untouched.

The civil rights approach traditionally advocated by the National Association for the Advancement of Colored People (NAACP), and by newer groups like the Congress on Racial Equality (CORE) and the Southern Christian Leadership Conference (SCLC), is inadequate, too. For the civil rights movement is based on two assumptions: that "the Negro problem" is predominantly a white man's problem; and that the problem will be solved by giving Negroes full civil rights. It makes little attempt, therefore, to solve the Negro's "Negro problem." But "the Negro problem" is as much a black man's as a white man's problem.

The growth of Negro militancy in the area of civil rights has evoked a good deal of finger-wagging on the part of whites, who, like John Fischer of *Harper's*, believe that Negroes should place more emphasis on self-improvement. This view is particularly common among members of ethnic groups whose acceptance in American society is recent and still a little tentative, and who resent the growing Negro demands for equality. "There is a widespread feeling among the minorities," Stewart Alsop and Oliver Quayle reported in "What Northerners Really Think of Negroes" (*Saturday Evening Post*, September 7, 1963) "that the Negroes, in the words of Mr. Ray Yoshiyama of Gardena, California, 'haven't worked their way up.' " What these minority-group members are saying, in effect, is that *we* faced severe discrimination (Yoshiyama spent his boyhood in a World War Two detention camp), but that we scraped and saved and worked and studied, and that, by God, we *earned* the status we now enjoy; why don't the Negroes do the same? Why don't they *prove* their right to equality?

One cogent answer to this argument, of course, is that neither the Declaration of Independence nor the Constitution suggests that equality be earned. It is a right of citizenship, and Negroes need make no apologies for demanding now what they have always been entitled to, and what they have been denied for three hundred and fifty years. But the question is a good deal more complex. It is essential that whites understand the reasons for the Negroes' single-minded pursuit of civil rights, and that they understand the fury they arouse in Negro audiences when they suggest more emphasis on self-improvement.

This understanding requires just a bit of historical perspective. The NAACP, which until recently *was* the civil rights movement, and which still dominates it, was founded and shaped by two principal forces. One was the revulsion felt by a small group of white liberals—Mary White Ovington, William English Walling, Dr. Henry Moskowitz, Jane Addams, Henry Garrison Villard, Rabbi Stephen Wise, among others—over the outbreaks of anti-Negro violence during the first decade of the century. The other was the great debate at the end of the nineteenth and beginning of the twentieth century between Booker T. Washington and W. E. B. Du Bois over the proper goals and strategy for Negro activity. That debate helped create a climate of opinion which, until today, has made the call for self-improvement and the demand for civil rights seem like opposites, and which, in Negro minds, has indissolubly tied any call for self-improvement to abject surrender, accommodation, and "Uncle Tomism."

In this day of intense competition for Negro leadership, it is hard to imagine the total monopoly Booker T. Washington enjoyed for almost a third of a century. No white philanthropist made a grant to a Negro cause, no public official appointed a Negro to office or took a position affecting Negroes without consulting first with Washington. Washington gained this status in part by the force of his own personality, in part by his skill in cutting possible rivals down to size, but in good measure because he told white Southerners and Northerners what they wanted to hear. For Washington urged Negroes to improve themselves economically before seeking political or social equality. When Negroes had demonstrated their worth by producing industrious workers and successful businessmen, he argued—when they were "prepared" for equality—whites would be willing to grant them "all privileges of law." The best course of action in the meantime would be to emphasize the sort of education that would make Negroes an efficient labor force.

Everything followed logically from that premise; Washington was above all a "realist," a politician dealing with "the art of the possible." On the one hand, he reasoned, Negroes lacked the resources to build a network of vocational schools; on the other hand, white Southerners would not grant that support, unless they were convinced that a docile labor force would result. Expediency demanded, therefore, that Negroes accept the prevailing caste system and accommodate themselves to it. Washington had built his career on precisely this sort of expediency; three years after he opened Tuskegee Institute in 1881, the Alabama State Legislature—convinced that Washington would not oppose the status quo—granted the school an annual appropriation.

But Washington was as much a moralist as a politician. His own life demonstrated—or so it seemed to him—that starting at the bottom gave a man an opportunity for moral development that those starting higher on the ladder were denied. Indeed, Washington at times seemed almost pleased that whites had made it possible for Negroes to start out with absolutely nothing. A program that began as mere expediency, therefore, was rapidly elevated into an absolute principle—in Du Bois' phrase, "into a veritable way of life." By the time Washington delivered his famous speech at the opening of the Cotton States and International Exposition in Atlanta in 1895, expediency and morality had become fused into one. The great theme of the speech was the exhortation—delivered to white and black alike—to "cast down your bucket where you are."

> Our greatest danger is that in the great leap from slavery to freedom we may overlook the fact that the masses of us are to live by the productions of our hands, and fail to keep in mind that we shall prosper in proportion as we learn to dignify and glorify common labor and put brains and skill into the common occupations of life; shall prosper in proportion as we learn to draw the line between the superficial and the substantial, the ornamental gewgaws of life and the useful.
>
> No race can prosper till it learns that there is as much dignity in tilling a field as in writing a poem. It is at the bottom of life we must begin, and not at the top. Nor should we permit our grievances to overshadow our opportunities.

> To those of the white race who look to the incoming of those of foreign birth and strange tongue and habits, were I permitted I would repeat what I say to my own race, "Cast down your bucket among those people who have, without strikes and labor wars, tilled your fields, cleared your forests, builded your railroads and cities, and brought forth treasures from the bowels of the earth. . . .

And, Washington solemnly promised that if the whites would only follow his advice to use Negro rather than European immigrant labor, "you and your families will be surrounded by the most patient, faithful, law-abiding, and unresentful people that the world has ever seen.

> As we have proved our loyalty to you in the past, in nursing your children, watching by the sick-bed of your mothers and fathers, and often following them with tear-dimmed eyes to their graves, so in the future in our humble way, we shall stand by you with a devotion that no foreigner can approach, ready to lay down our lives, if need be, in defense of yours, interlacing our industrial, commercial, civil and religious life with yours in a way that shall make the interests of both races one. In all things that are purely social we can be separate as the fingers, yet one as the hand in all things essential to mutual progress . . .
>
> The wisest among my race understand that the agitation of questions of social equality is the extremest folly, and that progress in the enjoyment of all the privileges that will come to us must be the result of severe and constant struggle rather than of artificial forcing. No race that has anything to contribute to the market of the world is long in any degree ostracized. It is important and right that all privileges of the law be ours, but it is vastly more important that we be prepared for the exercise of these privileges. The opportunity to earn a dollar in a factory just now is worth infinitely more than the opportunity to spend a dollar in an opera-house.

The speech earned Washington a tumultuous ovation; when he concluded, Governor Bullock of Georgia rushed across the platform to congratulate him; newspapers throughout the country praised the speech editorially and printed it in full; President Grover Cleveland sent him a letter of congratulations. Washington had become a hero to the whites. He still is a hero to segregationists like David Lawrence, the ultra-conservative political columnist and editor of *U.S. News & World Report,* who quoted at length from the Atlanta Exposition speech in a September, 1963, column attacking the Negro protest movement.

In the view of most thoughtful Negroes, however, Washington's strategy was as ill-advised in 1895 as it seems today. Indeed, this most "practical" and "realistic" of politicians was in fact impractical and unrealistic. For one thing, Washington's moralistic infatuation with the soil and with manual labor, and his concern over the "evils" of urban life and the "impracticality" of liberal education blinded him to the enormous changes that were taking place in the American economy. ("I would much rather see a young colored man graduate from college and go out and start a truck garden, a dairy farm, or conduct a cotton plantation, and thus become a first-hand producer of wealth," he said, "than [become] a parasite living upon the wealth originally produced by others, seeking uncertain and unsatisfactory livelihood in temporary and questionable positions.") The result was to leave Negroes completely unprepared for the Great Migration to the cities that had already gotten underway when Washington delivered his Atlanta Speech. (See chapter II.) As Du Bois put it thirty years later, "My opposition to Dr. Washington was . . . based upon the fact that he taught Colored children to use certain tools which were almost always obsolete by the time they had finished their course."

More important, Washington failed to understand the emasculating effects of the Southern caste system; indeed, he helped create it. That is to say, by urging Negroes to give up any interest in political power and to abandon any effort to secure their civil rights, Washington strengthened the forces which were moving toward total disfranchisement of the Negro and erection of a legal system of segregation. Nor did he ever understand that the Jim Crow system he urged Negroes to accept made impossible the initiative he was trying to create—that submission and accommodation served only to sap Negro manhood and to destroy Negro aspirations. Indeed, as late as 1912, Washington was telling whites that "we are trying to instill into the Negro mind that if education does not make the Negro humble, simple, and of service to the community, then it will not be encouraged."

Inevitably, therefore, Negro voices rose to attack Washington's doctrine. The most eloquent was that of Du Bois. "Mr. Washington represents in Negro thought the old attitude of adjustment and submission," Du Bois wrote in 1903 in *The Souls of Black Folk,* "but adjustment at such a peculiar time as to make his program unique . . . In other periods of intensified prejudice all the Negro's tendency to self-assertion has been called forth; at this period a policy of submission is advocated. In the history of nearly all other races and people, the doctrine preached at such crises has been that manly self-respect is worth more than land and houses, and that a people who voluntarily surrender such respect, or cease striving for it, are not worth civilizing." And so Du Bois called on Negroes to "unceasingly and firmly oppose" Washington's doctrine.

The issue was joined. Washington had indissolubly linked the idea of self-improvement to that of accommodation and submission. Now, Du Bois' voice began to be heard in defense of Frederick Douglass' older strategy of "assimilation through self-assertion." "By every civilized and peaceful method," he argued, "we must strive for the rights which the world accords to men." In 1905, he issued a personal call to a number of sympathetic Negro intellectuals to create a new organization to counter Washington's monopoly on Negro leadership and to "organize thoroughly the intelligent and honest Negroes throughout the United States for the purpose of insisting on manhood rights, industrial opportunity and spiritual freedom." The result was the formation of the "Niagara Movement." At the movement's second annual meeting in 1906, held at Harper's Ferry to pay tribute to the memory of John Brown, Du Bois stated the militants' goals:

> We want full manhood suffrage and we want it now . . . We want discrimination in public accommodation to cease . . . We claim the right of freemen to walk, talk, and be with them that wish to be with us . . . We want the Constitution of the country enforced . . . We want our children educated . . . And here on the scene of John Brown's martyrdom we reconsecrate ourselves, our honor, our property to the final emancipation of the race which John Brown died to make free . . . We are men! We will be treated as men. And we shall win.

The Niagara Movement was short-lived and seemingly accomplished little. It was racked by internal discord and handicapped by sniping from the Negro press, which Booker T. Washington controlled (and some of which he subsidized or bribed to keep on his side). Washington's own opposition, moreover, cut the movement off from the few wealthy or influential whites who might have been sympathetic. The movement was handicapped also by the fact that its members were psychologically isolated from the great mass of Negroes in the United States. If Washington overemphasized the importance of jobs and underemphasized the need for civil rights, Du Bois and his colleagues of the Niagara Movement made the opposite mistake. Washington wanted to teach every Negro a humble trade; the result was to keep Negroes humble. Du Bois was relatively disinterested in the mass of Negroes; in his view, salvation would come through the education and training of an intellectual elite, the so-called "Talented Tenth." He himself was an aristocrat with little interest in social action and no inclination to make contact with the masses of poor and uneducated Negroes.

Even so, the long-run impact of the Niagara Movement was as great as its short-term accomplishments were small. As the first national organization to insist, without qualification, that Negroes be granted the same civil rights that whites enjoyed, it laid down a strategy of protest that was to guide Negroes and whites for a long time to come: an attempt to invalidate racist laws through sponsoring and financing test cases; and an attempt to organize a political lobby supported by articulate public opinion. For the Niagara Movement fell apart in 1909, just as a group of white liberals was organizing the National Negro Committee. Du Bois and several of his associates joined with Miss Ovington, Villard, Walling, Dr. Moskowitz and other white liberals in organizing the new group—whose name was changed in 1910 to the National Association for the Advancement of Colored People. At the 1910 conference, Du Bois was elected Director of Publications and Research, and as editor of the monthly magazine, *The Crisis,* he dominated the organization for the next twenty years.

To a considerable degree, therefore, the civil rights movement developed as a reaction against the accommodation and "Uncle Tomism" of Booker T. Washington. But this reaction represented considerably more than just a clash of personalities; to use the jargon of the sociologists, the formation of the NAACP was a response to a "felt need." In the decade preceding the Springfield riots of 1908—the event that precipitated formation of the NAACP—an average of two Negroes a week had been lynched, and terror had become a principal means of forcing the Southern Negroes back into their servile place. It was not the only means; as we have seen in chapter II, this was also the period in which the Jim Crow system developed, and in which Negroes were systematically deprived of their franchise. In this atmosphere, it would have been surprising had the NAACP *not* considered the establishment and protection of civil rights to be the dominant problem.

Nor is it hard to understand why civil rights has remained

the NAACP's main preoccupation. In this day of racial change and Negro self-assertion, it is difficult to recall the atmosphere of terror and intimidation under which the great majority of Negroes lived only twenty or thirty years ago. As recently as 1930, for example, well over half the Negroes of the United States were still living in the rural areas of the Old Confederacy, and more than half the remainder were in the cities and towns of the South. By 1940, the rural proportion had dropped a bit, but two-thirds of all Negroes were still living in the Deep South. And what was life like for them? Here is Gunnar Myrdal's clinical report as of 1944: *

> It is the custom in the South to permit whites to resort to violence and threats of violence against the life, personal security, property, and freedom of movement of Negroes. There is a wide variety of behavior, ranging from a mild admonition to murder, which the white man may exercise to control Negroes. While the practice has its origin in the slavery tradition, it continues to flourish because of the laxity and inequity of the administration of law and justice . . . [The spirit of slavery has] prevailed in the complex of laws protecting the planters' interests—labor enticement laws, crop lien laws, vagrancy laws—by which the states sanctioned the actions of the police and the courts in virtually upholding peonage . . .
>
> But quite apart from laws, and even against the law, there exists a pattern of violence against Negroes in the South upheld by the relative absence of fear of legal reprisal. *Any white man can strike or beat a Negro, steal or destroy his property, cheat him in a transaction and even take his life, without much fear of legal reprisal.* [Emphasis added] The minor forms of violence—cheating and striking—are a matter of everyday occurrence . . . Of course, there are certain checks on violence . . . Public opinion in the South tends to frown upon any white man who acquires the reputation for being consistently mean or dishonest . . . But the general attitude is one of laisser faire: if a planta-

* Myrdal, *op. cit.*

tion owner cheats or beats his Negro tenants, "that's his business"; if a Negro is the victim of a sudden outburst of violence, "he must have done something to deserve it." Above all, the Negro must be kept in his "place."

He still is kept in his place in most of Mississippi and Alabama, where governors openly defy the Federal Government, and in the small towns of Georgia, South Carolina, and indeed most of the states of the Old Confederacy. It is no criticism of the NAACP, therefore, to say that its program does not constitute a panacea; Negroes could not hold their heads aloft if first priority had not been given to the demand for equal treatment.

And yet the fact remains that a good deal more is needed, particularly as Negroes become residents of the big cities of the North rather than the villages and towns of the South. For one thing, the "traditional" civil rights approach does not come to grips with prejudice that is unsupported by legal discrimination. Northern whites are perfectly willing to grant Negroes their formal rights as citizens; but they have been unwilling, so far, to grant the social acceptance that would make those rights meaningful. In interviewing a national sample of Northern whites for the *Saturday Evening Post,* Stewart Alsop and Oliver Quayle discovered a common pattern of talk:

> "The colored got rights, just like us whites, *but* I don't see why we got to mingle together."
>
> "They're human beings just like the rest of us, *but* I wouldn't want one living next door."
>
> "Sure, they deserve a break, *but* look what happens to property values when they move into a neighborhood."

Almost every statement of sympathy or support was accompanied by a "but" that revealed deep-seated hostility or fear. Public opinion analyst Louis Harris reached the same conclusion in a larger series of interviews he conducted for

Newsweek. While whites outside the South were in favor of expanding Negroes' formal rights—for example, they favored the Civil Rights bill then being debated in Congress—their prejudice almost always showed when the questioning was pushed far enough. "There is some point at which most white Americans draw the line at the prospect of closer association with Negroes," *Newsweek* reported. That point usually involved physical association, for example, Negroes moving into a white neighborhood.

The net effect has been the great Northern invention, de facto segregation. For the last ten years, one Northern city after another has passed new laws and strengthened old laws forbidding discrimination in housing, employment, and the like. It would be a gross exaggeration to say that these laws have had no effect. In New York, for example, Negroes now shop quite freely at the midtown department stores, whereas before World War Two most stores strongly discouraged a potential Negro clientele. And Negro sales clerks are conspicuous in virtually every store catering to the mass market and even in some appealing only to a luxury clientele. Yet the fact remains that having destroyed the last vestiges of de jure segregation, Negro civil rights groups find themselves up against the much more difficult, and much more frustrating, problem of de facto segregation of neighborhoods and consequently of schools.

More important, the emphasis on civil rights does not begin to deal with the Negro's "Negro problem." The NAACP's preoccupation with rooting out white discrimination and insuring equal treatment for Negroes has led it, consciously or otherwise, to see "the problem" as exclusively a white man's problem, which will be solved when whites grant Negroes the rights which are morally and legally theirs. This emphasis on changing white behavior and attitudes and laws in turn has led the organization to eschew any attempt to involve the great mass of Negroes in action on their own behalf. Perhaps the most telling criticism of this failure ever made was contained in one of the memoranda Dr. Ralph

Bunche (now a member of the NAACP's board of directors) wrote in 1941 while assisting Gunnar Myrdal in the preparation of *An American Dilemma:* "The NAACP does not have a mass basis. It has never assumed the proportion of a crusade, nor has it ever, in any single instance, attracted the masses of people to its banner. It is not impressed upon the mass consciousness, and it is a bald truth that the average Negro in the street has never heard of the Association nor of any of its leaders. It has shown a pitiful lack of knowledge of mass technique and of how to pitch an appeal so as to reach the ears of the masses." Asked to comment on Bunche's criticism, Roy Wilkins, then Assistant Secretary of the NAACP and editor of *The Crisis*, replied that "we recognize our lack of skill at mass appeal, and I believe we are on our way to doing something about it." Walter White, the Executive Secretary, also conceded that "we have not yet found the formula for selling to the public the nature, the extent, the details, and the significance of the Association's program." But White was less optimistic than Wilkins. "Some have suggested that we might follow the example of Marcus Garvey and others in the utilization of fancy titles and robes," he continued. "The Association, however, has felt that reverting to some of these methods of attracting the masses would do more harm in the long run to the organization, than good."

White's reply to Bunche's criticism reveals the very weakness Bunche was criticizing: a strong distaste for the techniques that seemed to be necessary to "attract the masses" and, by implication, a decision to forgo the attempt altogether. Garvey, a West Indian Negro who emigrated to the United States in 1916, founded the first and in many ways the most successful mass-based Negro movement. Millions of Negroes were stirred by Garvey's call for African unity and his appeal to race pride. "Up, you mighty race," Garvey thundered to men and women who had always thought themselves worthless, "you can accomplish what you will . . . The Negro of yesterday has disappeared from the scene of human activities and his place is taken by a new Negro who stands erect, conscious of his manhood rights and fully determined to preserve them at all costs."

If Garvey was a hero to the uneducated, improverished Negroes of the large cities, he was a repugnant mountebank and charlatan and dangerous demagogue to virtually every educated Negro. For one thing, Garvey's appeal to pride in blackness was accompanied by a demand for racial separatism (he even praised the Ku Klux Klan) and a denunciation of Negroes of mixed blood, which included virtually all Negro intellectuals. For another, middle-class Negroes who had spent a large part of their time and energy trying to escape the stereotype of the childlike buffoon could hardly avoid being repelled by Garvey's posturing and posing. He had himself proclaimed Provisional President of the African Republic and appeared in public in a resplendent uniform complete with plumed hat, accompanied by deputies bearing such titles as Supreme Potentate and the like. The Faithful followers were rewarded with membership in honorary orders like the Knights of the Nile and the Distinguished Service Order of Ethiopia. Worst of all, Garvey's organization was characterized by constant bickering and monumental mismanagement and chicanery. His Black Star Line, formed to demonstrate the value of self-improvement and especially of Negro business activity, managed to dissipate completely its $750,000 capital in less than three years, ending in bankruptcy with a cash balance of $31.12. (Nearly forty thousand Negroes had bought shares in the company.) In 1923, Garvey was convicted of using the mails to defraud* and was sent to the federal penitentiary in Atlanta. He was pardoned and deported in 1927 and died in London in 1940 in almost total obscurity.

---

* In the opinion of his biographer, Edmund D. Cronon (*Black Moses: The Story of Marcus Garvey,* Madison, Wisconsin: University of Wisconsin Press, 1962) and other scholars, Garvey was innocent of any intent to defraud. His crime—like that of Warren G. Harding—was placing confidence in his almost unbelievably venal subordinates.

Garvey appeared, built his movement, and faded from the scene in just seven tumultuous years, yet his impact was profound and lasting. To large numbers of Negroes, he brought a desperately needed message: that their blackness was a badge of honor, not of shame. As Professor Harold Issacs has said, "The inner shame over blackness was by no means exorcised, but after Garvey it was never again quite the same as it had been." But Garvey's racist appeal served to widen the already large breach between "the Talented Tenth" and the rest of the Negro population. And his bizarre posturing and parading, together with the collapse of his Black Star Line, created a distaste for mass movements that was evident twenty years later in Walter White's defense of the NAACP's narrow appeal.

The distaste lingers. To be sure, Roy Wilkins was willing to admit, twenty years ago, that the NAACP lacked skill at mass appeal. It still does. Wilkins is brilliant, articulate, thoughtful, but pallid; he utterly lacks the "charisma" (or ability to evoke mass support) that marks such diverse personalities as Rev. Martin Luther King and Elijah Muhammad. In a sense, Wilkins' thoughtfulness is his curse. He has a temperament that sees issues in all their complexity; he lacks the capacity to define problems in the simple, stark, all-or-nothing way necessary to arouse people from their apathy. His appeal, in short (and it is a considerable appeal), is cerebral, not emotional. There is a measure of truth in Adam Clayton Powell's prideful boast that whereas he is surrounded with admirers wherever he goes in Harlem—with almost every step there is a "Hi, Adam" from someone—Wilkins could walk down Lenox Avenue from 155th Street to 110th Street (the length of Harlem) without being hailed.

The problem transcends that of personality, however; it goes to the heart of what constitutes a mass movement. Walter White's reply to Bunche's criticism was particularly revealing in this context: "We have not yet found the formula *for selling to the public* the nature, the extent, the details, and the significance of the Association's program," he wrote

Myrdal, as if building a mass movement depended only on successful public relations. [Emphasis added] Wilkins betrays the same blindness. "You have to give it to CORE and Martin King," he has said. "They know how to dramatize their wares; people know what they have to sell. Somehow we have failed to do this; people don't know about our apples and peaches and potatoes. And because they don't know, they conclude we do not have anything for sale." But mass movements (or at any rate, mass movements among disadvantaged peoples) are built not on skill in selling "apples and peaches and potatoes" to a passive, inert audience, but on the ability to articulate a people's real, if unconscious, grievances, and to propose a course of action that conquers their apathy and converts them from an inert mass to an active movement. To see the role of leadership as one of establishing proper goals and then of "selling" them to the public is to misunderstand completely the nature of mass leadership.

And what are the sources of discontent among "the black masses"? Not segregation per se, certainly, for lower-class Negroes are too contemptuous and too fearful of white culture. Squalid housing, a narrow range of job possibilities, frequent unemployment, low pay, exploitation (whether real or imagined) by landlords, shopkeepers, and employers, police brutality—these are the grievances that animate the Negroes who live in the big-city slums. But these are issues the NAACP considers outside its purview. "The grievances themselves are genuine enough," Dr. John Morsell, Assistant to the Executive Secretary, has written in *The Crisis*. "The police are frequently brutal, other Negroes are often insensitive to the needs of the disadvantaged, and exploitation is not unknown on the part of landlords, shopkeepers and employers." But "*for the very reason that these are essentially class, not racial grievances*," Dr. Morsell continued, "*they cannot properly be top priority items in organizational programs which are committed to the struggle against racial wrongs*. Such problems are thus not within direct reach of the organized efforts in which aggrieved Negroes are accustomed to think of themselves as being (actually or potentially) involved on a personal basis." [Emphasis added] Dr. Morsell is right, of course, in suggesting that problems of bad housing, poor jobs, and so on, involve questions of social class, not just race—though he exaggerates the former and underestimates the latter. But the Negro poor are not able to make such fine distinctions; they know only that they are black, and that they are exploited and cheated. To rule their concerns out of bounds is to abandon in advance any hope of building a mass base.

▼

2

The failure of the NAACP to stir the emotions has encouraged the growth of a number of new organizations, the most prominent being "direct action" organizations like CORE, SCLC, and the Student Non-Violent Coordinating Committee —SNCC or "Snick." Enthusiasts like the militant journalist Louis E. Lomax have hailed these movements as evidences of a "Negro revolt"—a revolt directed as much against the established Negro leadership as against the so-called "white power structure."

The revolt is not as far-reaching as Lomax and others would like to think. The energies which CORE, SCLC, and "Snick" have mobilized have been directed, for the most part, at the same goals sought through quieter means by the NAACP: desegregation of lunch counters, railroad and bus terminals, washrooms, drinking fountains, and more recently, employment of more Negroes in stores and factories.* To a considerable degree, moreover, the newer organizations have felt free to use dramatic means like sit-ins and street demonstrations because they felt confident the NAACP and the separate NAACP Legal Defense and Education Fund stood ready to defend all those who might be arrested. The legal expenses that resulted from the Freedom Rides, for example, were roughly fifteen times as great as the cost of the Rides themselves, and in the Birmingham demonstrations in the spring of 1963, in which hundreds were arrested, the NAACP took care of all the legal work. Roy Wilkins could hardly be blamed for his outburst in the summer of 1963 complaining that the NAACP was receiving less than its fair share of credit or support. "Day in and day out," he said, "we're working for integration, not in one spectacular flash, but steady, steady all the time. Who tackles the sticky stuff after the headlines die down?" Wilkins asked rhetorically. "I'll tell you who tackles it. The NAACP. Nobody else can do this. We have organization and ability to proceed. Who carries it out and on? The NAACP. Who inspires it? Dr. King."

Yet differences in means can sometimes be as important as differences in ends. The defect of the traditional NAACP approach is not that it is ineffective but that, in Lomax's phrase, it achieves its goals by "doing the job for the people, rather than having the people do the job themselves." The upshot, all too often, is that when the NAACP has won a victory through the courts or through negotiation, few Negroes come forward to claim the right. The main contribution of the newer protest groups is that they *have* involved large numbers of Negroes in action on their own behalf. Not only

* Rev. Martin Luther King has spoken at times as though he had other goals in mind as well. "We have become so involved in trying to wipe out the institution of segregation, which certainly is a major cause of social problems among Negroes," he pointed out in 1961, "that we have neglected to push programs to raise the moral and cultural climate in our Negro neighborhoods." But the politics of protest have kept him completely immersed in the fight against segregation.

have Negroes been involved, but they have also shown courage and iron self-discipline that has contributed enormously to Negro self-pride. The fear is gone; Negroes throughout the country began walking straighter when the bus boycott began in Montgomery and the sit-ins in Atlanta and the demonstrations in Birmingham. "Got the white folks shaking," an unemployed laborer in Chicago told Louis Harris in July, 1963. "It showed those white folks we ain't gonna take that stuff no more." Indeed, four Negroes in ten told Harris they had participated in mass protests of one sort or another. The figure was a gross exaggeration; it is doubtful that as many as one in ten have actually had a hand in sit-ins, picketing, or street demonstrations.* But the answer revealed the new climate prevailing in the Negro community. Not too many years ago, most Negroes would have felt safer denying participation in racial demonstrations.

Important as the demonstrations have been to Negro morale, however, it would be a mistake to exaggerate their impact. They have contributed a great deal to Negro self-pride —but not enough to conquer apathy, not enough, certainly, to stir the great bulk of slum dwellers into action on their own behalf. Indeed, Louis Lomax, the chronicler of "the Negro revolt," occasionally seems puzzled at the superficiality of the results to date. Writing about Montgomery, Alabama, for example—the birthplace of the "revolt"—Lomax asks why "such a deep-rooted movement as the Montgomery boycott resulted in nothing more than the integration of the buses." In fact, the boycott did not do that, either. Integration came as a result of an NAACP suit filed six months after the boycott began. Nor was the movement as deeply rooted as it appeared at the time; as soon as the original leaders left the scene, the movement dissipated. In 1962, for

* The sponsors of the March on Washington were delighted that 200,000 people, coming from all parts of the country, participated. Yet there are 400,000 Negroes living in the city of Washington, D.C., alone, and several million more within a few hours' driving time.

example, less than a year after Rev. Ralph Abernathy had left his Montgomery church for a pastorate in Atlanta, the SCLC held a state-wide conference in Montgomery. The leaders hoped to climax the three-day meeting with a mass rally in one of Montgomery's Negro churches. Not a single church was willing to lend its facilities for the rally—not even the church Reverend Abernathy had headed, where a year before a group of Freedom Riders had spent the night besieged by a white mob outside. And by 1963, most Negroes in Montgomery had returned to the old custom of riding in the back of the bus.

The protest movement is as important for what it has done to whites, however, as for what it has done to Negroes. White Southerners have always rationalized their discriminatory practices with the fiction that "their Nigras" really preferred it that way—that if it were not for "agitators" from somewhere else, the local Negro populace would be perfectly content to maintain the status quo. The sit-ins and street demonstrations have destroyed that fiction; they have forced whites to face the reality of Negro anger and discontent, for it was "their Nigras" who were sitting-in and marching and singing and protesting.* The demonstrations have done even more: they have forced a startling reversal of roles. Twenty years ago, Myrdal observed that "The Negro's entire life, and consequently, also his opinions on the Negro problem, are . . . to be considered as secondary reactions to more primary pressures from the side of the dominant white majority." Today, the reverse is true. As James McBride Dabbs, president of the Southern Regional Council has observed, "The Negro now has leadership in the South. It is he who makes the move and the white man who responds, or more accurately, reacts."

* For that reason, Southerners sympathetic to the Negro cause were generally very critical of the strategic wisdom of the Freedom Rides. Since most of the Freedom Riders came from the North and returned to the North when the rides were over, they permitted Southerners to revive the old myth about outside agitators.

Not always, though. In Albany, Georgia, for example, the white business and political leaders decided on all-out resistance, and several years of demonstrations have not led to the desegregation of a single facility. The Birmingham demonstrations in the spring of 1963 had important national consequences—for example, the decision of the Kennedy Administration to press for a Federal civil rights bill. In Birmingham itself, however, the results were pitifully small: desegregation of a few lunch counters, employment of a handful of Negroes.

And yet the demonstrations in Birmingham represent a major watershed in the history of United States race relations. For one thing, they demonstrated, so that no one could doubt it any longer, the depth of Negro discontent, the extent of Negro anger and hate, and the ease with which Negro anger and hate can flare into violence. More important, the demonstrations raised that anger to a new pitch. When the police dogs were unleashed in Birmingham, every Negro in America felt their teeth in the marrow of his bones. The explosion of anger and hatred that resulted for a moment, at least, broke through the traditional apathy of the poor and created an almost universal desire to act. It will take more than a single event, of course, to destroy the apathy and hopelessness. But Birmingham did mark the entry of the Negro poor into the protest movement; this is its most important consequence. The riots in that city at the time of the demonstrations, and following the various bombings of homes, motels, and churches, were waged not by the disciplined cadres of relatively well-educated "middle-class" Negroes but by the apathetic poor who had previously remained completely on the outside, and whose potential for violence frightened Rev. Martin Luther King's lieutenants as much as the whites. (See page 122.)

The protest movement will never be the same again. It is bound to become more militant; many of the Negro poor are intolerant of "moderation" and contemptuous of the doctrine of non-violence which Dr. King has tried to convert from a strategy into a philosophy. Within a single week during the torrid summer of 1963, for example, Dr. King was pelted with eggs in Harlem, James Meredith was publicly rebuked by an NAACP official, and Rev. Joseph H. Jackson of Chicago, president of the National Baptist Convention, the largest single Negro church group, was booed off the platform at an NAACP rally and threatened with bodily harm for having called for a halt to anti-segregation demonstrations. For a time at least, as Dr. King himself pointed out, the Negro leaders' position recalled Mahatma Gandhi's famous remark, "There go my people. I must catch them, for I am their leader."

The entry of the poor is forcing a change in the protest movement's goals as well as its means. The great mass of Negroes are more concerned with where they work than with where they eat; winning the right to eat at a desegregated lunch counter is small consolation to men who cannot afford the price of the meal. Thus, after Birmingham, the emphasis began to shift from civil rights to jobs. And the danger of violence began to concern Negro leaders as much as whites.

This change in direction and temper is likely to continue, though certainly not without interruption; mass apathy is too deeply rooted to be more than just temporarily pierced by a single event, like the Birmingham demonstration, or even a series of events. But the change is rooted in something much more fundamental than the immediate anger evoked by Bull Connor's police dogs or the famous photograph of three Birmingham policemen pinning a lone Negro woman to the ground. The growth of black nationalism is bringing to the surface the most fundamental questions of Negro goals. More and more Negroes are beginning to wonder if they really want to eat at the white man's lunch counter after all.

▼

3

The question the black nationalists are raising, in short, is whether Negroes really want integration—more to the point, whether they *should* want integration, whether they should keep banging on the doors of a white society that much of the time seems determined to keep them out. "Is it necessary to integrate oneself into a burning house?" the playwright Lorraine Hansberry (author of *Raisin in the Sun*) has asked with considerable bitterness, using a metaphor adopted by James Baldwin. "The question is openly being raised among all Negro intellectuals, among all politically-conscious Negroes," Miss Hansberry adds, with considerable exaggeration. "And we can't quite get away from it." To be sure, the question is rhetorical; Negroes really have no choice, for there is only one house—there is only one United States, and there can be no solution of the Negro problem anywhere but in that United States or in any way other than full integration of the Negro into the main stream of American life. Yet the question *is* being asked, and widely.

It always has been asked; there always has been a certain dualism in Negro thought: an urge toward separatism co-existing with the demand for integration. There is no Negro who at some time or other has not wanted to shout to white America, "If you won't let me in, for God's sake let me out." The migrant from the Mississippi Delta "wants out" when he throws his beer can out the window of his Chicago tenement. The most educated, the most sophisticated, the most successful Negro on occasion feels the same way. "There comes a time," James Weldon Johnson wrote in 1934, "when the most persistent integrationist becomes an isolationist, when he curses the white world and consigns it to hell. This tendency toward isolation is strong because it springs from a deep-seated natural desire—a desire for respite from the unremitting gruelling struggle; for a place in which refuge might be taken."

The "tendency toward isolation" has been more than just an occasional silent fit of anger or expression of despair. For the last two centuries, individuals and organizations have emerged periodically to argue that there was no place—could be no place—for Negroes in the United States and to urge Negroes to seek their salvation elsewhere. In 1787, the free Negroes of Newport, Rhode Island, formed the Free African Society to promote repatriation to Africa. In 1815, Paul Cuffee of Boston, who was both a Quaker and a successful entrepreneur, took a shipload of free Negroes to settle in Sierra Leone. Cuffee had started out as a militant integrationist who refused to pay taxes until Massachusetts recognized his right to vote. Martin Robinson Delaney, a Harvard-educated physician, novelist, and pamphleteer, underwent the same conversion. Delaney gained prominence in the 1830s as an opponent of the American Colonization Society, which wanted to transport American Negroes to Africa. By the 1850s, however, he had himself become an advocate of migration. "I am not in favor of caste," Delaney wrote in answer to criticism from William Lloyd Garrison, "and would as willingly live among white men as black"—if he could enjoy the same rights. "If there were any probability of this," he continued, "I should be willing to remain in the country, fighting and struggling on . . . But I must admit that I have no hopes in this country—no confidence in the American people. . . ."

Like a good many other Negroes, Delaney's hopes were revived with the outbreak of the Civil War and the issuance of the Emancipation Proclamation. Those hopes were shattered a decade later, when political expediency dictated the withdrawal of Federal troops from the South and the end of Reconstruction. By 1885, Bishop Henry McNeal Turner, who had been a chaplain in the Union Army and a member of the Georgia state legislature, had given up all hope for the Negro in the United States:

> There is no manhood future in the United States for the Negro. He may eke out an existence for generations to come, but he can never be a man, full, symmetrical and undwarfed . . . The whites will not grant social equality to the Negroid race . . . [Hence] I believe that two or three million of us should return to the land of our ancestors, and establish our own nation, civilization, laws, customs, style of manufacture. . . ."

The migration movement never caught hold, of course; most Negroes were unwilling to surrender their fight for equality in the land of their birth. But the separatist idea gained support again at the end of World War One, when Marcus Garvey called upon Negroes to drop their futile fight for equality in America and instead "to plant the banner of freedom on the great continent of Africa."

> If you cannot live alongside the white man in peace, if you cannot get the same chance and opportunity alongside the white man, even though you are his fellow citizen . . . then find a country of your own and rise to the highest position within that country . . . If Europe is for the Europeans, then Africa shall be for the black peoples of the world . . . The other races have countries of their own and it is time for the 400,000,000 Negroes to claim Africa for themselves. . . ."

Garvey is dead and largely forgotten.* But the Africans have now claimed Africa for themselves, as the Asians have

* Not entirely! Garvey exerted considerable influence on the growth of African nationalism, partly through personal contact with Africans studying in London during his years of exile there, partly through his writings. "Of all the literature I studied," Kwame Nkrumah has written of his years in the United States, "the book that did more than any other to fire my enthusiasm was *The Philosophy and Opinions of Marcus Garvey.*"

claimed Asia for themselves. More than a hundred years ago, Martin Delaney told a convention of free Negroes in New York, "The white races are but one-third of the population of the globe—or one of them to two of us—and it cannot much longer continue that two-thirds will passively submit to the universal domination of this one-third." Indeed, the domination has ended; the "us" of whom Delaney spoke are now lining up against the "them," as the voting in the United Nations General Assembly frequently indicates. (The Assembly now has fifty-six African and Asian member states —50.4 per cent of the total membership—compared to eleven states when the UN was founded.)

The rise of the colored peoples around the world has had an enormous impact on American Negroes. One result—not the only one, certainly—has been to stimulate the growth of a number of black nationalist groups. The most important, so far, is the Black Muslim movement headed by Elijah Muhammad.

The Muslims deserve very careful attention. Their importance is not due to their numbers: membership certainly does not exceed 100,000 (Professor C. Eric Lincoln's estimate) and may be closer to 50,000 (Professor Morroe Berger's estimate), and in any case it has not grown since about 1960. What makes the Black Muslims important is that they spring from and speak to a number of basic forces in Negro life—forces which have gained considerable strength in recent years.

For one thing, the Muslims are drawing upon the separatist streak which, as we have seen, runs deep in Negro thought. But the Muslims have elevated separatism into a religious doctrine and thereby have given it a new twist. Negroes are told to abandon all notions of integration, all hopes of becoming part of American society not merely because white Americans will never give them a fair shake, but because the white man is *incapable* of treating them fairly —more important, because the white man is a devil who is doomed to destruction, and soon. "The white devil's day is over," Elijah Muhammad tells anyone who will listen. "He was given six thousand years to rule. His time was up in 1917. These are his years of grace—seventy of them. He's already used up most of those years trapping and murdering the black nations by the hundreds of thousands. Now he's worried, worried about the black man getting his revenge."

He should be worried, for according to Muslim doctrine, revenge is very near. Allah postponed the Battle of Armageddon in order to give the brainwashed American Negroes more of an opportunity to separate themselves from the white devil. They had better separate soon, for Elijah sees signs all around "that the time of God's coming is upon us." Unless the white man repents and accedes to Muslim demands for a separate territory all for themselves, "all of you who are sitting here, your government, and your entire race will be destroyed and removed from this earth by Almighty God. And those black men who are still trying to integrate will inevitably be destroyed along with the whites; only the faithful will be saved." *

---

* The Muslim's mythology is no less credible than that of the Southern white racists. Here, for example, is an excerpt from a text which the White Citizens Council of Mississippi has officially suggested for the third and fourth grades in all Mississippi schools:

> God wanted the white people to live alone. And He wanted colored people to live alone. The white men built America for you. White men built America so they could make the rules . . . The white man has always been kind to the Negro. We do not believe that God wants us to live together. Negro people like to live by themselves. Negroes use their own bathrooms. They do not use white people's bathrooms. The Negro has his own part of town to live in. This is called our Southern Way of Life. Do you know that some people want the Negroes to live with white people? These people want us to be unhappy. They say we must go to school together. They say we must swim together and use the bathroom together. God has made us different. And God knows best. Did you know that our country will grow weak if we mix the races?

The Muslims, in short, are more than just another separatist movement: for a Negro to accept Muhammad's teaching is to hitch a ride with the wave of the future. Indeed, Malcolm X, former Minister of the New York mosque, argues that the movement cannot be understood except in a world-wide context. The civil rights groups, says Malcolm X, look only at the United States, and thereby doom the Negro to perpetual minority status; by linking their movement to the world-wide rise of the colored nations, the Muslims convert the Negro into a member of a majority, and a majority that feels it has all the forces of history on its side. There was great glee among the Muslim leaders, for example, when Mao Tse-tung issued a call in the fall of 1963 for "sensitive persons of all colors of all the world—black, white, yellow, brown—to unite against the racial discrimination of United States imperialism. . . ." The official Muslim newspaper *Muhammad Speaks* hailed China as "the first major nation in world history to take official notice of the oppression of American Negroes and extend moral support to them," and unleashed a violent attack on Roy Wilkins of the NAACP for having spurned the Chinese Communist offer of support.* The Muslims have established highly cordial relations with

---

And for the fifth and sixth grades, the Citizens Council recommends this:

> . . . One of the main lessons in the Old Testament of our Bible is that your race should be kept pure. God made different races and put them in different lands. He was satisfied with pure races so man should keep the races pure and be satisfied. BIRDS DO NOT MIX. CHICKENS DO NOT MIX. A friend had 100 white chickens and 100 reds. All the white chickens go to one side of the house, and all the red chickens go on the other side of the house. You probably feel the same way these chickens did whenever you are with people of a different race. God meant it to be that way.

* "We await the opportunity," Wilkins replied to Mao in a sarcastic statement, "to send felicitations to Chinese citizens gathered in a huge demonstration in your nation's capital to protest living conditions under your government."

the Arab representatives at the UN, who are delighted with the Muslims' virulent anti-Semitism. Orthodox Moslems in the United States have generally looked askance at Elijah for his racism, his claim to be "The Messenger of Allah," and his spurious history of how the white devil temporarily gained power. But the Muslims are now trying to establish much closer ties with the world of Islam. Elijah Muhammad's youngest son has just spent several years of study at Egypt's Al-Azhar University, the Harvard of the Moslem world. On his return, young Akbar Muhammad brought the residents of Harlem "a message from our African brothers": "Spokesmen from African states," he reported to a street rally, "told me to tell you that if you unite, they are ready to help us win our freedom. They are ready to help us with arms, men and know-how!"

Beside appealing to the separatist strain in Negro thought, however, the Black Muslims are digging deep into the well-springs of Negroes' hatred of the white, and making the most of it. At meetings around the country, for example, the Muslims have put on a morality play, *The Trial,* written by Louis X, a former popular singer and musician who now is minister of the Boston temple. A jury of twelve Negroes hears an eloquent prosecuting attorney deliver the indictment:

> I charge the white man with being the greatest liar on earth! I charge the white man with being the greatest drunkard on earth . . . I charge the white man with being the greatest gambler on earth. I charge the white man, ladies and gentlemen of the jury, with being the greatest peace-breaker on earth. I charge the white man with being the greatest adulterer on earth. I charge the white man with being the greatest deceiver on earth. I charge the white man with being the greatest troublemaker on earth. So therefore, ladies and gentlemen of the jury, I ask you, bring back a verdict of guilty as charged.

The jury does not take very long to reach its verdict.

The Muslims have gained a wide and approving audience by articulating feelings which most Negroes share but fear to voice in public. Witness the admiring cab driver quoted in chapter III, who told photographer Gordon Parks that "That Malcolm ain't afraid to tell Mr. Charlie, the FBI or the cops or nobody where to get off." * (This was before Malcolm X, in effect, had tried to tell Elijah Muhammad himself where to get off and had been forced out of the movement as a result.) The cabbie was not a Muslim himself—he was unwilling to curb his appetite for pork or women in accordance with Muslim doctrine—but he had concluded that the Muslims "make more sense to me than the NAACP and Urban League and all the rest of them put together."

It is not just the poor and the uneducated who cheer Malcolm X on, however. Parks himself—a deeply sensitive man who is a composer and a novelist as well as a distinguished photographer—found that the Muslim message struck such a responsive chord that he was forced to re-examine the moral convictions he had developed during the course of his life. Parks held firm to his belief in the universality of man. Nevertheless, part of the Muslim message stayed with him. "I wouldn't follow Elijah Muhammad or Malcolm X into a Black State," he wrote in his moving *Life* article on the Muslims. "I've worked too hard for a place in this present society . . . Nevertheless, to the Muslims I acknowledge that the circumstance of common struggle has willed us brothers. I know that if unholy violence should erupt—and I pray it won't—this same circumstance will place me, reluctantly, beside them. Although I won't allow them to be my keeper, I am, inherently, their brother."

Nor is Parks' experience at all unique; a great many Negroes who are deeply committed to the integration move-

---

* This, of course, is also the basis of Adam Clayton Powell's popularity among Harlem residents. "Adam flies off the handle," one constituent puts it, "but he gets white folks told."

ment somehow find themselves responding to Malcolm X's revelations of white duplicity. It takes no leap of the imagination to understand why. "The brutality with which Negroes are treated in this country," James Baldwin has said, "simply cannot be overstated, however unwilling white men may be to hear it. In the beginning—and neither can this be overstated—a Negro just cannot *believe* that white people are treating him as they do; he does not know what he has done to merit it. And when he realizes that the treatment accorded him has nothing to do with anything he has done, that the attempt of white people to destroy him—for that is what it is—is utterly gratuitous, it is not hard for him to think of white people as devils." When the Muslim ministers talk, Baldwin argues, they articulate that suffering for all the Negroes listening. As the psychologist Kenneth B. Clark expresses it, the Muslims preach a dangerous doctrine "because the basic premises are true . . . They are not inventing nor for that matter are they even exaggerating or distorting the basic fact. White America has permitted a system of cruelty and barbarity to be perpetrated and perpetuated on citizens of dark color, and the Muslims are very effective in saying this over and over again."

The Muslims strike a responsive chord for another reason: they not only articulate the anger and hatred that every Negro feels, but they promise revenge as well. The desire for vengeance may not be the most admirable human trait, but it is one of the most common. The weakness of Rev. Martin Luther King's movement—in the opinion of some psychologists, its fatal flaw—is that it asks more of Negroes than any but a handful of men can ever give. For Dr. King is asking Negroes not just to forgo violence, not just to forgo hatred; he is demanding that they actually *love* their oppressors. It is doubtful whether the masses of *any* oppressed group can sublimate their bitterness and resentment to that extent—particularly not Negro Americans, who are "acculturated" enough to acquire the white Southern tradition of aggression and violence. Hence the widespread admiration for Dr. King is mixed, as has been noted, with a good deal of resentment. Lower-class Negroes do not want to be represented to the whites as non-violent. Their anger has been suppressed for too long, and they are deriving too much pleasure from the discovery that it is the white man who is afraid of them rather than they who are afraid of the white man. Malcolm X loses no opportunity, therefore, to attack King as a castrating Uncle Tom who teaches Negroes not to fight back, who urges them to suffer peacefully. "It's not possible to love a man whose chief purpose in life is to humiliate you," Malcolm argues, "and still be what is considered a normal human being." (Malcolm misjudged the Negro mood during the Birmingham demonstrations, however, and angered a good many Negroes by calling Dr. King "a chump.")

But the Muslims do more than simply vent Negro anger and frustration. For all the fanciful past which Elijah Muhammad has constructed and the equally incredible future,* the real emphasis of the movement is on the here and now; despite the demand for a separate black state and the prediction of white doom in the Battle of Armageddon that is to come, Elijah and Malcolm's main objective is to improve the position of the Negro in the United States. Whether consciously or unconsciously, their ideology is designed to accomplish that end.†

Elijah's message is clear and simple: Negroes can look to no one but themselves for their salvation; they must pull themselves up by their own bootstraps—in a favorite phrase of Elijah's, they must "wake up, clean up, and stand up" be-

* There is more truth to Muslim doctrine than most whites (or Negroes, for that matter) realize, however. There were highly civilized black Moslem states in West Africa; while most of the Africans brought here were not Moslems, some were. (See chapter VI.)

† For a much more detailed analysis of the Muslim movement, *see* E. U. Essien-Udom, *Black Nationalism,* Chicago: University of Chicago Press, 1962; C. Eric Lincoln, *The Black Muslims in America,* Boston; Beacon Press, 1961; and Morroe Berger, *op. cit.*

fore they can hope to become free and independent. For formal freedom is meaningless; true freedom—substantive freedom—cannot be conferred upon people who do not want it, or who are not willing to work, if need be to sacrifice, in order to attain it. Nor can equality be bestowed upon people who do not feel equal or who do not act equal. "We know that we are inferior to you here in America," Elijah Muhammad tells white interviewers. "We cannot say that we are equal; we can't do it because we're not. We have undergone such treatment that it has absolutely made us inferior to you, and therefore we cannot be your equal"—not the white man's equal, that is to say, until the black man has learned who he is, until he has overcome his "slave mentality."

The real enemy, therefore, is not the white man but the Negro—the Negro who has been taught by white oppression and discrimination to despise himself and who is unable, therefore, to help himself. "The worst crime the white man has committed," says Malcolm X, "has been to teach us to hate ourselves." For self-hatred has produced the crime, the drug-addiction, the alcoholism that infest the Negro community; self-hatred is responsible for the apathy that keeps Negroes ignorant and poor and that makes them blame every failure on "the man"; self-hatred is responsible for the idealization of everything white that leads Negroes to despise their own kind and makes them unable to work together except for "funerals, food, and fun." Elijah asks:

> What is the nature of interpersonal relationships among Negroes? How do Negroes relate themselves to one another? How do they relate themselves to their community? The Negro's relationship with one another is utterly deplorable. The Negro wants to be everything but himself. He wants to be a white man. He processes his hair. Acts like a white man. He wants to integrate with the white man, but he cannot integrate with himself or with his own kind. The Negro wants to lose his identity because he does not

> know his own identity. He lives in the black belt because the white man says he cannot move. He takes no interest in the community. As far as it is possible, the Negro does not want to be identified with other Negroes. How can he integrate with the white man when he has not learned how to integrate with himself or with other Negroes? *

Solution of the Negro problem, therefore, must start with the Negro himself. The civil rights groups, Malcolm argues, are concerned with changing the white man's image of the Negro; the Muslims are interested only in changing the black man's image of the Negro. "If we do that," Malcolm X argues, "the whites will change their opinion automatically." But "we can't change the white man's opinion of the black man until we change our image of ourselves."

Muslim ideology is directed to that end. The Garvey movement, Malcolm X explains, demonstrated that Negroes *could* unite—but not on any basis that Negro intellectuals could accept, nor on any basis that would fail to frighten whites. The only thing that can bring Negroes together, in Malcolm X's view, is their color, for slavery destroyed their original culture and severed them from their past.

And so the Muslim leaders use color to persuade Negroes that they are the white man's equal. They simply turn the doctrine of white supremacy on its head; they play on the Negro's inescapable consciousness of color and his hatred of the white man to create a sense of identity and direction that will enable him to rise out of the *anomie* that is the Negro slum.† For the black man, Elijah tells his listeners, quoting Allah, is "The Original Man . . . He is the first and the last, the maker and owner of the universe; from him comes all—brown, yellow, red, and white." The black man was created with the universe "sixty-six trillion years ago," and he is

---

* In Essien-Udom, *op. cit.*, p. 305.

† The Muslims' inverted racism serves another function: it permits them to propound a doctrine of self-improvement that, coming from any other group, would be denounced as pure "Uncle Tomism."

"by nature divine." The white man's history goes back a mere six thousand years, and he is a devil by nature, created "out of the weak of the Black Nation" by Yakub, "a black scientist in rebellion against Allah."

Hateful and incredible as the Muslim ideology may be, it serves its function well; the Muslims are remarkably effective in changing Negro behavior. As James Baldwin has said in *The Fire Next Time,* "Elijah Muhammad has been able to do what generations of welfare workers and committees and resolutions and reports and housing projects and playgrounds have failed to do: to heal and redeem drunkards and junkies, to convert people who have come out of prison and to keep them out, to make men chaste and women virtuous, and to invest both the male and the female with a poise and a serenity that hang about them like an unfailing light." Every serious student of the movement has reached substantially the same conclusion. Psychiatric social workers in Harlem Hospital in New York, amazed by the Muslims' success in rehabilitating drug addicts, have approached Malcolm X for his advice and his assistance, and the Negro Probation Officers Society of New York invited him to explain the Muslims' approach to addicts at a meeting in April, 1964. (Malcolm X himself is a reformed drug addict and criminal who was converted while he was in a maximum security prison.) Indeed, one of the great ironies of the current scene is the fact that a movement preaching a pathological hatred of everything white and middle class and Christian has been remarkably successful in producing models of white-middle-class behavior and exemplars of the Protestant ethic.

Yet middle-class respectability is precisely the behavior Elijah is trying to produce. A whole panoply of rules and regulations is designed to root out any behavior that conforms to the old "Sambo" stereotype, and to instill a rigid discipline and self-control. Muslims are forbidden to eat pork, corn bread, and a long list of other favorite Negro foods.

Overeating the permitted foods is frowned upon as well; an overweight Muslim may be punished by a fine. (To prevent overeating—and to instill self-discipline—Muslims are enjoined to eat only one meal a day.) Alcohol and tobacco are completely forbidden as is gambling, and a Puritanical code of sexual behavior is demanded and enforced. The religion makes a fetish of cleanliness; Muslims are required to rinse their mouths and wash their hands, feet, and forearms before beginning their prayers—and they are required to pray five times each day. Most important of all, perhaps, women are required to play a subordinate role as wife, mother, and homemaker. In Malcolm X's view, the persistence of matriarchy lies at the heart of the Negro problem. "Negro women don't realize the destructive role they play in continuing the matriarchy established by slavery," Malcolm X observes, though he concedes that they are not entirely to blame; white society has made the woman the breadwinner and removed the male from his normal role as head of the house.

Muslim men are able to assume the male role because the movement demands hard work, thrift, and self-reliance. They must dress neatly, keep all appointments punctually, and respect authority, even white authority. The Muslims' separatist philosophy places great emphasis on the creation of Negro businesses in order to create jobs independent of the whites. "If the white man says to you, 'Johnny, go back home, I have no work for you today,' you go back home and wait for the white man to send for you when he sees fit," Elijah says in chastisement. "You must learn to make jobs for yourselves so that the next time the boss tells you he does not have any work for you, you can tell him that you are going to do some work for yourself."

Although the bulk of the members undoubtedly still work for white employers, the Muslims have established restaurants, barber shops, laundries and dry-cleaning establishments, clothing factories, grocery stores, and other small businesses in most of the cities in which they are active. There are few experiences more impressive than spending an afternoon with Malcolm X at the Muslim Restaurant in Harlem, and seeing the steady procession of lean, handsome, courteous young men who come to deliver a message or to obtain a decision on some matter; each is flawlessly groomed in a gray-flannel suit, his shoes shined, and his head erect. The contrast between these tautly disciplined, ascetic, completely controlled young men, and the shapeless, unstable, unrestrained life in the streets around them drives home, as perhaps nothing else can, the impact Elijah Muhammad has had on at least a small segment of the Negro community.

The Muslims are not nearly as free of white culture as their statements suggest, however. The Muslim grocery stores, for example, offer "Shabazz Saving Stamps" to lure the customers in.* The movement's official newspaper, *Muhammad Speaks,* now carries an advice-to-the-lovelorn column, "For And About You," conducted by Harriet Muhammad. (In one column, a man in love with a woman married to an "extremely irresponsible, unfaithful, disrespectful, abusive" man is urged to visit the local mosque for guidance.) There are times, in fact, when *Muhammad Speaks* reads almost like a parody of the white popular press—perhaps because the movement, like any ambitious white organization, has engaged the services of a public relations firm. Thus, an advertisement in the December 20, 1963, issue for the "incomparable Shabazz Restaurants," which are Muslim-owned, urged readers to "Discover the Art of Gracious Dining in Pleasant Surroundings During the Holiday Season." (Lest there be any doubt as to which holiday season was meant, the ad contained a picture of a sprig of holly.) The same issue carried a feature story plugging the Shabazz Restaurant in Chicago. "A soft-spoken young woman

* "Shabazz," a word of unknown origin—it is neither Arabic, Persian, Turkish, nor Hebrew—is enormously popular among Muslims, who use it as a last name and as a name for their businesses.

who has served the public as a waitress for more than twelve years considers Chicago's recently opened Shabazz Restaurant as having 'the most pleasant and ideal atmosphere I've ever worked in,'" the article begins. "Mrs. Eva June Morgan is in a position to make such a comparison," it continues, reading as though it had come off the Muslim PR firm's mimeograph machine. "June, as she is known to the thousands fortunate enough to have met her as a waitress, has been in restaurant, or, as she termed it, 'service' work, since 1951. 'For me, it was love at first sight,' she told *Muhammad Speaks*. 'Making people happy seemed an ideal way to earn a living, and a waitress performs one of the most important functions known to man—she feeds him.'"

There are signs, moreover, of a softening of the Muslim's demand for total separation from white America. At the 1963 Muslim convention, Elijah Muhammad authorized members to register and vote; in the past, voting had been forbidden as a form of recognition of the legitimacy of the United States. (One of Elijah's sons served a term in jail for refusing to register for the draft.) Most remarkable of all, the Muslims joined the period of public mourning after the assassination of President Kennedy. "We, with the world, are very shocked at the assassination of *our* President," Elijah's statement began. [Emphasis added] And when Malcolm X went ahead with a public meeting despite Elijah's ban and rejoiced at the President's death, he was publicly rebuked and suspended indefinitely. In March, 1964, Malcolm X pulled out altogether, organizing his own mosque as the core of a black nationalist movement designed to attract Negroes "regardless of their religious or political beliefs." Malcolm's emphasis is on the here and now; he clearly hopes to become a major factor in the civil rights struggle. (He asked civil rights leaders to forgive his past attacks on them and offered his co-operation to them.) "I am and always will be a Muslim," he announced. "I still believe that Mr. Muhammad's analysis . . . is the most realistic and that his solution is the best one . . . But separation back to Africa is still a long-range program, and while it is yet to materialize, 22 million of our people . . . still here in America need better food, clothing, housing, education and jobs right now."

How much of an impact Malcolm will make remains to be seen; it could be very large. His emphasis on political black nationalism ("we must control the politics and the politicians of our community; they must no longer take orders from outside forces") and his advocacy of self-defense against white violence ("the little Negro they thought was passive will become a roaring lion") strike a responsive chord among many Negro intellectuals as well as slum dwellers (see pages 152-153). Until now, however, his ability to command an active following was limited by the cultish restraints of the Black Muslim religion: Many Negroes who agreed with Malcolm's attacks on the whites were unwilling to join the Muslims because of the demand that they give up women, smoking, drinking, etc. "As long as the Muslims keep saying 'you must be more virtuous than Caesar's wife,'" Prof. Kenneth B. Clark observed in the fall of 1963, "I don't think I would worry about their mass attraction. I'll start worrying when they modify their demands . . . and make them more consistent with what the Negro is able to respond to." This modification is precisely what Malcolm seemed to be offering—and a great many Negro leaders in addition to Professor Clark are worrying as a result.

VI

LOST AND FOUND: AFRICA AND THE NEGRO PAST

What is Africa to me:
Copper sun or scarlet sea,
Jungle star or jungle track,
Strong bronzed men, or regal black,
Women from whose loins I sprang
When the birds of Eden sang?
One three centuries removed
From the scenes his fathers loved,
Spicy grove, cinnamon tree,
What is Africa to me?

—COUNTEE CULLEN

1

Most discussions of Malcolm X and the Black Muslims have seen them as a threat to the white community. Certainly the danger of violence, inspired by Malcolm or led by him, can't be discounted, particularly if the white reaction to Negro advances itself takes the form of violence, as it has in Mississippi and Alabama, and to a lesser and more sporadic degree, in Philadelphia and Chicago and other Northern cities. While the number of Muslim members is small and static, there are many "fellow travelers" who may be attracted by Malcolm's movement, and there is every reason to believe that Negro anger and impatience will increase rather than diminish in the next several years.

But the Muslims represent a much greater threat to the leaders of the Negro community and to that community's dominant institutions, for their existence bears testimony to these leaders' failure, thus far, to capture the imagination and allegiance of their constituents. Even more, the Muslims' success in transforming the lives of its members dramatizes the failure to date of the traditional institutions—the Negro church, the civil rights groups, the white settlement houses—to make any real headway with the psychological, social, and economic problems of the Negro poor.

The growth of black nationalism, moreover, exposes the real differences of opinion, and the very real conflicts of interest, that exist around the question of integration. A good many Negro businessmen and politicians, for example, might be hurt by integration; their livelihood and their status derive from the existence of segregation. Hence their advocacy of integration tends to diminish as its existence draws nearer. The problem is posed for politicians in quite concrete terms when, for example, there is discussion about the best location for a new public housing project: should it be built within the existing Negro community, in which case it will almost certainly be segregated; or should it be built on available land somewhere else in the city, which might lead to depopulation of the politicians' district?

The more important problem is a good deal subtler: what do Negroes really mean by "integration"? As C. Eric Lincoln asks the question, do Negroes want "true integration," or do they want what he terms "a conspicuous, superficial integration which relieves them of the self-hatred and insecurity that come from second-class citizenship, but which also relieves them of the responsibility that full participation would mean." Too many Negroes, Professor Lincoln fears, prefer the latter; when the Atlanta Negro community won the right to attend the Atlanta Symphony concerts and to eat in a few leading downtown restaurants, for example, a good many upper-class Negroes concluded that the battle at long last had been won. What else, they wondered, was there left to do?

Atlanta, needless to say, is still a highly segregated city. So are New York—and Washington and Detroit and Los Angeles, for that matter. But what are the hallmarks of "true" integration? Does it imply the disappearance of the Negro community and the all-Negro churches, fraternal orders, and other institutions; does it require the redistribution of the Negro population more or less evenly throughout the white community? Or is integration compatible with the perpetuation of a distinctly Negro community? Is perpetuation desirable, or simply inevitable? What attributes of the Negro community are worth preserving? Is there a specifically Negro culture that is worth preserving, or are so-called Negro culture traits simply an outgrowth of Jim Crow? Should kudos be granted to Negroes who move into previously all-white neighborhoods—or alternatively, should any onus be attached to people who prefer to remain in all-Negro enclaves? Is an all-Negro neighborhood necessarily a ghetto? Is an all-Negro school necessarily inferior?

The answers are by no means obvious; they require nothing less than a redefinition of what it means to be a Negro in the United States and a new appraisal of the ways in which Negroes can best relate to whites. The redefinition is long overdue; perhaps because achievement of integration has always seemed so far away, Negroes have given surprisingly little thought to what they actually mean by the term—to what kind of relationship they really want with whites or, for that matter, with other Negroes. The ideology of the civil rights movement, as we have seen, developed at the beginning of the century, when liberal thought was dominated by the notion of "the melting pot." In fact, Israel Zangwill's influential play, *The Melting Pot,* in which the term originated, opened on Broadway the year before the NAACP was founded.

But the crucial thing about the melting pot was that it did not happen: American politics and American social life are still dominated by the existence of sharply-defined ethnic groups.* To be sure, these groups have been transformed by several generations of life in America; the immigrants of three or four or five generations ago would be unable to recognize the Italian-Americans, the Irish-Americans, the Jewish-Americans of the 1960s; the latter groups, in turn, would disavow kinship with their ancestors. And yet the ethnic groups are not just a political anachronism; they are a reality. The WASPs (White Anglo-Saxon Protestants), the Irish-Americans, the Italian-Americans, the Jewish-Americans do differ from each other in essential ways. They vote differently, raise their children differently, have different ideas about sex, education, religion, death, etc.† And so if Negroes are to assimilate, if they are to integrate with the white American, the question has to be asked: with *which* white American? With the WASP? Or with the Irishman? The Italian? The Slovak? The Jew? For in truth there is no "white American"; there are only white Americans.

More to the point, the experience of the European ethnic groups suggests that integration need not mean assimilation,

* For a discerning analysis of the role of ethnic groups in American life, *see* Nathan Glazer and Daniel P. Moynihan, *Beyond the Melting Pot,* Cambridge, Mass.: MIT Press and Harvard University Press, 1963.

† In an article describing the rapidly growing phenomenon of the public dance for single men and women—as many as 150 such affairs are held on a single weekend in New York—*The New York Times* reported that separate dances for persons of Irish, German, Polish, Greek, Italian, and Hungarian extraction are advertised in neighborhood papers and in the foreign-language press.

that integrating the Negro into the main stream of American life does not depend—indeed, cannot depend—on "making color irrelevant by making it disappear as a fact of consciousness." Consciousness of color is not likely to disappear unless color itself disappears, or unless men lose their eyesight. For color is not merely a political fact, as James Baldwin argues; on the contrary, it is a social and personal reality, just as being Protestant or Catholic or Jewish is a reality, just as being Italian or Irish or German is a reality. One of the contributions the Muslims have made is their insistence that solution of "the Negro problem" cannot depend on the Negro's disappearance.

This is not to say that the attempts of Professor Handlin or Professor Hauser to equate the Negro migration with the European migrations are correct. It is infinitely harder for white Americans to accept the fact of color than it was for their fathers or grandfathers to accept the fact of ethnic difference. And it is vastly harder for Negro-Americans to come to grips with their Negro-ness than, say, for Jewish-Americans to come to grips with their Jewishness, or Italian-Americans to come to grips with their Italian-ness. (Neither group, in fact, has completely resolved the complex conflicts that still exist between being an Italian or a Jew and being an American.) Negroes are both more than an ethnic group and less: though their color makes them far more identifiable than any ethnic group, they lack the common history and cultural traditions which the other groups share. The Negro's central problem is to discover his identity, or to create an identity for himself. What history suggests is that when the Negro solves his problem of identity, he will have gone a long way towards finding the means of relating himself to every other American group.

▼

2

Solution of the problem of Negro identity seems much closer than appeared likely only a few years ago. The biggest factor in this change has been the rise of the African states, which is making it possible for American Negroes to admit their relationship to Africa—which in fact is encouraging them to reconstruct their history and restore the cultural ties to Africa destroyed by slavery. It is hard to exaggerate the importance of Africa for the problem of Negro identity in the United States. Today, Africa is contributing enormously to Negro self-pride; yesterday, Africa contributed even more to Negro self-hate.

To understand why, it is necessary to recall the image of Africa that prevailed just a few years ago—the image which, indeed, still dominates most white thinking. Africa, in this view, is the Dark Continent, "a continent without history," a place of savagery and ignorance whose people had contributed nothing at all to human progress. "All the continents begin with an 'A' except one," begins a chapter of V. M. Hillyer's *A Child's Geography of the World*, a favorite when I was a child, and still a popular children's book. "Asia is the largest continent. Africa is the next largest. But Africa was an 'In-the-Way' continent," the chapter continues. "It was in the way of those who wanted to get to Asia. Everyone wanted to get *around* Africa. No one wanted to get *to* it. Sailors have been shipwrecked on its shores, but few lived to tell the tale of jungles, of wild animals, and wild black men. Africa was called the Dark Continent because no one knew much about it or wanted to know about it . . . On one edge—along the Mediterranean Sea—white men lived, but south of that edge was a great desert that men feared to cross, and south of that wild black men and wild animals. . . ."

Public school textbooks were even more deprecating. In the texts used when today's adult Negro population attended school, the inevitable pictures of "the five races of man" almost always showed the African man at his most primitive. In contrast to "the Emersonian white man in his study, the Japanese aristocrat, the Malay nobleman, and the Indian chief—all obviously selected to depict the highest social rank in each case," Professor Harold R. Isaacs has written, the "African" appeared as "a prehistoric figure of a man, naked, stepping out of primeval ooze, carrying an ante-deluvian club and shield." * One text, Isaacs reports, classified the states of man as "savage" ("all black or red"), "barbarous" ("chiefly brown"), "half-civilized" ("almost wholly yellow"), and "civilized" ("almost all belong to the white race.") Movies were even more devastating: Hollywood almost invariably showed Africa as a land populated by half-naked cannibals.

Against this debasing picture of "the African," the Negro child had no defense; he had no way of knowing that the picture happened to be false. On the contrary, this "evidence of the black man's inferiority," as Isaacs puts it, "was borne in upon him with all the weight and authority of the all-knowing, all-powerful, all-surrounding white world," thereby confirming the sense of his own worthlessness that white attitudes and actions had already established. This confirmation played an important, frequently a crucial, role in the development of Negro children's conception of themselves. In the interviews with a hundred seven leading Negroes that formed the basis of *The New World of Negro Americans,* Isaacs found "that in nearly every instance" the early discovery of the African background had been "a prime ele-

* Anyone concerned with the impact of Africa on Negro consciousness is indebted to Professor Isaacs for *The New World of Negro Americans* (New York: John Day, 1963).

ment" in shaping the individual's knowledge of and attitude toward himself and his world—so much so that most of the subjects could recall the details of the pictures and the names of the texts with agonizing clarity forty, fifty, and even sixty years later!

In general, therefore, Africa served to alienate the Negro not just from America but from the whole human race. In self-defense, he tried to dissociate himself from Africa. As the Negro historian Carter G. Woodson, a pioneer in the study of Negro history in Africa and in the United States, put it in 1937, Negroes "accept as a compliment the theory of a complete break with Africa, for above all things, they do not care to be known as resembling in any way 'these terrible Africans.'" Negroes not aware of the academic debate over just how many African cultural traits had survived did, however, emphasize their Indian or white ancestry, if they had any. And they proceeded to use "African" as an epithet and an insult. If a Negro had dark skin and kinky hair, lighter-skinned Negroes would wither him with a "You look like a black African." Indeed, to call someone a "black African" became an even greater insult than to call him a "nigger."

The key word was "black." For a Negro to dissociate himself from Africa meant, after all, to dissociate himself from the African's color, hair, features—from the Negroidness that stared at him from the pictures in the public-school textbooks and that assaulted his senses from the movie screen. But in the last analysis, dissociation was impossible, the perverse fact of color remained. And so the Negro's rejection of Africa was, at bottom, a rejection of himself.

African independence is profoundly altering American Negroes' relation to Africa and to themselves. Few Negroes can fail to feel a flush of pride as jet-black African ambassadors, presidents, and prime ministers are received at the White House or take their places in the United Nations. Negroes who had shuddered inwardly at the mention of

Africa are developing an interest in African art and poetry; men who had fled from blackness are pondering the meanings and debating the attributes of *Negritude;* adolescents and young adults whose idols had been some entertainer or athlete now worship the memory of Lumumba or make a hero of Nkrumah. And ordinary Negro women who a short time ago were buying hair-straighteners and skin-bleaches now wear the new "African look" in hair styles.

Negroes of all social classes and all educational levels, moreover, are developing an interest in African history. They are discovering, as a result, that their past—or at least that part of their past which belongs to Africa—is a lot easier to accept than they had thought. For Africa does have a history which enables black men to hold their heads aloft. We do not know nearly enough about that history, to be sure, but we know considerably more than most people (or most scholars, for that matter) realize. And what we do know makes it clear that Arnold Toynbee erred grievously when he wrote that of all the races of mankind, "The Black races alone have not contributed positively to any civilization."*

The contribution of the black race may have started at the very beginning; there is some evidence to suggest that Elijah Muhammad's claim that the black is "original man" may not be as wide of the mark as it sounds. A number of distinguished archaeologists, anthropologists, paleontologists, and other "prehistorians," now believe that human life first developed in Africa. As the eminent Oxford anthropologist L. S. B. Leakey, puts it, "Africa's first contribution to human progress was the evolution of man himself." Professor

---

* Toynbee's error may be due less to outright prejudice than to a century-old tradition that has simply excluded Africa from serious historical or archaeological study. Thus, the 600-page Somervell abridgement of Toynbee's *Study of History* contains no more than three indexed references to Africa. The tradition continues: a recently published 1,300-page study called *The World of The Past* contains no section on any part of Africa save Egypt.

Leakey's view is based on fossils and skeletons he has discovered in Africa. The evidence, needless to say, is circumstantial, but it is persuasive nonetheless. The distinction between man and other primates is that man makes and uses tools. The earliest toolmaker so far known is a creature called Zinganthropus, discovered by Professor Leakey in northern Tanganyika. Zinganthropus lived nearly two million years ago, and was more apelike than human; thousands of generations of evolution were needed before he came to resemble what we call *Homo sapiens*, whose brain is more important than his brawn and whose hands are more useful than his teeth. As the historians Roland Oliver and J. D. Fage have put it, "there is little doubt that throughout all but the last small fraction of this long development of the human form, Africa remained at the center of the inhabited world."* All the so-called "pebble tools" that have been discovered so far have been found in Africa or close by, and far more "hand axes" (the next tool to be developed) have been found in Africa than anywhere else.

However vague the evidence may be concerning the origin of man in Africa, it is clear that black men played a far greater role in the civilizations of antiquity than most historians have acknowledged. What we call "civilization" began at about the same time, some seven thousand years ago, in Mesopotamia and in Egypt. Whether the Mesopotamians were black is open to question, though there is some evidence indicating that they were. But there is no doubt that black men played a significant role in Egyptian civilization from the very beginning. The Egyptians were, in all probability, a mixed breed; in their own paintings, they depicted themselves as black, reddish-brown, or yellow; white-skinned figures usually represented foreigners or slaves. Examination of skeletons and other remains, moreover, indicate that a substantial proportion of the Egyptian population

* R. Oliver and J. D. Fage, *A Short History of Africa,* Baltimore: Penguin Books, 1962.

—perhaps a third or more—was clearly Negroid. And Herodotus described the fifth-century B.C. Egyptians as "black and curly-haired."

There was contact, extending over millenia, moreover, between the Egyptians and the Ethiopians, who considered themselves the spiritual fathers of Egyptian civilization.* Diodorous Siculus, the Greek historian of the first century B.C., wrote that "The Ethiopians conceived themeslves to be of greater antiquity than any other nation; and it is probably that, born under the sun's path, its warmth may have ripened them earlier than other men. They supposed themselves to be the inventors of worship, of festivals, of solemn assemblies, of sacrifices, and every religious practice." There was a good deal in Greek legend to support the Ethiopian claim. The *Iliad* speaks of the Gods feasting among the "blameless Ethiopians," and Homer elsewhere praises Memnon, king of Ethiopia, and Eurybates:

> Of visage solemn, sad, but sable hue,
> Short, wooly curls, o'erfleeced his bending head . . .
> Eurybates, in whose large soul alone,
> Ulysses viewed an image of his own. . . .

The Old Testament, whose historical reliability is being validated more and more by the findings of archaeology, provides perhaps the best evidence of the role black men played in the development of ancient civilization. Chapter X of Genesis, for example, catalogues the principal races and nations known at the time, describing them all as branches of one great family owing common ancestry to Noah. (This chapter is thus the first assertion of the unity of the human race, a concept which follows logically from the Hebrew belief in the Unity of God.) "These are the groupings of Noah's descendants," says the author of Genesis,

* In antiquity, "Ethiopia" referred to the Egyptian Sudan, as well as to the land on *both* sides of the Red Sea.

"according to their origins, by their nations; and from these the nations branched out on the earth after the Flood." The Israelites themselves claimed direct descent from Shem, the first Semite and Noah's oldest son. The Medes, the Greeks, the Scythians, and the Cimmerians, among others —"the maritime nations"—were descended from Japheth, Noah's youngest son. Noah's middle son, of course, was Ham. His name in Hebrew—*Cham*—means black; it also means Egypt.*

The Biblical language itself thus shows clearly that the ancients viewed Egypt as a black society. Lest there be any doubt of the role of black men in that period, the author of Genesis continues by listing the sons of Ham. The oldest was *Cush,* the Biblical name for Ethiopia and, down to the present, the vernacular Hebrew term for a black African. (Genesis reports that in addition to a number of other children, Cush "begot Nimrod, who was the first man of power on earth. He was a mighty hunter by the grace of the Lord," not to mention his having been the founder of Babylonia. The Israelites clearly believed that the Babylonians and Assyrians were of African origin—a belief shared by some contemporary historians.) The other children of Ham included *Mizraim,* the most common Biblical name for Egypt; *Put,* or Libya; and *Canaan,* a name derived from a root meaning "to be low;" and referring originally to the low-lying coast of Phoenicia and the lowlands of the Philistines, later to all of western Palestine.

It was Ham's son Canaan, incidentally, and not Ham himself, upon whom Noah laid his famous curse, "a servant of servants shall he be to this brethren." For centuries, the so-called "curse of Ham" (Genesis, IX, 25-27) has been cited to prove Biblical justification for Negro slavery and inferiority. Rarely has a greater hoax been perpetrated, for Noah's

* For direct references to Egypt as "the land of Ham" (in Hebrew, *eretz Cham*), see Psalms CV, verses 23 and 27, and CVI, verse 22, which describe the Israelites' slavery in Egypt and the Exodus.

curse is completely unambiguous: "And he said: Cursed be Canaan; A servant of servants shall he be unto his brethren. And he said: Blessed be the Lord, the God of Shem; and let Canaan be their servant. God enlarge Japheth . . . And let Canaan be their servant." In short, the curse was laid not on Ham and his descendants, *i.e.*, on the black race, but on Canaan—the traditional enemy of the ancient Israelites.*

What happened to end the large, perhaps central, role which Africa played in world progress for some five or six thousand years or more?† In Professor Leakey's opinion, Africa lost this role for two reasons: the expansion of the desert "cut off Africa from the rest of the world" (except for the Nile); and the African climate reduced human incentive by providing an abundance of food, and reduced capacity because of an abundance of disease. The truth undoubtedly is a good deal more complex. For one thing, the Sahara was nothing like the obstacle to communication that so many historians assume; on the contrary, the trans-Saharan trade connecting North Africa with the western Sudan, and

* The erroneous belief that Ham was cursed stems in part from the ambiguity of the verses immediately preceding the curse, in part from mistranslation. They are usually translated: "Ham, the father of Canaan, saw his father's nakedness and told his two brothers outside. And Noah awoke from his wine and *knew what his youngest son* had done unto him." [Emphasis added] The first verse does suggest that the sin (of looking at Noah's nakedness) was committed by Ham—but the text curiously identifies Ham as "the father of Canaan." The fact that it was Canaan and not Ham who was guilty seems clear from study of the next few verses. For one thing, the curse is clearly directed at Canaan, not at Ham. For another, the line preceding the curse is invariably translated incorrectly. It should read "and Noah knew what his *grandson* had done unto him." The Hebrew word *beno hakatan* may either be translated "his youngest son" or "his grandson" (the later meaning is similar to the French *petit fils.*) But "grandson" is the correct—indeed, the only possible—translation in this instance, for Ham was *not* Noah's youngest son. Japheth was the youngest; Ham was the middle son. (*See* Genesis VI, 1; VII, 13; IX, 18; X, 1.)

† Archaeologists have unearthed a primitive abacus in the Congo that is appoximately 8,000 years old—probably the world's oldest.

through the Sudan, with the Gold Coast, continued on a large scale down to the nineteenth century, and indeed is still carried on. For another, the expansion of the desert does not explain the decline of Egypt—once the pinnacle of civilization and of wealth, now one of the poorest and most backward of lands. Indeed, few things in history are as dimly understood as the causes for either the rise or the fall of the great civilizations.

Be that as it may, the fact remains that although Africa lost its leadership, it did not sink into savagery or barbarism. On the contrary, Negro cultures and cultures led by mixed groups of Negroes, Berbers, and whites flourished in West and Central Africa and on the eastern coast until the sixteenth century, and in lesser degree down to the establishment of European hegemony in the nineteenth century.* These societies were known to the Europeans of their day; knowledge of them disappeared in modern times in part because black Africa has no written history, and our literate age tends to assume that an absence of written record means an absence of anything worth recording. But knowledge of African culture and history disappeared also because, as Du Bois put it, "the world which raped it had to pretend that it had not harmed a man but a thing."

In good measure, however, the history of black Africa was obscured by the interpenetration of Moslem and Negro cultures during the Moslem ascendance that ran from the seventh to the sixteenth centuries. It is now clear that much of what had been considered the history of Arab or Moslem or Moorish societies was the history of Negro and Negroid people as well.† The term "Arab" or "Moor" was applied to

---

* I am indebted to Professor Morroe Berger of Princeton University for his help in interpreting African history, especially its Moslem elements.

† *Cf.*, Morroe Berger, *op. cit.;* Oliver and Fage, *op. cit.;* Basil Davidson, *The Lost Cities of Africa,* Boston: Atlantic Monthly Press, 1959; J. D. Fage, *An Introduction to the History of West Africa,* Cambridge, England: Cambridge University Press, 1962; W. E. B. Du Bois, *Black*

anyone professing the faith of Islam; the large proportion of Negroid blood among the Berbers and other peoples of North Africa is evident to anyone who has traveled in the area. Thus, Elijah Muhammad's identification of Negroes with Islam and the Arabic world, while grossly exaggerated, reveals a truth that has been generally ignored and unknown.

From its beginnings, in fact, Mohammedanism contained substantial Negroid elements. One of the greatest figures in the development of Islam, for example, was Bilal-i-Habesh, or Bilal of Ethiopia, a liberated slave who became Mohammed's closest friend, and to whom Mohammed yielded precedence in Paradise. Mohammed adopted another Negro, Zayd bin Hareth, as his son; Zayd became one of the Prophet's greatest generals. The Moorish army which invaded and conquered Spain included a great many Negroes and dark-skinned Berbers as well as "white" Arabs; if Shakespeare's *Othello* is any indication, the Europeans considered the Moors to be Negroes. Thus, Othello's color is described as "sooty," and Iago refers unflatteringly to "the thick lips." *

The main impact of Islam on the Negro peoples began in

Folk, Then and Now, New York: Henry Holt & Co., 1939, and *The World and Africa,* New York: The Viking Press, 1947; Henri Labouret, *Africa Before the White Man,* New York: Walker & Co., 1962; Lerone Bennett, Jr., *Before the Mayflower,* Chicago: Johnson Publishing Co., 1962.

* Shakespeare's play suggests how deep European prejudice against Negroes had already become—witness the horror and fury with which Desdemona's father receives the news of her marriage to Othello. (He is sure she must have been drugged by some magic potion.) But the play also demonstrates that however much Europeans may have frowned on miscegenation, their image of the Negro was as far from the "Sambo" stereotype as can be imagined: Othello—a former slave—is described as "the noble Moor" and as the greatest general of his day. (He convinces the Duke of Venice that he did not use any magic to win Desdemona's love by explaining that she fell in love with him while overhearing him tell the story of his military exploits.)

the eleventh century, when a Puritanical sect of Berber warriors, the Almavorids, crossed the Sahara, conquered the ancient empire of Ghana,* and converted to Islam the rulers (but not much of the population) of the whole fertile belt that stretches across Africa from the Western Sudan to the hills of Ethiopia. At the time of the Almavorid conquest, Ghana was noted for its wealth throughout the Arab world; the Arab geographer El Bikri reported in 1067 that the king of Ghana had a nugget of gold so large that he could tether his horse to it. After the conquest, however, Ghana went into a decline.

The next great empire to emerge in the Sudan was Mali. Its history goes back to the seventh century, but Mali became important in the thirteenth century when a Moslem convert, Sundiata, came to power, and reached its apex in the fourteenth century under Mansa (Emperor) Musa, who ruled from 1307 to 1332. Mansa Musa put Mali on the map† through his pilgrimage to Mecca in 1324, which was carried out with incredible pomp and style; the enormous store of gold he took on the journey was a source of awe throughout the Moslem world and much of Europe as well. On his return, he brought with him an Arab poet and architect who built mosques in Timbuctu and other cities. Twenty years after Musa's death, Ibn Battuta, the John Gunther of the fourteenth century, spent nearly two months in Mali. Its inhabitants, he reported, "are Moslems, punctilious in observing the hours of prayer, studying books of law, and memorizing the Koran." The women were "of surpassing beauty." All in all, Ibn Battuta, who visited virtually every state from Africa's west coast straight across to China, was impressed with what he saw in Mali:

* Ancient Ghana was located considerably north and west of present-day Ghana. The state, which included most of present-day Senegal and part of Mali, was founded in about the fourth century A.D. by North African Berbers.

† Quite literally so: the first map of West Africa ever drawn in Europe, in 1375, showed Mali and its "Land of the Negroes."

> The Negroes possess some admirable qualities. They are seldom unjust, and have a greater abhorrence of injustice than any other people. Their sultan shows no mercy to anyone who is guilty of the least act of it. There is complete security in their country. Neither traveler nor inhabitant in it has anything to fear from robbers or men of violence. They do not confiscate the property of any white man who dies in their country, even if it be uncounted wealth. On the contrary, they give it into the charge of some trustworthy person among the whites, until the rightful heir takes possession of it. . . .

In short, Mali was a state whose organization and civilization compared favorably with those of the Moslem kingdoms or indeed the Christian kingdoms of the same epoch.

One hundred and sixty years later, this part of the Sudan was still the site of a flourishing civilization, though the Mali empire had been replaced by a former vassal, the kingdom of Songhay, whose capital was seven hundred miles to the east. Timbuctu had become a city of perhaps 100,000 inhabitants; its University of Sankore was famous throughout the Moslem world for the study of law and surgery. Leo Africanus, a member of the Papal Court of Leo X, the Medici Pope, visited Mali in about 1510 and was considerably impressed.* "The people of this region," he reported "excel all other Negroes in wit, civility, and industry, and were the first that embraced the law of Mohammad." In Timbuctu itself, he reported, there were "great stores of doctors, judges, priests, and other learned men that are bountifully maintained at the king's costs and charges. And hither are brought diverse manuscripts or written books out of Barbary, which are sold for more money than any other merchandise." (Timbuctu's intellectual and cultural life was

---

* Leo Africanus was an Arab Moslem who was captured in Spain. Impressed by his learning, his captors presented him to Pope Leo who freed him, converted him to Christianity, and made him a member of his court.

carried on in Arabic, since the African languages had never been committed to writing.) But Leo's visit came near the end of Sudanese glory. At the end of the sixteenth century, the Songhay empire was destroyed by an invasion from the North—this time by Moors who, possessing gunpowder, had no trouble subduing the black population. From the time the capital of Gao fell in 1591, the Sudan went into a decline from which it never recovered. Once the central government was destroyed, the Songhay empire dissolved into tribal kingdoms. The Sudan became a battleground, fought over by Tuareg nomads infiltrating from the desert and pastoralists coming from the west.

The history of the forested southern half of West Africa—what the Europeans called Guinea—is more obscure than that of the Sudan, since it was not visited by the Arab authors who wrote about the Sudan between the eighth and fifteenth centuries. By the thirteenth century, however, the Negroes of Guinea had begun to develop states rather similar in pattern to those of the Sudan, and when the European slave traders came, they dealt with highly organized, and militarily powerful states.* The societies of the Guinea area, though agricultural, were also urban in character; settlements ranged from small villages to substantial towns. Most of these towns were barred to Europeans until the nineteenth century, when the Europeans finally succeeded in penetrating beyond the coastal strip. The town of Benin, in what is now Nigeria, was an exception; Benin was one of the "ports of trade" to which the European slave traders were restricted. Sixteenth- and seventeenth-century European traders, whose descriptions survive, quite clearly regarded Benin as a great city, quite comparable with the major European cities of the time. In 1602, for example, a Dutch trader reported that:

* *Cf.*, Oliver and Fage, *op. cit.*, and Karl Polanyi, Conrad M. Arensberg, & Harry W. Pearson, eds., *Trade and Market in the Early Empires*. Glencoe, Ill.: Free Press, 1957.

> The town seemeth to be very great; when you enter into it you go into a great broad street, not paved, which seems to be seven or eight times broader than Warmoes street in Amsterdam . . . At the gate where I entered on horseback, I saw a very high bulwark, very thick of earth, with a very deep broad ditch . . . Without this gate there is a great suburb. When you are in the great street aforesaid, you see many great streets on the sides thereof, which also go right forth . . . The King's Court is very great, within it having many great foursquare plains, which round about them have galleries, wherein there is always watch kept. I was so far within the Court that I passed over four such great plains, and wherever I looked, still I saw gates upon gates to go into other places . . . It seems that the King has many soldiers; he has also many gentlemen, who when they come to court ride upon horses. . . .

Today, Benin is best known for its magnificent bronze art, which exerted a powerful influence on Picasso and other contemporary painters. The rulers of such states as Benin and Dahomey maintained their authority over large areas, and as noted, were able to keep the Europeans out until the late-nineteenth century. In the middle of the nineteenth century, when Dahomey was still under African control, the English trader and writer, John Duncan, was impressed by the country's law and order. "During my stay at Abomey," he wrote, "I was never asked by any individual for an article of even the most trifling value, nor ever lost anything, except what was stolen by my people from the coast. The Dahoman laws are certainly severe, but they have the desired effect."

▼

3

Looking at the broad sweep of African history, it seems clear that Negroes need not feel ashamed of their race on account of its past. There are, to be sure, enormous gaps in our knowledge of African history, and a great many mysteries as well. Why did the culture of the Western Sudan atrophy after the sixteenth century? (The region did not come under European control until the nineteenth century.) And why did black Africa never develop a written language?

The point at issue, however, is not whether black African civilization was the equal of European or Arabic civilizations, whatever "equal" may mean; we understand too little of the reasons for either the rise or the fall of any of the great civilizations of the past. If progress requires the stimulation that comes from contact with other cultures, as many historians and anthropologists believe, then black Africa commands particular respect: it has been more isolated from contact with other cultures than any other society save the Indians of North and South America. And how do we measure one culture against another? Were the pagan (or the Moslem) blacks, for example, the moral inferiors of the whites who came from Catholic Spain and Portugal or Protestant England and Holland to trade in human flesh? And if black Africans failed to develop a written language, what are we to make of African art; how do we rate a culture in which esthetic expression is an experience in which the entire population participates? (In Africa, as Lerone Bennett, Jr., has observed, art "was not for art's sake, but for life's sake.")

Whether African societies were "better" or "worse," "more civilized" or "less civilized" than the societies developed by white men, in short, is not really germane. What is crucial is simply the fact that Negroes can hold their heads aloft in the knowledge that men of black skin have contributed to human progress, that they have created and maintained societies and civilizations of a high order. Having been denied a place in history for so long, it is essential that Negroes be allowed to claim their rightful place in the story of mankind. It is equally important that white men understand that Negroes do in fact have that place.

If Negroes are to claim the past that is rightfully theirs, however, they will have to assume the risks that go with it. Acquisition of a past is necessary, but it is also perilous—for it means an end to innocence. Just as the Negro past shows beauty and grandeur, so does it show meanness, cruelty, injustice. The Europeans, after all, did not invent the slave trade; they exploited and expanded a commerce that Africans had been carrying on from time immemorial, and diverted it into new channels. (Slaves had always been one of the staples of the trans-Saharan trade.) Indeed, the European slave traders themselves almost never enslaved an African, for they were not permitted to enter the interior. They were, instead, restricted to the coastal trading settlements by the African kings and emperors who wanted to keep the monopoly of the slave trade in their own hands. It was Africans who waged war periodically in order to enslave other Africans, and it was Africans who chained the slaves together and marched them hundreds of miles to the sea, to be sold to the Europeans for guns or cloth.

The attempt to establish kinship with contemporary Africa raises even deeper problems. It is only when he visits Africa that the American Negro realizes how much of an American he really is and how wide is the cultural gap between him and the African Negro; it is only when he visits Africa that the American Negro realizes how deep are the wounds that Africa has inflicted on him. Richard Wright's experiences provide a case in point. When friends first suggested that he go to Africa, Wright wrote:

> I heard them, but my mind and feelings were racing along another and hidden track. Africa! Being of African descent, would I be able to feel and know something about Africa on the basis of a common "racial" heritage? . . . Or had three hundred years imposed a psychological distance between me and the "racial stock" from which I had sprung? . . . Am I African? Had some of my ancestors sold their relatives to white men? What would my feelings

> be when I looked into the black face of an African, feeling that maybe his great-great-great-grandfather had sold my great-great-great-grandfather into slavery? Was there something in Africa that my feelings could latch onto to make all of this dark past clear and meaningful? Would the Africans regard me as a lost brother who had returned? . . . According to popular notions of race, there ought to be something of "me" down there in Africa. Some vestige, some heritage, some vague but definite ancestral reality that would serve as a key to unlock the hearts and feelings of the Africans whom I'd meet. . . .

The key did not work; Wright's meeting with Africa was disastrous, for his mind and tastes were too American. He was horrified to find that belief in magic was not limited to the uneducated; he was shaken by what he saw of African culture; and he found that Africans regarded him as a stranger to be evaded or fooled. "I found the African an oblique, hard-to-know man who seems to take a kind of childish pride in trying to create a sense of bewilderment in the minds of strangers," Wright reported. "I found the African almost invariably underestimated the person with whom he was dealing; he always placed too much confidence in an evasive reply, thinking that if he denied something, then that something ceased to exist. It was childlike." More important, perhaps, he found a universal distrust; "This fear, this suspicion of nothing in particular came to be the most predictable hallmark of the African mentality that I met in all of the Gold Coast, from the Prime Minister down to the humblest 'mammy' selling *kenke* on the street corners." *

Wright traveled to Africa in 1954, when African independence was just beginning, but his experience seems to be repeated by many Negroes who "return" for any length of time. They discover an enormous cultural gap, far beyond anything they have been prepared for: they are troubled by telephones and plumbing that do not work, by appoint-

* *Black Power, A Record of Reactions in a Land of Pathos,* New York: Harper & Row, Publishers, Inc., 1954.

ments that are not kept and promises that are not fulfilled, if indeed they are even remembered the next day—in short, by hundreds of factors, large and small, that remind him that Africa is not really "home." "It's ridiculous," one American Negro in Africa told Harold Isaacs, "but I had never before realized how much of my life had nothing to do with the race problem at all. I mean just the way you do everything you do, what you mean when you say something, and how you understand what the other fellow means."

Nor are the difficulties of communicating the only things that serve to alienate the American Negro in Africa; he is upset also by the corruption and brutality of much of African political life. (Nkrumah has been jailing political opponents since he first came to power, under a law that permits him to hold men for four years—recently extended to eight—without trial or charges.) Nor does it take much sensitivity to see that the new black ruling classes frequently are as contemptuous of their subjects, and as condescending toward them, as was the most arrogant white colonial. Thus it is not surprising that American Negroes who visit frequently find it more upsetting than rewarding. Almost every American Negro he met in Africa in 1960, Isaacs reports, had "discovered that he was much more alien in Africa. Whether he liked it or not, he found that he was American, and that in Africa he became an American in exile."

It is in the United States, in short, and only in the United States, that American Negroes will be able to resolve their problem of identification. To be sure, Negroes must recapture their African past, because denying them a place in history has been one of the means whites have used to keep them down; and they must find some basis on which to relate to Africa, because denying that relationship has been central to Negro self-hatred. But building a bridge to Africa past and Africa present is simply a means of erasing the old stigma of race; it is not a base on which Negroes can erect a new identity. For American Negroes have been formed by the United States, not by Africa; Africa gave them their color, but America gave them their personality and their culture. The central fact in Negro history is slavery, and Negroes must come to grips with it, must learn to accept it—to accept it not as a source of shame (the shame is the white man's) but as an experience that explains a large part of their present predicament. Only if they understand *why* they are what they are, can Negroes change *what* they are. Identity is not something that can be found; it must be created.

It is clear, however, that pride in race must play a part in the new identity. The Negro is not struggling to become free, Ralph Ellison argues, simply in order to disappear. For one thing, he cannot disappear; to argue, as does a liberal intellectual like Norman Podhoretz, that "the Negro problem can be solved in this country in no other way" than through assimilation and miscegenation is to argue that no solution is possible for several centuries. Equally important, Negroes are beginning to think that maybe they do not *want* to disappear, that perhaps there are specifically Negro values and cultural traits that should be kept.

This new pride in race must be carefully nurtured, for it is not yet deeply entrenched. The process is bound to lead —has already led—to a considerable degree of racial self-consciousness, indeed, to out-and-out race chauvinism. Whites who encounter it tend to react with surprise or indignation: how can Negroes, who have been (and who still are) the victims of racial persecution, now turn around and talk about mystical notions like Negritude, "soul," and the like? The answer is simple: the reaction to centuries of being ashamed and humiliated by the color black is not likely to be a calm and dispassionate analysis of racial characteristics. Only by swinging in the opposite direction can the pendulum find the center. But Negro self-consciousness is not entirely irrational; to some degree it involves what the French existentialist philosopher and playwright Jean-Paul Sartre calls "anti-racist racism." Before differences can be abolished, they must be respected; given past history, neither Negroes nor whites will learn to respect blackness unless the virtues of being black are emphasized and over-emphasized. Once racial differences are respected, however, people can proceed to ignore them, or to transcend them. Thus, Solly Saunders, the hero of John Oliver Killen's novel, *And Then We Heard the Thunder*, is transformed by reading a copy of Richard Wright's *Twelve Million Black Voices* which his race-conscious sweetheart had sent him.

> The photography by Edwin Russkam together with Wright's overpowering word images awoke inside of Solly emotions long asleep and almost forgotten. Sometimes he would be reading a passage, or sometimes a face would stare at him from the pages, and he would hear the voices, and he would feel a trembling in his stomach and a fulness in his own face, and he would feel his own blackness deeply, and be proud to be a black man.

This pride in self dissolves Solly's hatred of the white.

> One day he was reading the book, and it suddenly came to him, and he said to himself, if I'm proud of me, I don't need to hate Mr. Charlie's people. I don't want to. I don't need to. If I love me, I can also love the whole damn human race. Black, brown, yellow, white. . . .*

The danger, of course, is that the pendulum does not always come back to center; anti-racist racism does not necessarily lead to a belief in the common humanity of man. The bitterness of Killens' novel shows that clearly enough; Killens' hero may have been able to overcome his suspicion and hatred of every white man, but Killens himself was not. More to the point, the two mass movements that have been most successful in developing self-pride among Negroes—the Garveyites and the Black Muslims—did so in large meas-

* Killens, *op. cit.*

ure by preaching undying hatred of everything white. The problem is not peculiarly Negro; on the contrary, one of the central questions of our time is whether any group, be it a religion, a nationality, or a race, can instil a commitment among its members without at the same time derogating other groups. It is fortunate, perhaps, that the search for Negro identity is coming to a head at a time when the great religions of the West are seriously grappling with this problem—when they are discovering, in fact, that faith without prejudice *is* possible.*

As they struggle to create an identity for themselves, Negroes inevitably find the present particularly painful to live through. They are caught in the tensions of two worlds. For a great many Negroes, as we have seen, segregation had become a crutch on which they leaned very heavily; the concept of Negro inferiority relieved them of the need to compete in a sternly competitive society, and absolved them of responsibility for their behavior or their fate. For other Negroes, segregation provided a convenient scapegoat to excuse their personal failures.

But now the crutch is being broken and the scapegoat cast aside; the old identity is being destroyed before the new one has been completed. The winds blowing from Africa (and from within the United States as well) are forcing Negro Americans into new and uncharted territory—into a terrain that terrifies as much as it invites. Clearly the conditions of life have changed, the opportunities have broadened enormously. Yet just as clearly, the white world is still mined against the Negro. Or is it? One is never really sure; part of the price of being a Negro in America is a degree of paranoia. The obstacles are no less frightening for being imagined—and many are real enough, for the United States has a long, long way to go before discrimination disappears.

---

* *See,* for example, Bernhard E. Olson's pioneering examination of Protestant religious school curricula in *Faith and Prejudice,* New Haven: Yale University Press, 1963.

Hence the Negro must keep his guard up while adjusting to the new world that is opening. All this, moreover, while he is still searching for his identity, while he is still struggling to assimilate and understand the varied messages with which his mind and heart have been assaulted, to put the pieces together in a way that makes sense.

The result is a terrible strain as old customs and habits and patterns of thought are eroded and the familiar and the unfamiliar merge in a kaleidoscope of changing impressions. "The tensions among Negroes," says Harold Isaacs, "become less and less the tensions of submission and endurance, and more and more the tensions of change and self-assertion. But both kinds of tension continue to co-exist in almost every Negro individual . . . they jostle each other in a constant and bruising inward turmoil as each person seeks to discover the new terms of life—the older person fighting both to hold on to and to throw off the older habits of mind and outlook; the younger person trying to find the new ground to stand on amid all the tangled fears and angers and despairs and exhilarations." No Negro can remain as he was; the poverty-stricken Negro in the Mississippi Delta and his cousin in the Chicago slum, the lawyer or doctor holding his head up high in an integrated suburb of New York, and the president of a Negro college in the South, who still must bow and scrape to keep his school alive—all are being forced to see themselves and to see others in new and unsettling ways.

VII

POWER, PERSONALITY, AND PROTEST

We wish to plead our own cause. Too long have others spoken for us.

—Editorial in *Freedom's Journal,*
March 16, 1827

1

By itself, however, all the race pride in the world will not solve the Negro's crisis of identity. In the last analysis, what Negroes need more than anything else is to be treated like men—to believe, in their hearts, that they *are* men, men who can stand on their own feet and control their own destinies. Asked what it is that Negroes want, spokesmen from Frederick Douglass to W. E. B. Du Bois to James Baldwin have answered in almost identical terms: Negroes want to be treated like men.

"Negroes want to be treated like men." The request sounds simple enough. Yet as James Baldwin has put it, "People who have mastered Kant, Hegel, Shakespeare, Marx, Freud, and the Bible find this statement utterly impenetrable." They find it impenetrable because they do not realize how patronizing they really are in dealing with Negroes, how little they know about Negroes, and how little effort they have expended in trying to learn. And so they tell a forty-five-year-old porter, "You're a good boy, Jimmy," and feel pleased with their generosity of spirit; or they tell a heavy-set Negro housekeeper, "You look just like Aunt Jemimah," and think they have bestowed a great compliment, or they shake a Negro's hand or call him "Sir" or "Mister," and congratulate themselves on the "tolerance" they have shown. The self-congratulations shows through and is resented.

Nor is the patronizing limited to the uneducated or even to the unsophisticated. "At lilac evening," the beatnik author Jack Kerouac has written, "I walked with every muscle aching . . . wishing I were a Negro, feeling that the best the white world had offered was not enough ecstasy for me, not enough life, joy, kicks, music. . . ." Kerouac was writing out of admiration, of course—but in his self-conscious search for values superior to those of the white world he needs to reject, he comes surprisingly close to the old "Sambo" stereotype of the happy, musical, sexually-superior Negro; and Negroes read it as an insult, not a compliment. "I would hate to be in Kerouac's shoes if he should ever be mad enough to read this aloud from the stage of the Apollo Theater," James Baldwin commented to a *Time* reporter.

But how *not* to patronize Negroes? This is a real question for a great many whites with deep convictions about equality and justice. At times, there seems to be no way; *whatever* one says or does is received with hostility. James Baldwin has gone so far as to state flatly that "there is no role for the white liberal. He is our affliction." In Baldwin's cosmology, in fact, there seems sometimes to be no decent white of any sort, and no way a white can prove his decency: If you are hostile, you are a racist; if you express friendship of sympathy, you are a fuzzy liberal, part of "the chorus of the innocents"; and if you commit yourself to action, this merely proves that you are a condescending white using Negroes to purge your own conscience, or trying to raise Negroes to your level. In expressing these sentiments, Baldwin claims to be consciously exaggerating; his aim, as an artist, is to anger—and through angering, to force the white liberal to examine his own attitudes and purge himself of the patronizing sense of superiority that Baldwin feels makes real discourse difficult. (There was a time, however, when Baldwin wanted to be heard as a *man,* not as a Negro.) Other Negro writers and intellectuals have their anger under much less control. Indeed, the pose they strike brings to mind an old vaudeville gag about a passenger in a Pullman dining car, who becomes very abusive when told there is no French pastry for dessert. At the next town, the train is halted while a waiter runs to a bakery and returns, panting, with a platter bearing an elegant assortment. The passenger looks at the pastry for a moment and then waves the waiter away, saying, "I'd rather be angry." Sometimes it seems as though Baldwin, Killens, *et al* *would* rather be angry—and the natural white reactions is to be angry in return.

But something more than anger is needed if communication between the races is to be restored—or rather, to be established, since there never has been real communication. To be sure, Baldwin sometimes appears guilty of the same sin with which he charges whites: of seeing men of a different color not as individuals but as stereotypes—as nameless, faceless men. And indeed, Baldwin charges every white with the guilt of every other white, past and present. This is more than any man is likely to accept; the individual white answers Baldwin's charge with indignation, refusing to accept the guilt of others, insisting that he is guilty only of the sins which he himself has committed.

He may not be guilty of the sins of others; he is responsible. As Rabbi Abraham J. Heschel has reminded us, "an honest estimation of the moral state of our society will disclose: some are guilty, but all are responsible . . . In a community not indifferent to suffering, uncompromisingly impatient with cruelty and falsehood, continually concerned for

God and every man, racial discrimination would be infrequent rather than common."

It is the white citizens of America, therefore, individually and collectively, who bear the responsibility for establishing communication between the races. If they are to carry out that responsibility, they must understand what prompts the "unreasonableness" of the Negroes with whom they come into contact; they must understand why Negroes rudely reject their proffer of sympathy or help. A marvelously ironic scene in Jules Feiffer's comic novel *Harry, The Rat With Women,* helps provide that understanding. "Patronizing sons of bitches," a drunken Negro shouts to his white companions at a Greenwich Village party.

> All I give you is hate and all you give me back is understanding. You think that's what I want? I don't want you mothers to love me," he continues; "I know you're the enemy. You wouldn't hate me for being black, so I turned communist. You insisted I turned communist because of my bitter background and you gave me more love . . . So I turned queer! You insisted I only turned queer because I can't fulfill my normal role in a white society and you gave me more love. So I turned junkie because I never had a chance. And you gave me more love. Where is your White Love going to leave me? It won't let me have the power to make myself a communist, it takes away my free choice to be a queer, it robs me of the will to be a junkie. It does all for me; nothing left for me to do ever.*

"It does all for me; nothing left for me to do ever." This is the heart of the matter: that white philanthropy, white liberalism, white sympathy and support, no less than white bigotry and discrimination, have had the affect of preventing Negroes from standing on their own feet, from "exercising their full manhood rights," to use Du Bois' phrase.

---

* Jules Feiffer, *Harry, The Rat With Women,* New York: The McGraw-Hill Book Company, 1963.

Myrdal summed it up twenty years ago in the introduction to *An American Dilemma*, when he pointed out that "practically all the economic, social and political power is held by whites."

> It is thus the white majority group that naturally determines the Negro's "place." All our attempts to reach scientific explanations of why Negroes are what they are and why they live as they do have regularly led to determinants on the white side of the racial line. In the practical and political struggles of effecting changes, the views and attitudes of the white Americans are likewise strategic. The Negro's entire life, and, consequently, also his opinions on the Negro problem, are, in the main, to be considered as secondary reactions to more primary pressures from the side of the dominant white majority.

The "Negro revolt" cannot be understood, therefore, except as a long-suppressed reaction against this imbalance of power—an imbalance which whites take for granted, but which Negroes have always resented. "We wish to plead our own cause. Too long have others spoken for us," the first editorial in the first Negro newspaper to be published in the United States proclaimed in 1827. "You whites have always decided everything," a young black nationalist leader told me accusingly a hundred thirty-five years later; "you even decided when to set us free."

And indeed whites *have* decided everything—sometimes in malice, sometimes with the best intent, frequently because Negroes were unable or unwilling to decide for themselves. The reason varies; what is crucial is that Negroes never have had the sense of controlling their own destinies; they have never had the feeling that they were making, or even participating in, the decisions that really counted, the decisions that affected their lives and fortunes. Even those actions which advanced the Negro cause, the Emancipation Proclamation for example, were usually taken for reasons having little to do with Negro interests and needs. Hence they tended to heighten rather than lessen the Negro's sense of anger or dependency. "The tragedy," writes Saul Alinsky of Chicago, "is that Negroes, lacking the opportunity and trapped by insurmountable circumstances, could not themselves come to grips with the issue of equality; that none of the issues were resolved on their merits or by the power of the oppressed. They were always a by-product of something 'more important.' This series of situations left many Negroes more or less as by-products of themselves and inevitably diluted their dignity and strength."

▼

2

Negroes cannot solve their problem of identity, therefore—they cannot achieve their manhood—until they are in a position to make or to influence the decisions that affect them, until, in a word, they have power. For in the last analysis, self-hate stems more from Negroes' unequal position relative to power than from any lack of knowledge of self. The Negro's problem, that is to say, is not one of "acculturation," nor even of identity in the usual sense, but of power. As Professor Dan W. Dodson of New York University has said, it is "impossible for a . . . member of a group which is powerless in the community to grow to maturity without some trauma to his perception of himself." Thus, the principal solution to the problem of Negro personality and identity is the acquisition of power: political, social, and economic. The fact that Negroes constitute so large, and so rapidly growing, a proportion of the population of large cities provides an opportunity for the acquisition of political power no other ethnic group ever had, except in isolated instances —for example, the Irish in Boston.

Negroes are well aware of this fact, and they are determined to make the most of it. They are aware, also, of the fact that Africans, because of their political independence, are treated with a respect and deference still denied American Negroes. ("Africa has been black a long time," James Baldwin has written, "but American Negroes did not identify themselves with Africa until Africa became identified with power.") Hence a growing number of Negro-Americans are determined to harness the political power their numbers make possible, and to use it, in turn, to acquire social and economic power—to force their way into what they uniformly refer to as "the white power structure," that is, the vague and shadowy coalition of government officials, politicians, businessmen, and civic leaders who in legend, if not always in fact, make the crucial decisions. It is impossible to understand the dynamics of Negro protest activity except in terms of this determination to acquire power—a determination that stems from three hundred fifty years of being powerless.

Hence Negroes are demanding more than jobs or desegregation of lunch counters or integration of schools and neighborhoods. Negro leaders are determined that "the white power structure" recognize them and negotiate with them—that public officials, businessmen, and civic leaders come to the bargaining table not as patrons but as equals. They are insisting that whites recognize the leaders selected by the Negro community itself, whoever they may be or however distasteful the whites may find them. "I'm less interested in how many Negroes are selected for public office," says D. G. Gibson, the Negro political boss of Oakland, California, "than in how they were selected."

Gibson's interest in how Negroes are selected for office reflects considerably more than just a play for personal power (though Gibson certainly is not averse to power). His demand for a voice in selecting Negro officials reflects one of the most profound Negro concerns, a concern which white leaders must recognize if there is to be any racial peace. For nothing rankles Negroes quite so much as the white "power structure's" habit of choosing the Negro "leaders" whom it wants to reward or with whom it wants to deal. The habit is strongest in the South, of course, where the almost total lack of communication between the races makes it easier for whites to deal with Negroes through colored intermediaries, *i.e.*, through straw bosses of their own choosing.* And the whites naturally enough have chosen only Negroes willing to accommodate themselves to white interests. On their side, the Negroes have had no choice but to recognize the leaders whom the whites had selected. In a society as dependent on personal relationships as the South—a society in which, for Negroes, the rule of law was so weak—Negroes have needed men who could establish contact with the influential whites, who could gain favors or personal protection or, perhaps, by winning white favor and confidence, persuade the whites to build a needed school or hospital, or meet some other urgent need.

But Northerners have been in the habit of picking Negro "leaders," too, and many still consider this one of their prerogatives. In the fall of 1962, for example, a group of businessmen in Oakland became concerned over the extent of Negro unemployment and the possibility of a boycott or picketing by Negro militants, and decided to take the initiative themselves in developing a program to open up new jobs for Negroes. So far, so good. But when it came time to sit down and discuss alternatives, the businessmen did not call on the Negroes who would be most likely to organize a

* "When the white people want to influence Negro behavior or attitudes in one direction or another," Myrdal observed, ". . . to get the Negro farmers to plant a garden around their shacks, to screen their windows, to keep their children in school, to cure and prevent syphilis, to keep Negroes more respectful to the whites, to prevent them from joining trade unions, and to frighten them against 'outside meddlers' or 'red' seducers—the natural device . . . is to appeal to the 'community leaders.' These leaders are expected to get it over to the Negro masses, who are supposed to be rather passive."

boycott or call out the pickets. "We didn't want any of those emotional fellows from the NAACP," Norris Nash, vice-president of Kaiser Industries and ad hoc chairman of the businessman's group, explained. "We wanted sound men who would be willing to ignore the past and just concentrate on the future, so we asked Mr.——— to get a group together. He's a sound man," Nash added. "In fact, he's the whitest Negro we have in town." He also happened to be an employee of the city government, and consequently unable to display as much independence as someone deriving his livelihood from the Negro community.

The result was as predictable as it was unfortunate. The grass-roots Negro leaders in Oakland, all of whom were Democrats close to D. G. Gibson, interpreted the move not as an attempt to help Negroes, but as a plot by a group of businessmen to attract Negroes to the Republican Party. For if the program were to work—if it were to create job opportunities—Mr.———, the "whitest Negro in town," would replace D. G. Gibson as the man to see when a Negro was in trouble.* Instead of gaining the support of the Negro leadership, therefore, the businessmen aroused bitter anger and violent opposition.

The point, of course, is not whether the indigenous Negro leaders of Oakland were shortsighted in fighting the businessmen's program. (Ultimately, in point of fact, they recognized the potential value of the program, and the businessmen recognized their need for grass-roots Negro support, and so a modus vivendi was worked out.) What is crucial is that whites must learn to curb their ingrained habits of authority and paternalism if there is to be genuine communication between the races. For their own well-being, and even

---

* The Negro's suspicions had at least some basis in fact: a statement of objctives issued by the businessman's committee was almost identical with a statement issued the week before by a local Republican group.

more for the well-being of the community, businessmen and civic leaders must realize that when they talk only to the eight or ten most prosperous or most socially polished Negroes in town, they are not really talking to the Negroes at all, and that as a result they can be badly misled as to the temper and desires of the Negro community.

Equally important, the Negroes' demand for recognition is a crucial part of the struggle to overcome the devastation that the past three hundred fifty years have wrought on Negro personality. The apathy, the aimlessness, the lack of interest in education that characterize the Negro lower classes, and the crisis of identity that afflicts Negroes of all classes, stem from their sense of dependency and powerlessness—their conviction that "Mr. Charlie" controls everything, Negro leaders included, and that he has stacked the cards so that Negroes can never win. Negroes must gain a sense of potency and power if they are to stand erect as free men. Hence when businessmen or government officials or civic leaders say they are willing to grant some of the Negro demands, "but not if we're pushed too hard," they are missing the point. Negroes want to achieve their aims by their own efforts, not as a result of white beneficence. The crux of the matter may be summed up in the difference between the words "conversation" and "negotiation." Whites are accustomed to holding conversations with Negroes, in which they sound out the latters' views or acquaint them with decisions they have taken. But Negroes insist more and more on negotiations—on discussions, as equals, designed to reach an agreement, designed "to come to terms especially in state matters," as *Websters Third New International Dictionary* defines the word. To negotiate means to recognize the other party's power. When whites negotiate with Negroes, therefore, it not only helps solve the Negro's "Negro problem," it helps solve the white man's "Negro problem" as well; for whites begin to see Negroes in a different light—as equals, as men.

Negotiations aside, Negroes need to express their anger in a variety of ways—in word and deed, in picketing and marching, in singing and shouting. "The Negro has many pent-up frustrations," Rev. Martin Luther King wrote to eight Birmingham clergymen who had publicly urged him to call off the Birmingham demonstration. "He has to get them out. So let him march sometime: let him have his prayer pilgrimage to the city hall; understand why he must have sit-ins and freedom rides. If his repressed emotions do not come out in these non-violent ways," Dr. King added, "they will come out in ominous expressions of violence."

The point is not that demonstrations provide a cheap form of therapy (though such is at least partially the case), but that having suppressed their rage these many years behind a mask of servility or humility, Negroes must prove their new-found courage to themselves, as well as to the whites. When the poor Negroes of Montgomery stopped riding the buses, and when the college students in a dozen cities started sitting-in at lunch counters, many Negroes in the United States walked a little straighter; and whites began to see Negroes in a somewhat different light. The truth is that people can gain their freedom and self-respect only in the process of fighting for it. Thus, the very militancy and stridency that whites find so upsetting is indispensable if Negroes are to shuck off their traditional dependency and become truly free and equal, if they are to learn to respect themselves, and to be respected by whites. When whites express a yearning for "responsible" Negro leadership, therefore, the question must be asked: Responsible to whom?

A great many Negroes believe their leaders have been too responsible to white interests and insufficiently attentive to Negro needs; they believe that only men who are in no way beholden to whites are free to represent them without fear or favor. A crucial part of "the Negro revolt," therefore, is the attempt to replace the "Uncle Toms" and the "racial diplomats" of yesteryear with a new breed of "race men."

Indeed, the Negro revolt is directed as much against the old-line Negro leadership as against the white community. The revolt has already radically altered the style of Negro leadership: leaders have no choice but to assume a post of intransigent militancy. ("If I compromise," A. Philip Randolph is supposed to have said, "they'll picket me.") And so almost all Negro spokesmen now endorse the "Now, All, Here" theme made popular by Rev. Martin Luther King: "We want our Freedom *now:* we want it *all;* we want it *here!*"

There always has been a strain between the Negro community and its ostensible leaders. The reason, Ralph Bunche suggested more than two decades ago, was that "The Negro hates the Negro role in American society, and the Negro leader, who acts out this role in public life, becomes the symbol of what the Negro hates." In Southern communities in particular, but in the North as well, Negro leaders were humble and self-demeaning in the presence of whites. (There are stories of Negro college presidents being asked to sing and dance by groups of whites to whom they were appealing for funds.) The leaders saw no other option. For one thing, they owed their leadership to the whites, who held all the power. But even if the leaders had any taste for protest, they knew they would get no support from the Negro community, which was afraid to express the anger it really felt. Without the backing of mass protest, leaders had no weapons save flattery and servility with which to advance the Negro cause—to get a new school built, or a hospital; to obtain civil service jobs for Negroes, etc. But the Negro community assuaged its own sense of shame by turning on its leaders for their servility, attacking them for being "Uncle Toms," "handkerchief heads," "white men's niggers," and the like, and accusing them of trading their dignity and honor for some personal benefit.

As often as not, the accusations were true: in the South, as Myrdal and others have pointed out, Negro leaders frequently were a venal lot. In general, the scarcer a commodity, the more ruthless the struggle to possess it. No commodity is quite so scarce in the Negro community as power, and so the candidates for leadership—ministers, doctors, lawyers, businessmen—tended to fight for the occasional scraps of white recognition, using whatever weapons lay at hand. And since those who obtained power knew they would be resented by their constituents, they felt little loyalty to them—and the constituents felt even less loyalty to the leaders. Hence the attainment of power did tend to corrupt. As Ralph Bunche said in 1942, "The Negro leader often quickly puffs up when given power. He 'struts' and puts up a big front, or puts on 'airs,' often indulges in exhibitionism . . . For leadership itself is a form of escape." The result was (and all too often still is) an atmosphere of rivalry, envy, and mutual backbiting that defiled the whole community, and that gave whites the opportunity to neutralize whatever power Negroes may have had by playing off one faction against another.

Even where Negro leadership was honest and sincere, it tended to be highly ineffective. Some leaders—businessmen in particular—were reluctant to take the risks that militance might involve, for example, having a loan application turned down by the local bank, or having an outstanding loan called. Other leaders were so flattered at being consulted by whites that any thought of protest they might have harbored simply melted away. And still others, who led comfortable lives within the ghetto, simply wondered what more Negroes might want.

The city of Atlanta provides an excellent case in point. The city has long enjoyed a reputation for harmonious race relations, despite a pattern of segregation as rigid as that in any other large Southern city. In the 1962-63 school year, for example, after the city had basked in national praise for the dignified way in which it integrated its schools, a grand total of forty Negro students were actually enrolled in white schools. Atlanta achieved its reputation, and in fact maintained racial peace, by a disarmingly simple device: on any question involving both races, the city's white civic business leaders took care to summon a small cadre of Negro politicians and businessmen for consultation. As an Atlanta correspondent for *Time* wrote:

> The Negroes, overjoyed and terribly grateful at being included in the pow-wows of the whites, didn't seem to mind that they never really achieved very much in the way of specific benefits. In this relationship of fine balance, hammered out by the astute Mayor William B. Hartsfield, both sides knew exactly where the power and influence and last word really lay, but both were willing—for their own reasons—to play out the show. For the Negroes it was a form of eagerly-sought acceptance; for the whites it was an insurance policy against trouble that carried a very cheap premium. And as the years passed and the Negro population grew until it could control the outcome of city elections by bloc voting, the old ties still bound and the Negro community continued to listen to its old, established leaders who continued to toe the white line.

They are not listening now; the old leadership has been pretty well shoved aside by a younger and far more militant group. The revolt actually began with the student sit-ins and boycott in 1961, which the old-line leaders tried first to prevent and then to limit; when the adult leaders reached an agreement with city officials and businessmen that called for only the most token sort of lunch-counter desegregation, the students refused to go along—and they carried the bulk of the Atlanta Negro community with them. The displacement of the old leadership was completed in January of 1963, thanks to the new mayor, Ivan Allen, Jr., who had succeeded the perennial Mayor Hartsfield on his retirement, and who failed completely to gauge the undercurrents of dissatisfaction among the younger Negro businessmen and professional men. In an effort to ease the tensions that had arisen when Negroes bought homes in an adjoining white neighborhood, Allen created a buffer zone between the two communities by closing two streets and erecting a steel barricade.

Allen was simply following in the tradition established by his predecessor, who had used the same device before with the approval of the old-guard Negro leaders. (A similar barricade was erected in the same section of the city in 1961, Hartsfield's last year as mayor, with no publicity at all.) Allen assumed that Negroes would go along again, particularly since he had offered to rezone 250 acres of industrial land for residential purposes, thereby providing the space the Negroes needed. Instead, the erection of the barrier aroused an enormous hue and cry; Negroes compared the barricade to the Berlin Wall and threatened political retaliation. (Allen had been elected by Negro votes, receiving a minority of the votes in the white sections of the city.) Allen responded in the traditional way: he called on the leaders of the Atlanta Negro Voters League and the Empire Real Estate Board to meet with representatives of the white property owners "to work out solutions" to the problem of Negro residential expansion.

But erection of the barricade proved to be a catalyst that welded a new Negro leadership group together; the old-line leaders had no choice but to go along. To Mayor Allen's amazement, the heads of the Atlanta Negro Voters League and the Empire Real Estate Board curtly declined to come to City Hall, informing him that their organizations would be represented by the newly-formed All Citizen's Committee for Better City Planning. And the latter group—comprising the Atlanta chapter of the NAACP, the Atlanta chapter of the SCLC, the Committee on Appeal for Human Rights (the Atlanta students' movement), the local chapter of SNCC, and four or five other Negro organizations—in turn refused to enter into any negotiations until the barricade was taken down.* Dr. C. Miles Smith, co-chairman of the All-Citizens

* The barricade came down a few weeks later as a result of a court injunction which the city decided not to appeal. The new quarterbacks were not much more successful than the old, however; a year later, they were threatening new sit-ins and demonstrations unless public accommodations were desegregated.

Committee and president of the Atlanta NAACP, made no bones about the change in leadership and in goals. "It's a matter now of a new team coming into the game," he told reporters. "We're saying 'your team's done fine, but it's getting tired. New blood is coming in. We're going to take the ball from here.' We haven't ruled out the older element," he added, "but we have placed them in an advisory status. We don't mind them being the coaches, but we want to take the ball and be the quarterbacks." As *Time*'s correspondent reported, "It's an amazing turn of events in Atlanta."

The same turn of events is occurring in a number of northern cities, where the problem of leadership is far more complex. Negroes are free to vote; consequently, Negro political power is potentially very large. Negroes are now well aware of this potential; and some may even overestimate it. But they also know that their power has not grown in proportion to their numbers, and that what power they have has not been used to force social change or alter the conditions under which they live, or even to dramatize the problems of discrimination and segregation. In some cities, New York for example, Negro factionalism has made it easy for white politicians to play one group off against another, and so neutralize Negro power. Elsewhere whites have maintained control by political incorporation, *i.e.*, by "co-opting" potential leaders into the regular party organization, where the need to maintain unity would make them moderate or abandon any race demands.

Chicago provides an excellent example of how Negroes can be co-opted into inactivity. United States Representative William Dawson has been a powerful figure in Chicago politics since 1939, when he led his machine from the Republican to the Democratic Party and was rewarded by being made committeeman of the Second Ward. (In Chicago, political power is vested in the ward committeemen.) Bit by bit, Dawson gained control of four other wards which, together with his second ward, contained the bulk of the

Negro population of Chicago's South Side. As a result, Dawson has been a key member of the inner circle of the ruling Democratic machine. But he has been unable or unwilling to use that power to advocate any basic measures to improve the Negro's lot—fair employment or open housing legislation. Nor has he used his position to drive home the degree of Negro discontent or to dramatize the problems fostered by segregation.

The reasons are clear enough. The basic unit of representation in Chicago is the ward, the relatively small and therefore racially and ethnically homogeneous neighborhood. (The average population of a Chicago ward was 72,000 in 1950, compared to almost 300,000 in a New York City Council district.) The ward system has made it relatively easy for Negroes to get elected to public office; Negroes have served in the Board of Aldermen since Oscar de Priest was elected in 1913.* But the same system has made it much easier for the opponents of Negro progress to gain representation. There is a long history of antagonism between Negroes and Chicago's tightly-knit Irish, Polish, and Italian enclaves, whose aldermen also belong to the Democratic Party. Dawson's problem was that militant advocacy of race goals of a far-reaching sort would arouse strong opposition from these ethnic enclaves, hence would create serious strains and conflicts within the Party. In order to maintain his power within the Democratic organization, therefore, Dawson had to give up such advocacy. As Professor James Q. Wilson has commented, "Dawson, before being co-opted into the Democratic Party, was an outspoken and vigorous champion of race causes. Once inside an organization that was strong and which manifestly held the key to the future, race matters

* In cities where councilmen are elected on a city-wide basis, *e.g.*, Detroit, Los Angeles, Oakland, Negroes find it very difficult to elect anyone. Oakland, where Negroes are 25 per cent or more of the population, still has no Negro member of the Council. Los Angeles got its first Negro councilman in 1963.

were subdued. He was able to provide a plausible . . . rationale to account for the change: The future of the Negro was bound up with political advancement and power. This could best be obtained by working within the Democratic Party and accepting, as a cost, what one could not immediately change."

The cost was too high: Dawson surrendered far more than he has obtained for the Negro community. What Dawson obtained were the traditional benefits of the big-city political machine: low-paying jobs for a lot of followers; political intervention with the police and with bail bondsmen, social workers, housing officials, and other bureaucrats whose decisions can affect a poor constituent's life; and a slice of the "melon" in the form of public housing projects, welfare payments, and the like.*

What Dawson surrendered was the pride and dignity of his community; he threw away the opportunity to force Chicago's political and civic leaders to identify and deal with the fundamental problems of segregation and oppression. The result, as Professor Wilson described it in 1960, was that in Chicago, "influential whites regard Negroes as a collective problem, but not as individually interesting phenomena. The presence of the Negro is a fact; it must be dealt with when necessary, but few whites regard it as a condition which must or can be significantly altered." Though Negroes constituted more than 25 per cent of the city's population, neither the Mayor nor the civic leaders saw any need to take major action to improve the Negroes' lot. As Wilson bitingly put it, "An analysis of 'how things get done' on behalf of Negroes in Chicago is made more difficult

* For all Dawson's influence, however, Negroes have secured surprisingly few high-level jobs. In 1960, for example, there were only three Negro judges in Chicago and no Negroes in high administrative positions; whereas New York, with a Negro population only about one-third larger, had seventen Negro judges, with Negroes also holding cabinet and sub-cabinet level jobs, *e.g.*, borough president, welfare commissioner.

by the fact that so few things seem to get done at all." For "*there is no Negro organization, and no group of Negro leaders, who are in a position to, or want to, force these larger issues by mounting a massive, vocal, and sustained demand for race goals.*" [Emphasis added]

There is now—and as a result, the lid has been blown off the tightly-sealed box that was Chicago politics. In retrospect, it seems clear that Dawson's political "practicality" was as great a disservice to the white as to the Negro community. It kept the white political and civic leadership innocent of any knowledge of the hatred that was festering in "Bronzeville," and so left them totally unprepared for the bitter and violent revolt that developed in the torrid spring and summer of 1963.

The revolt was foreshadowed by the formation, in 1961, of The Woodlawn Organization, the first successful attempt anywhere in the United States to mobilize the residents of a Negro slum into a large and effective organization.* One of the first of many dramatic moves undertaken by TWO, as it is called, was a campaign in August, 1961, to get the usually apathetic Woodlawn residents registered to vote; in a show of strength, a caravan of forty-six chartered buses took some two to three hundred TWO members down to City Hall to register, instead of having them register in their own districts. Dawson understood the potential threat immediately; Dawson lieutenants posted in the bus-loading area warned residents that if they boarded the buses, they would forfeit their right to future favors. "We've had enough favors; now we want our rights," replied the Woodlawnites.

The revolt TWO had started caught fire throughout "Bronzeville" in the aftermath of the Birmingham riots in the spring of 1963. The amiable and well-meaning Mayor Richard Daley, who had fancied himself something of a hero

---

* For an analysis of the significance of The Woodlawn Organization, *see* chapter X.

in the Negro community, suddenly found himself harried day in and day out by sit-ins and threatened sit-ins, by school boycotts, marches on City Hall, mass picketing, and any number of other harassing techniques; the climax came during the national NAACP convention, where Daley was booed and hissed as he got up to speak. (The local NAACP chapter had long been a docile appendage of the Dawson machine.) The six Negro aldermen, all loyal members of the Dawson machine, found themselves derided and scorned as "The Silent Six" for their failure to speak out in support of open housing and fair employment bills sponsored by an independent liberal white alderman, and for approving appointment of a school board member regarded as a segregationist by Negro militants. And the Democratic Party leadership found itself under bitter attack because whites continued to control the party machinery in several wards that once had been all-white, but that now were virtually all-Negro.

By the fall of 1963, the Negro revolt—supported by a coalition of white Protestant and Catholic church groups—had grown so strong that Mayor Daley felt obliged to take dramatic action: he forced a bitterly resentful City Council to pass a strongly-worded open housing law. But it was too late. Negroes were still angry and dissatisfied. "Dick Daley is a man surrounded by tame Negroes," one militant leader commented. "The mayor of this city doesn't need silent Negroes—he needs an action committee." But Chicago's tightly-knit Polish, Irish, and Italian enclaves were also angry; feeling threatened by the explosive growth of the city's Negro population, they thought action had gone much too far. The three-time mayor seemed without a friend. And Representative Dawson looked more and more like a leader without a following.

Much the same process is going on in other cities. In St. Louis, a group of "young Turks" decided, in 1959, to challenge the monopoly of Negro leadership which the late Jor-dan Chambers had enjoyed for twenty-five years (Chambers died in 1962). Two of the group won seats on the Board of Aldermen, and one of them, Assemblyman William L. Clay, has been leading an attack on the established Negro leadership ever since. Clay claims to represent "a new group of Negroes who feel they should speak for themselves and not parrot someone else"; he bitterly accuses the older generation of Negro leaders of being too responsive to white interests, or to their own welfare. The white "power structure," as he puts it, "has contained Negro political strength by taking care of a few men." Because the Negro wards provide the margin of victory for local and national Democratic candidates, Clay argues, Negro politicians should help select *all* the local candidates, not just the Negro candidates. All too often, in his judgment, politicians have supported Democratic candidates who were opposed or indifferent to Negro interests, *e.g.*, a candidate for the school board who owned a restaurant which refused to serve Negroes. And their desire to avoid splitting the party—or to hold on to their patronage—kept the Negro legislators from introducing controversial "race" legislation.

There is no question about Clay's independence. When he dislikes the Democratic candidate, he backs the Republican. He even has opposed Negroes who, in his view, are not sufficiently militant; for example, when Fred Weathers, heir apparent to Chambers' dynasty and perhaps the wealthiest Negro in St. Louis, ran for public office in 1962, Clay backed his white opponent. Though Weathers was endorsed by both St. Louis newspapers and backed by the Negro Establishment, he did poorly in Negro wards and went down to defeat. Clay has also introduced open occupancy and other civil rights legislation, and he has conducted an investigation of Civil Service hiring practices which revealed widespread discrimination. In general, he has pushed the older Negro leaders into a more militant posture, in turn forcing a middle-of-the-road mayor into much stronger advocacy of

Negro rights and appointment of considerably more Negroes to public office.*

In Los Angeles, where in 1960 Professor Wilson found Negroes unable to create any effective political organization, a wave of political activity suddenly swept the Negro community in 1962 and 1963. For the first time, Negroes were able to elect men to the City Council, and they mounted a very vigorous campaign for seats on the all-white school board. This political ferment, in turn, led to appointment of Negroes to such high positions as police commissioner and postmaster general. This Negro political renaissance was led by younger men who made no attempt to hide their impatience with their elders. Thus, in an unconscious piece of irony, Loren Miller, leader of the old guard, who only four months before had bid "Farewell to Liberals" in a much-discussed article in *The Nation,* publicly begged the new generation of Negro activists to be a little more gentle in elbowing his generation out of the way. "It dawned on me last week that my generation is being replaced in whatever it is we call leadership in the Negro community," Miller wrote in February, 1963, in the *California Eagle,* a weekly paper of which he is the publisher. Miller professed to welcome the change ("We could do with some new thinking and . . . some new wisdom"). But "those who are on their way out," he plaintively reminded the new generation, "do deserve some thanks." The rash of appointments of Negroes to high office "didn't just happen. Today's crop," he told the thoughtless youngsters, "is the harvest of yesterday's labor."

The revolt against the established Negro leadership creates a good many problems for both whites and blacks. For one thing, the new militancy has not overcome the old rivalry and backbiting. In a good many instances, white civic and business leaders have been besieged by a number of

* In January, 1964, Clay was sentenced to six months in jail and fined $1,000 for his part in a demonstration designed to force a St. Louis bank to hire more Negroes.

organizations, each purporting to be the true spokesman for the Negro community and each denouncing the others as a bunch of "Uncle Toms." The organizers of the 1963 National Conference on Religion and Race, for example, received warnings from several Negro church groups that the Conference would be denounced and boycotted unless *its* organization was recognized as the only representative Negro church group. The clergymen were able to resolve this particular conflict. But there are times when it is nearly impossible for whites to determine who does speak for the Negro community. The best solution is to assume that no single group ever does represent an entire community.

Sooner or later, moreover, Negro militants will have to face up to the dilemma posed by their desire, on the one hand, to become a part of the "power structure," and their determination, on the other, to remain free of white control. For if Negroes are to be elected and appointed to high office—if they are, in fact, to enter the "power structure" and help shape the decisions that count—they will have to give up a good deal of their freedom to criticize and protest. This is the price of power. No member of a city, state or federal administration can expect to keep any influence over that administration if he is always denouncing it; to be an effective advocate of Negro interests within the power structure, he must abandon his role as social actionist. He cannot have it both ways.

▼

3

Negroes' determination to speak and act on their own behalf has produced the greatest strain where it was least expected: in the alliance that bound Negro organizations, civil rights and civil liberties groups, interfaith organizations, church groups, and trade unions together in a great liberal coalition. Quite suddenly in 1962 and 1963—or so it seemed to the white liberals—they found themselves under bitter attack and heard themselves denounced in terms usually reserved for the most rabid southern racists.

The reasons lie deep in the history of the civil rights movement—particularly in the fact that the movement has been dominated by whites until fairly recently. For all the reasons discussed in chapters IV and V, there was a vacuum of Negro leadership and Negro support that could be filled only by whites. Thus, the NAACP was founded by whites because the Niagara Movement was falling apart, and whites provided much of the leadership and financial support until recent years.* Whites still provide most of the funds raised by Martin Luther King's Southern Christian Leadership Conference; for all his charismatic appeal, he has been unable to raise more than a fraction of the funds he needs from the Negro community. Equally important, the civil rights organizations depended on political support from white liberals—trade unions, civil liberties organizations, interfaith organizations, church groups, and the like. Negroes depended on the liberal coalition because their own strength was too slight to offer any chance of victory. As Myrdal said twenty years ago, Negroes, because they are only 10 per cent of the population, "can never cherish the healthy hope of coming into power. A Negro movement can never expect to grow into a democratic majority in politics or in any other sphere of American life." The result, Myrdal suggested, "is a sense of hopelessness in the Negro cause." Since "it is a political

* The NAACP proper now draws most of its revenues from Negroes; income comes largely from membership dues, and the membership is predominantly Negro. The separate NAACP Legal Defense and Education Fund, however, whose budget is about as large as that of the NAACP proper, still draws most of its revenue from white contributors.

axiom that Negroes can never . . . attain more in the short-term power bargain than white groups are prepared to give them," Negroes remained the junior, and usually silent, partner in the great liberal coalition, deferring to white judgment on strategy and tactics.

However unavoidable, this relationship had unfortunate consequences for both the black and white partners. The white allies acquired the habit of speaking for, and doing for, the Negroes. And the Negroes, consequently, were never able to break the habit of having things done for them. As Professor James Q. Wilson wrote in *Negro Politics*,* Negroes tended to be "the objects rather than the subjects of civic action. Things are often done for, or about, or to, or because of Negroes, but they are less frequently done *by* Negroes."

But Negroes always resented the relationship; their dependence on their white allies created an underlying animus that was no less real for being carefully suppressed. Besides resenting their dependency, Negroes have never really trusted their white allies; they have always had a nagging suspicion that the whites were holding them back, that they could gain more, and faster, if they were only free to act on their own. "They are betraying us again, these white friends of ours," one of the Negro participants shouted during the meeting at which the NAACP was founded; and other Negroes have echoed this cry ever since. In the lengthy monograph on Negro organizations and leadership which he prepared for Gunnar Myrdal in 1942, for example, Ralph Bunche delivered a stinging attack on the NAACP's interracial composition:

> The interracial make-up of the NAACP, is an undoubted source of organizational weakness. There can be no doubt that the Negro leaders in the organization have always kept a weather eye on the reactions of their prominent and influ-

* James Q. Wilson, *Negro Politics*, Glencoe, Ill.: The Free Press, 1960.

> ential white sponsors . . . These white sympathizers are, in the main, either cautious liberals or mawkish, missionary-minded sentimentalists on the race question. Their interest in the Negro problem is motivated either by a sense of "fair play" and a desire to see the ideals of the Constitution lived up to, or an "I love your people" attitude. Both attitudes are far from touching the realities of the problem.* But the evident concern for the opinions of the white supporters of the organization, especially on the part of the National Office, has been a powerful factor in keeping the Association thoroughly "respectable," and has certainly been an influence in the very evident desire of the Association to keep its skirts free of the grimy bitterness and strife encountered in the economic area . . . The liberal . . . recognizes and revolts against injustices, but seeks to correct them with palliatives rather than solutions; for the solutions are harsh and forbidding, and are not conducive to optimism and spiritual uplift.

The point is not whether this animus against white supporters was justified. In large measure it was not; at the time Bunche wrote, the NAACP depended on white support because it could not get support from Negroes. Indeed, the apathy and disinterest of the Negro community was revealed dramatically in 1948, when the NAACP raised its minimum dues from $1 to $2—and lost half its membership as a result; membership did not return to the old level until the early 1960s. What is crucial is that Negroes *did* resent and distrust their white allies long before they felt secure enough to express it. And their resentment, while not particularly admirable, certainly is understandable; people who are permanently on the receiving end come to hate their benefactors, as the United States is discovering with its foreign aid program. "The politics of life do not provide for equality

---

* Ironically enough, when Adam Clayton Powell attacked the NAACP in similar terms in 1963, Dr. Bunche denounced him as a racist as dangerous as the Southern white racists.

when one is always in the high position of the magnanimous giver and the other in the low position of the grateful receiver," Saul Alinsky has written. "This kind of relationship is devoid of that dignity essential to equality."

If Negroes are to gain a sense of potency and dignity, it is essential, therefore, that they take the initiative in action on their own behalf. For the moment, at least, it is far more important that things be done *by* Negroes than that they be done *for* them, even if they are not done as well. Whites will have to learn that most difficult lesson of parenthood: to allow one's children to become adults. Whites, that is to say, will have to abandon their tradition of command and their habit of speaking for, and acting for, the Negroes. Their role must be limited: to stimulate indigenous leadership and activity, and then to retire to the sidelines—to retire to the sidelines even if the black neophytes are making mistakes. To the suggestion that Negroes are too inexperienced to get things done properly, some Negroes are likely to retort with the remark of Jomo Kenyatta: "If there is going to be a mess, let it be a black mess." Given the historical pattern of dependency, in short, there seems to be no way of avoiding a certain amount of race chauvinism; it is ironic but nonetheless necessary that, for a time at least, organizations working on behalf of Negroes be led and manned largely by Negroes. This does not mean that Negroes do not want help from white liberals. They expect it—but on their own terms. Negroes "are too sophisticated to believe that liberals can resign [the] battle . . . out of pique at the rejection of their leadership," Loren Miller wrote in 1962. But their message, as Miller reported it, was exceedingly blunt: "To liberals a fond farewell, with thanks for service rendered, until you are ready to re-enlist as foot-soldiers and subordinates in a Negro-led, Negro-officered army under the banner of Freedom Now."

There is a certain cynicism in Miller's position, to be sure, Negroes who are the most vociferous in denouncing white paternalism are sometimes the first to demand help from their white allies in getting some favor or some concession from "the power structure." And some Negro leaders use "white liberals" as whipping boys to impress the rank and file with their militancy. But Negroes cannot have it both ways; if they really want to limit whites to the role of "foot-soldiers and subordinates in a Negro-led and Negro-officered army," Negroes will have to assume a larger share of the financing of that army than they have been willing to do up to now. For if they continue to rely on white financing, they almost certainly will have to submit to a measure of white control.

But liberals, for their part, could do with a good deal of soul-searching as well. Much of the Negro cynicism about white liberals stems from their discovery that all too many ardent advocates of integration turn out to be for integration only in someone else's neighborhood or someone else's school district or someone else's trade union. "Negroes are dismayed," Loren Miller writes, "as they observe that liberals, even when they are in apparent control, not only do not rally their organizations for an effective role in the fight against discrimination, but even tolerate a measure of racial discrimination in their own jurisdictions." The trade union movement, of course, is the worst offender in this regard. Discrimination by the railroad and building trades union is notorious. But some of the most liberal unions have also been guilty of discrimination; Walter Reuther's United Automobile Workers, for example, didn't abolish separate seniority systems for Negro and white workers in southern factories until a few years ago. And none of the liberal unions have made any real effort to develop Negro leadership: trade union leaders are no more willing than businessmen or politicians to share any of the power they now enjoy. When men like Walter Reuther or David Dubinsky (or for that matter, the editorial writers of the *New York Times*) respond to Negro demands for representation with a pious insistence that union officers (or government officials) be selected purely on their individual merit, not because of their race or creed, Negroes understandably interpret the response as one more instance of white hypocrisy. Ethnic and religious considerations have been a major factor in public life for at least a hundred years; it is a little late to change the rules just at the point when Negroes are demanding in. The insistence that nothing but individual ability shall count comes with particular lack of grace from trade unionists: the demand for special treatment is, after all, the very foundation on which the trade union movement was built,* and the concept of group rather than individual rights is central to the unions' function.

There is another source of strain between Negroes and white liberals that is likely to take on more importance as the years go by: the fact that when the struggle for Negro rights moves into the streets, the majority of liberals are reluctant to move along with it. They are all for the Negroes' *objectives*, they say, but they cannot go along with the *means*. Rightly or wrongly, Negroes receive this sort of statement with a good deal of cynicism; as Bismarck once remarked, "When you say that you agree to a thing in principle, you mean that you have not the slightest intention of carrying it out in practice."

The problem is a real one. There is a fundamental difference in the situation of Negroes and of whites that leads almost inevitably to conflict over tactics and strategy: Negroes are outside the main stream of middle-class American life, whereas their liberal allies are on the inside. Hence the latter have a deep interest in preserving the status quo, in the sense of maintaining peace and harmony. The trade union movement, for example, is no more racist than any

---

* The preamble to the Wagner Act states that to redress the inequality of power between employers and employees, the latter must be given special protection to organize, compel the employer to bargain, etc.

other group, and probably less so; yet to the Negro, labor acts as a conservative establishment primarily concerned with maintaining the job monopolies of its members.

Other liberals want only to maintain the peace and comfort of the lives they now enjoy; they want racial change, all right, but without trouble or turmoil, and without upsetting the existing organizations and institutional arrangements. Indeed, the whole profession of "inter-group relations" is dedicated to the goal of preventing or minimizing tension and conflict, with persuasion the favored technique; the approach inherently assumes gradualism, since it takes some time to rid people of prejudice or to change their minds. But the Negro, as David Danzig has written in *Commentary,* is "no longer addressing himself to the white man's attitude of prejudice toward color, with the gradualism that this approach compels; he now confronts the white community on the issue of Negro rights and opportunities as a matter of politics, economic power, and justice." And so "whites whose ultimate perspective on race relations envisaged the gradual absorption of deserving Negroes one by one into white society are suddenly hard-pressed to come to terms with a demanding Negro community."

The point is that changes of the sort Negroes now demand, at the speed they insist upon, cannot be provided without considerable conflict: too many Americans will have to give up some privilege or advantage they now enjoy or surrender the comforting sense of their own superiority. There is nothing in American history, past or present, to suggest that Negroes can gain their rightful place in American society without direct confrontation. In Frederick Douglass' words, "If there is no struggle, there is no progress. Those who profess to favor freedom, and yet deprecate agitation, are men who want crops without plowing up the ground. They want rain without thunder and lightning. They want the ocean without the awful roar of its waters."

And so the years ahead are bound to be harsh and painful;

it would be naïve to pretend that any set of policies adopted by business, government, or civic groups can bring racial peace within the next few years. The most that can be hoped for is to establish some limitation on weapons and some minimum rules for participation. More to the point, we must learn that there are worse things than conflict; in Abraham Heschel's words, "so long as our society is more concerned to prevent strife than to prevent humiliation, its moral status will be depressing indeed."

▼

4

There is a danger, however, that in their new-found militancy, Negroes may become the victims of their own rhetoric. Negro leaders have already shown a tendency to react to labels rather than to substance; once a proposal has been called "soft" or "moderate," they feel obliged to attack it without regard to the merits of the case. Shortly before the assassination of President Kennedy, for example, virtually every national Negro leader had denounced the Kennedy Administration for opposing the "strong" version and supporting the "weak" version of the proposed Civil Rights Act, then before the House Judiciary Committee. Yet in certain important respects, the "strong" version was considerably weaker than the "weak" bill introduced by the Administration. For example, it omitted a provision that would have created Federal Registrars to insure Negro voting rights in counties where registration had been made difficult. In view of the importance Negroes attach to increased voter registration in the South, the universal attack on this "weak" bill may have been shortsighted.

And rhetoric can cut two ways. A slogan like "All, Now,

Here," for example, may be invaluable as a means of rousing the Negro poor out of their lethargy; indeed no method of getting an uneducated, disadvantaged, and disaffected group to seek freedom and power has ever been discovered save the old techniques of the trade union organizer: to capitalize on the peoples' frustrations, to "rub raw the sores of discontent," as Saul Alinsky puts it, until anger conquers apathy and people are stirred to act on their own behalf. ("Nice" people are always disturbed by the ungentlemanly tactics of those who seek power.) At the same time, however, the successful organizer must, wherever possible, avoid raising expectations that cannot be fulfilled; if defeat comes too soon and too often, it may produce an apathy even greater than before. A basic rule of organization, therefore, is to attack only when you have reasonable hopes of success. Negro leaders have not shown sufficient awareness of this rule, though they are learning from experience. For a time, in the spring and summer of 1963, a few modest successes, in Birmingham, for example, gave Negro leaders the heady feeling that a couple of blasts on the trumpet of direct action would break down all the remaining walls.

But the walls will not come down that easily. The problems faced by Negroes in the large cities of the North are enormously complex, and many of the Negro demands—*e.g.*, for preferential treatment in employment—bring them into direct conflict with the interests of white workers in protecting their own job monopolies, or of white property owners in maintaining segregation. Thus, a torrid summer of direct action in New York City, which included sit-ins in the Mayor's and Governor's offices, picketing of construction sites, lying down in the roadway in front of trucks to prevent their unloading, among other measures, produced very few jobs and very much frustration. By the fall, in fact, Negroes had begun to question whether "direct action" had any use at all. "You keep the demonstrators on the street for more than a month, and you have all those people arrested, and then what do you do?" Rev. Milton Galamison, leader of one of the protest groups asked.* "It's the general opinion among the most knowledgable people that a resumption of demonstrations wouldn't help. We are very frustrated at the moment."

The elections of November, 1963, demonstrated the extent and depth of white resistance to Negro demands. In Boston, for example, a school board member who had refused to concede the existence of de facto segregation and who had, as a result, become the prime target of the local NAACP, was re-elected with the largest vote accorded any candidate. (She ran 20 per cent ahead of the mayor, and received more than twice as many votes as the lone school board member who had sided with the NAACP.) In Philadelphia, the Democratic mayor was re-elected, but with the lowest plurality any Democrat had received in a decade. Italian and Irish wards that had given John F. Kennedy margins of three- and four-to-one in 1960, went Republican in the 1963 mayorality election—by unanimous agreement, because of resentment over concessions the Mayor had made to Negro demands.

Thus, the rhetoric of revolution which Negroes have self-consciously adopted may have unfortunate consequences: it may serve to mobilize the whites as well as the blacks. As one sophisticated analyst puts it, "If Negroes talk long enough about 'the white power structure,' they may succeed in creating one." While Negroes have tended to underestimate white resistance, they've overestimated the degree of unanimity among whites. This is not surprising; the further people are from power, the more monolithic and unrestricted they think it is; the closer they get, the more aware they become of conflicts of interest within the power structure, and the more conscious they are of the forces that

* Part of the problem was that demonstrations were staged by at least three or four competing groups, each purporting to be the true voice of the people.

inhibit the use of power. "The classic problem of the man on top in any political system," Richard Neustadt has written, is "how to be on top in fact as well as in name. It is a problem common to Prime Ministers and Premiers, and to dictators, however styled, and to those kings who rule as well as reign. It is a problem also for the heads of private 'governments,' for corporation presidents, trade union leaders, churchmen." By way of illustration, Professor Neustadt tells a story of President Truman contemplating in 1952 the problems that Dwight Eisenhower would have if he won the Presidential election. "He'll sit here," Neustadt quotes Truman as saying, "and he'll say, 'Do this! Do that!' *And nothing will happen.* Poor Ike—it won't be a bit like the Army. He'll find it very frustrating." And so Ike did. "The President still feels," an Eisenhower aide told Neustadt in 1958, "that when he's decided something, that *ought* to be the end of it . . . and when it bounces back undone or done wrong, he tends to react with shocked surprise." * Even John F. Kennedy, who had studied Neustadt's book and been briefed by Neustadt before taking office, told reporters that the greatest surprise of his first two years in office was the discovery that his power was far more limited than he had assumed. Indeed, the limitations of Presidential power was the main theme of a book written by Kennedy's closest assistant, Theodore Sorensen, a few months before the President's assassination.

Because they have been kept so remote from power, Negroes understandably exaggerate the power exercised by the "white power structure"; they see it as an undifferentiated bloc of corporate, civic, and political leaders acting in unison, out of identical motives, to reach common goals. In contrast, they see the Negro community as hopelessly divided among factions whose competing interests make united action difficult, if not impossible. Both views are distorted.

* Richard E. Neustadt, *Presidential Power: The Politics of Leadership*, New York: John Wiley & Sons, 1960.

Certainly there are sharp conflicts of interest within the white power structure—among the businessmen themselves (*e.g.*, between retailers and manufacturers), between the businessmen and the politicians, between the politicians and the civic leaders, and so on. When "the power structure" takes some action that Negroes construe as anti-Negro, therefore, as often as not it is because they were *not* thinking of Negroes, rather than because they were acting in concert against the Negro community. But if they find themselves labeled as conspirators frequently enough, the various individuals and groups making up the "power structure" may indeed begin to think and act in harmony on racial matters. It is important, therefore, to adopt a rhetoric that does not rule out conversation with individuals or groups whose assistance or assent is necessary for Negroes to gain their objectives.

VIII

THE CAT WITH THE SILVER SPOON

I sit on a man's back, choking him and making him carry me, and yet assure myself and others that I am very sorry for him and wish to lighten his load by all possible means—except by getting off his back.

—TOLSTOY

1

Negroes do need help; when all is said and done, they cannot go it alone all the time or in every circumstance. In most cities, white votes will be needed for some time if candidates favorable to the Negro cause are to be elected; failure to take white reaction into account may backfire. Politics aside, many of the problems Negroes face are simply too large for them to solve on their own; while Negro pressure may be necessary to force a change in the status quo, Negroes will need the co-operation or assent of governments, corporations, and trade unions. If more Negroes are to be employed, for example, business firms will have to be persuaded to employ them; if unskilled Negro laborers are to be equipped to hold jobs in our high technology economy, government or business is going to have to train them; if Negro youngsters are to have a chance, the public schools will have to educate them, for education is rapidly becoming the principal form of capital in the United States. Negroes are not equipped to maintain a public school system on their own; thus, it was the height of irresponsibility for a Negro leader like New York's Rev. Milton Galamison to say during a long radio interview on December 22, 1963, that if his timetable for integration is not adopted, he "would rather see [the public school system] destroyed; maybe it has run its course anyway, the Public School System."

Our attack on the Hauser-Handlin "acculturation thesis," in short, should not lead us into an equivalent blindness on the other side. It should be clear by now that acculturation alone will not solve the Negro problem: acculturation without power leaves the Negro in a cultural and political no-man's land. But power without acculturation can also be a blind alley. The heritage of slavery and discrimination have made all too many Negroes unable to cope with the complex demands of urban life in an advanced and rapidly changing technology. "Perhaps never in history has a more utterly unprepared folk wanted to go to the city," Richard Wright suggested in his "folk history" of the Negro in the United States. And in his autobiography, Wright brooded over the cultural barrier that separated the Southern Negro from the rest of Western civilization. "Whenever I thought of the essential bleakness of black life in America," he wrote, "I knew that Negroes had never been allowed to catch the full spirit of Western civilization, that they lived somehow in it but not of it. And when I brooded upon the cultural barrenness of black life, I wondered if clean, positive tenderness, love, honor, loyalty, and the capacity to remember were native with man. I asked myself if these human qualities were not festered, won, struggled and suffered for, preserved in ritual from one generation to another." *

Certainly Negroes from the rural South come from a "folk

* *Black Boy* (New York: Harper & Bros., 1945)—Wright's account of his own childhood—is perhaps the most searing description of the instability and ugliness of Negro family life ever published.

culture" that makes it exceedingly difficult for them—as for the Appalachian whites—to adjust to the large city. European peasants, who brought with them a stable culture and a strong family structure, were almost destroyed by the harshness of city life; Negroes, as we have seen, come with almost no tradition of stable family life. Negro leaders as diametrically opposed in their thinking as Whitney Young and Elijah Muhammad agree that Negroes will not be able to move up into American life unless major steps are taken to strengthen that weakest of all institutions, the Negro family. The role family weakness plays is clearly revealed in a story told by Edwin P. Stephenson, a dedicated Quaker who runs Neighborhood House in Richmond, California, about one of his social workers, himself a Negro, who was trying to convince an eighteen-year-old Negro youth that it *is* possible for a Negro to rise out of the slum and acquire the perquisites of American life without resorting to crime. By way of illustration, he pointed to the fact that the boy's new boss, a Negro, drives a Cadillac. "Yeah man," the youth replied, "but that cat was born with a silver spoon in his mouth." The puzzled social worker asked the young man what he meant. "I mean for one thing, that cat had a father; for another, his father taught him a trade," was the immediate answer.

Or consider this portrait of sixteen years in the life of a Negro woman—a highly intelligent high-school graduate with a year of college—and her two children, as revealed by the case history of one of the youngsters. (Names, date, and places have been disguised in order not to reveal the identity.)

> Lonnie Smith was born in November, 1947, in Scranton, Pennsylvania, the result of an unwanted, accidental pregnancy. His mother had been married a year before.
>
> *March, 1948:* Father divorces mother.
>
> *August, 1948:* Mother moves to Philadelphia with Lonnie.

November, 1948: Lonnie returns to Scranton to live with an aunt; mother rejoins him there in March, 1949.

August, 1949: Lonnie and mother return to Philadelphia, where Lonnie is boarded in an institution.

December 1949: Lonnie returns to aunt in Scranton; mother remains in Philadelphia until April, when she rejoins Lonnie in Scranton.

August, 1950: Lonnie and mother return to Philadelphia, where he is boarded again in the institution.

December, 1950: Lonnie and mother return to Scranton to live with aunt.

July, 1951: Lonnie and mother move to Detroit to live with mother's aunt, who had raised her; great-aunt is drug addict.

February, 1953: Lonnie and mother return to Philadelphia, where they live with another aunt.

September, 1953: Mother remarries; Lonnie returns to Scranton, where he begins school.

April, 1954: Lonnie returns to Philadelphia to live with mother and stepfather in one room.

January, 1955: Mother and stepfather move to another part of Philadelphia; because stepfather is drinking and while drunk, beating the mother, Lonnie moves in with an aunt.

July, 1955: Lonnie rejoins his parents, who have stopped fighting.

December, 1955: Mother and Lonnie return to Scranton because stepfather has taken up with another woman.

July, 1956: Lonnie and mother return to Detroit to live with mother's aunt.

October, 1956: Mother returns to husband in Philadelphia; Lonnie stays in Detroit.

May, 1957: Mother returns to Detroit; she and Lonnie live with mother's aunt.

October, 1958: Mother becomes pregnant and takes her own apartment with Lonnie. Brother born June, 1959.

March, 1961: Mother takes job as sleep-in maid, so Lonnie moves in with great-aunt, baby brother with another relative.

October, 1961: Mother, Lonnie, and baby move in with mother's aunt.

August, 1962: Mother and two children return to Philadelphia. Mother takes job as sleep-in maid; children live with still another aunt.

The case history is fairly typical of the kind of disorganization of family life that afflicts so many Negroes; in central Harlem, for example, only half the youngsters under eighteen live with both their parents. But the case history also suggests something of the strength and resilience of Negro life and character: Negroes raise families and live out their lives under conditions that would destroy a white middle-class family. "You know, I'd like to move all the people from Scarsdale, New York, right into my block," a Puerto Rican Negro told *New York Times* reporter Richard Hammer, "into the same apartments where some of them have to pay maybe seventy dollars for a couple of crummy little rooms for ten or eleven people and have to share a bathroom in the hall with the door falling off . . . I don't think these people from Scarsdale could take it." He is probably right; in sociological jargon, there must be enormously powerful mechanisms of "socialization" in Negro subculture to enable people to function in so destructive an environment. "In Scarsdale," the young man interviewed by Hammer continued, "the first things the kids learn are how to read and write; that's taken for granted. In my neighborhood, the first things the kids learn are how to fight and steal and not take any crap from anyone. We grow up knowing about narcotics, I mean we don't even remember when we didn't know about them, and everybody just takes that for granted." Thus, anthropologists and sociologists working in Hylan Lewis' "Child Rearing Project" in Washington, D.C., have been struck by the "copability" of so many Negroes—by their capacity to meet overwhelming problems with a certain style and *élan*—what James Baldwin calls the "vivacity" of Negro life. What is amazing, in short, is not that so few Negroes have risen out of the slum, but that so many have—that a Richard Wright, for example, could emerge from the hate and degradation and terror of his childhood, and become an enormously creative, if embittered, writer.

The fact remains that in a world in which having a father is equated with being born with a silver spoon in your mouth, help is needed. Many Negro families, for example, desperately need help and advice on how to handle their children. One of Hylan Lewis' most striking findings is that many Negro slum parents lose control over their children at an incredibly early age; rebellion begins about age five or six, and by ten or eleven at the latest, the children have already "won" the battle—their parents no longer can control them. Just why rebellion should begin so early remains something of a mystery; poverty alone does not explain it. But the harsh fact is that slum parents begin complaining "I can't do a thing with him" as youngsters reach age five or six,* and there is hardly a family with older children which does not have a son or daughter in trouble, and which is not mystified by it—which is not trying, without success, to understand why *their* child should have behaved in that way. Indeed, Dr. Lewis believes that a good many cases which the courts treat as parental neglect are in reality cases of parental inadequacy, *i.e.*, of children's successful early rebellion.

Negro parents need help in other crucial respects: how to talk to their children, how to play with them, how to dis-

* The "rebelliousness" of slum children is quite different—and far deeper—from the disobedience that passes for rebellion in white middle-class families.

cipline them, how to encourage them in school, how to provide education about sex, etc. Most low-income families, white and black, tend to be non-verbal, especially if they come from a rural background: they speak relatively little and then only in short sentences. Children do not know that their parents want them to succeed in school, because the parents have never expressed the thought. The monosyllabic character of conversation means a lack of stimulation; if parents learn that they can help their children by talking to them, asking questions, encouraging the children to ask questions, etc., they are generally delighted to cooperate. (But of this, more in the next chapter.)

A number of studies, moreover, have demonstrated that Negro parents have surprisingly high aspirations for their children—higher, in fact, than those held by white parents in the same socio-economic class. (If a white family is still lower-class by the third or fourth generation in this country, it "knows" that the cards are stacked against it; children from these homes have a toughness and cynicism that makes defeat inevitable.) All too often, however, the aspirations remain little more than vague and unfulfilled dreams, for neither the parents nor the youngsters have any notion of what, specifically, has to be done to fulfill the aspirations. There is no way they *can* know, unless someone tells them; for nothing in their experience enables them to know what it means to be a doctor or a lawyer or an engineer or a scientist, or what kinds of aptitudes are required. Indeed, parental ambitions for their children tend to be expressed in vague exhortations to "aim high," to "get enough education" or to "get a good education" so that the youngster can "get a good job"; what constitutes a good job or sufficient education is rarely specified. As one of Hylan Lewis' associates says, "There is lack of knowledge or clarity as to *how* children are to obtain the goals projected; and there is very little indication that the parents know what to do themselves in order to motivate the children. On the contrary, what seems to be the underlying theme is expressed in various ways in the idea that 'you can lead a horse to water . . .' There is communicated a kind of realism and pessimism, a kind of wise weariness that may appear to belie the very educational or career goals they express for at least some of their children."

Lack of knowledge about career choices, however, does not begin to account for what Eunice S. Grier of the Washington Center for Metropolitan Studies has aptly termed "the floundering phenomenon"—the aimless drifting that characterizes the lives of so many Negroes, even those with education, aptitude, and ambition. The disorganization of the family is reflected in a disorganization of Negro life itself—an absence, in all too many individuals, of the inner strength and self-discipline necessary if one is to be the master rather than the servant of his environment in a competitive society. This "disorganization" emerges very clearly in a study Mrs. Grier has made of the experiences of the male graduates of a Washington, D.C., high school—a school whose course work and orientation were aimed largely at preparation for college and whose student body was generally assumed to be capable of doing college work.* As Mrs. Grier describes them, the graduates were above average but not at the top of their class. (The top-ranking students in the class had all been girls—itself a reflection of the impact of matriarchy on student performance.) Almost all the young men were natives of Washington; the remainder had moved to the city in early childhood and had received all their education in District public schools. While not well-to-do, neither were they slum-dwellers with deprived backgrounds; almost half had one parent with some college training—a remarkable figure for a sample of Negro students—and most had grown up in stable, two-parent families. At the time of graduation, all the students Mrs. Grier could locate

* *In Search of a Future: A Pilot Study of Career-Seeking Experiences of Selected High-School Graduates in Washington, D.C.*, The Washington Center for Metropolitan Studies, 1963.

and interview—roughly half the total number—had intended going on to some form of higher education, and almost all were planning on careers in one of the professions, with a heavy emphasis on science and engineering. In point of fact, thirty-nine of the forty-six men took some post-high school training: seven of them went to technical training schools of some sort and thirty-two entered college.

Five years later, however, remarkably few of these young men had moved very far along the road toward realizing their ambitions. Of the thirty-two who had entered college, only seven had actually finished. Many of the remainder had started and stopped college several times; only three had abandoned college altogether, and of the rest, twenty-two still hoped to finish. Most were vague about the reasons for dropping out; the most common explanation was doubt about the wisdom or appropriateness of the course they had been following. In one way or another, they said they had become uncertain as to what they really wanted to do with their lives and had dropped out of college to think through more clearly what career they should pursue. Yet only three of the twenty-five with full-time and the ten with part-time work had jobs that bore any relation at all to their ambitions.* "The rest," as Mrs. Grier puts it, "viewed themselves as marking time until they were able to fulfill their true ambitions." All but one of the men, in fact, had had some job experience since graduation; rarely did the jobs bear any resemblance to the kind of work they hoped to do for the rest of their lives. All told, the group had held some fifty-six full-time jobs since graduation, most of which required little skill and provided even less status or personal satisfaction. Some twenty-four of the jobs had been clerical, mostly in the post office; nineteen men had held service jobs—as dishwashers, porters, bus-boys, or parking lot attendants.

What happened to keep so many of this promising group

* Eight were unemployed and actively seeking work—a remarkably high rate of unemployment for a group of this sort.

of young men from fulfilling any of their promise? Parental poverty kept some young men from entering college, and forced (or seemed to force) them to take the first job that came along. Inadequate guidance and counseling in high school lay at the root of some of the drifting: a substantial number of students, for example, had decided while in high school on careers in science or engineering because their guidance counselors had told them that these fields were open to Negroes; but they had taken no science courses in high school, and when they got to college discovered they had no aptitude or interest in these fields. And job discrimination certainly played an important role; as Mrs. Grier puts it, "only through the operation of discriminatory barriers, however covert and subtle, can their limited job achievement logically be explained."

Whatever the reasons, there is no doubt that "floundering" is a widespread phenomenon. Consider these excerpts from Mrs. Grier's case history of "Mr. A":

> Mr. A was graduated from high school in the second quartile of his class, with an average of 82. He was married in 1959 and now has one child. His wife, who has completed one year of college, is presently employed as a typist by the federal government. Mr. and Mrs. A live with his parents on a pleasant tree-lined street of small, older homes close to the Howard University campus.
>
> Mr. A was born in the District of Columbia and has lived there all his life . . . He has been interspersing employment with attendance at Howard University since he was graduated from high school in 1956. He entered Howard in September, 1956, and studied engineering full time for one year. He then dropped out of school and worked for several months as a semi-skilled worker for a construction contractor. He was paid an hourly rate of $1.50 . . . and averaged about forty hours a week over the seven-month period.
>
> He obtained the job through an older brother employed

> by the same firm. He left it in January 1958 intending to return to Howard for the spring semester, but did not do so. When asked by the interviewer why he did not, he evaded the question. Nor did he respond substantively to a question about why he had dropped out of school in the first place.
>
> He was unemployed during the spring except for one month when he worked as a parking lot attendant. He obtained this job through a friend employed at the same lot. His salary was $1.00 an hour . . .
>
> Mr. A returned to Howard in June, 1958, for the summer school session. He attended Howard from then until July, 1960. Although he has now been in college for a total of three full years, he has completed only two out of the four years of course work required for a degree in engineering . . . In August, 1960, Mr. A began work at the post office; he is currently employed there as a postal clerk . . . His salary began at $2.16 per hour for a forty-hour week.

In the last analysis, as Mr. A's case history suggests, the limited achievement of the group must be attributed to the disorganization of Negro life; Mrs. Grier's study confirms a pattern familiar to any close observer of Negro life. The "floundering phenomenon" was revealed also in a series of articles which the *New York Post* ran in 1963, profiling the careers of James Baldwin's thirty-three junior-high-school classmates. This was a class of intellectually gifted youngsters, chosen to complete three years work in two. Several of Baldwin's classmates had achieved a measure of success—in some cases, of distinction—in their careers. And yet the histories of many of them revealed the same pattern of aimless drifting from job to job and from career to career—starting college and then dropping it, starting and perhaps completing a technical training course, and then drifting again from job to job. Perhaps the greatest need Negroes have is for help in overcoming this disorganization, this state of *anomie* that destroys or distorts so many promising lives.

▼

2

Whatever else is done, it is clear that the Negro's "Negro problem" cannot be solved unless decent jobs are made available. For the Negro man, unemployment, underemployment, and, equally important, employment that is demeaning by its very nature, all serve to compound injuries that society and his own family have inflicted on him from birth. The difficulty Negro men experience in finding decent jobs—jobs that would accord them a measure of dignity and self-respect and permit them to play the male role of breadwinner—is central to perpetuation of the matriarchy and of the weakness of family relationships. Unemployment is demoralizing under the best of circumstances: one of the central facts of industrial society, the management consultant Peter F. Drucker has written, is that "social effectiveness, citizenship, indeed even self-respect depend on access to a job. Without a job a man in industrial society cannot possibly be socially effective. He is deprived of citizenship, of social standing, of the respect of his fellow men if not of his family, and finally of self-respect. No amount of economic relief can possibly offset the social destruction of chronic unemployment in an industrial society." *

Jobs are the fulcrum, therefore, on which a strengthening of the family, and through the family, of the Negro's role in American society, ultimately rests. This, as much as any other reason, is why so many Negro and white liberals believe that the Negro-liberal coalition must be restored: in their view, there can be no solution to the problem of Negro

* Peter F. Drucker, *The New Society,* New York: Harper & Brothers, 1949.

unemployment as long as unemployment remains high in the economy as a whole. But the liberals are understandably vague on precisely what this new coalition should *do*. Too many of them, for example, talk about programs for full employment as though all that were needed was the will to put the necessary programs into action.

But what kind of programs? The painful fact is that the reasons for the persistence of high unemployment in the United States are not at all obvious; on the contrary, they are rather mysterious. There are liberals, for example, who have taken as their text Gunnar Myrdal's *Challenge to Affluence,** which called for an all-out attack on what Myrdal terms "the sluggish and jerky development of the American economy." Myrdal's adjectives describe the economy of the middle and later 1950s—but not the American economy of the 1960s. On the contrary, the economy has been quite vigorous in recent years. As of the early spring of 1964, national output had been expanding without interruption for more than three years—the longest peacetime upturn in a quarter-century; the rate of economic growth has averaged nearly 5 per cent a year, which is considerably above the long-run rate of growth of the economy.† And yet unemployment has declined only one percentage point, from 6.7 per cent of the labor force in 1961, to 5.7 per cent in 1963. Some economists attribute this to a speedup in the rate of technological change, others believe that it is largely a residue from the sluggish performance of the economy during the 1950s and will be reduced if economic expansion continues; others are quite frankly puzzled.

In the absence of agreement over the causes of unemployment, there can be no agreement over the remedy; and

---

* New York: Pantheon, 1963.

† As this book went to press, most economists expected the expansion to continue until the middle of 1965—about as far ahead as they can peer. If their forecasts are realized, this would be the longest period of expansion in the peacetime history of the United States.

vague calls for a new Negro-liberal coalition fail to come to grips with the special problems that concern Negroes. Hence there is every reason for Negro organizations to concentrate their energies on an effort to expand *Negro* employment, quite apart from the overall problem of employment and economic growth. Whatever the causes, unemployment hits Negroes far more than whites: although they comprise only 10 per cent of the labor force, Negroes account for 20 per cent of total unemployment, and nearly 30 per cent of *long-term* unemployment (defined as unemployment lasting 27 weeks or longer). Indeed, unemployment is a major factor in the lives of Negroes: in 1961, for example, only 50 per cent of Negro men (compared to two-thirds of white men) worked steadily at full-time jobs. And Negroes are far more likely to be affected by under-employment; proportionately three times as many Negroes as whites work less than full time. Negroes tend to be paid less than whites, even for the same jobs—and Negroes are concentrated very heavily in low-paying unskilled and semi-skilled occupations. The result is that even the employed Negro man frequently is unable to support his family, with results that have already been described.

It is inevitable, therefore, that Negro organizations should use their power to try to increase job opportunities for Negroes *qua Negroes*. Indeed, Negroes are not content with equal opportunity any more; they are demanding preference, or "positive discrimination" in their favor. Some Negroes liken their position to that of a runner who is kept at the starting line until his opponents in the race are halfway to the finish line; merely "freeing him" to run will not enable him to catch up. More and more Negroes, therefore, are espousing "the doctrine of the debt," which holds that the United States owes the Negro something for two hundred fifty years of slavery and one hundred years of discrimination. "If those who make the decisions in this country are really sincere about closing the gaps," Whitney Young, director of the National Urban League, argues, "they must go further than fine impartiality. We must have, in fact, special consideration if we are to compensate for the scars left by three hundred years of deprivation, which actually represented special consideration of another sort." Hence Young is demanding special priority in employment, suggesting as a precedent the ten-point preference given veterans on civil-service exams after World War Two.

The Urban League is proposing that when a Negro and a white have equal qualifications for a job, the former should be given the preference. Militant Negro organizations are demanding considerably more; they are insisting, in effect, that business firms hire Negroes not because they are qualified but because they are Negroes. And they are developing a good deal of muscle to back up their demands for preferential hiring. The most widely used technique is the boycott, or "selective patronage campaign," as Negroes prefer to call it. "Don't buy where you can't work" campaigns were frequent during the 1930s, but they were sporadic and only occasionally effective. The contemporary use of the weapon began in the early sixties in Philadelphia. The campaign was organized and directed by a group of Negro ministers (some 400 ministers co-operated) with no formal organization. The ministers' technique is to approach one company at a time, usually a manufacturer or distributor of consumer products for which a number of competing brands are available—a bakery, a dairy, an oil company, a supermarket chain. If the company refuses to negotiate with the ministers, it is given an ultimatum to hire a specified number of Negroes in specified job classifications before a given date; if the demands are ignored, a boycott ensues. With four hundred ministers using their pulpits to announce the boycott, a substantial portion of the Negro population takes part. Some firms—Pepsi-Cola and Esso, for example—have come to terms without a boycott. Others held out—but generally not for long; Gulf Oil capitulated in twelve days, Sun Oil in three months.

All told, the ministers have won concessions from twenty-four firms so far. The technique has spread to Boston, New York, Atlanta, Detroit, and other cities, and is bound to be widely imitated. As Rev. Ralph Abernathy, Rev. Martin Luther King's chief lieutenant, says, "Not every Negro is able to go to jail, but every Negro can stop buying a particular brand of bread or milk or gasoline."

These efforts, which inevitably involve some sort of demand for special treatment, have drawn criticism from such diverse liberals as the late President Kennedy and the editorial writers of the *New York Times,* who periodically deplore what they call "racism in reverse." Perhaps the most thoughtful criticism has come from Professor Eli Ginzberg of Columbia University, author of *The Negro Potential.* In an address to the 1963 NAACP convention and elsewhere, Professor Ginzberg has questioned the present course of Negro social action on the grounds that Negro unemployment is due in only small measure to racial discrimination; the more important reasons, he argues are the handicaps of lack of education, training, and experience which Negroes share with other impoverished groups. The remedy, in his view, should come as "part of a national, not a racial program. In the past," Professor Ginzberg suggests, "the Negro has made significant gains when he has been included in important national efforts—the Revolutionary War, the Civil War, the New Deal, the CIO, World War Two, the expansion of public programs for health, education, and welfare. There is little prospect that white America will do much for the handicapped Negro group," he argues. "But we *can* expect our democracy to attend to its less fortunate citizens, Negroes included. All America needs a higher level of employment, more and better education, a closer approximation to true equality. To the extent that we move energetically toward these national goals, to that extent will the status of the Negro be improved."

Perhaps; but history provides little support for the belief

that Negroes will share automatically in the general welfare, and Negro militants are likely to view the suggestion that they abandon their strategy of self-interest in favor of a search for the common good as just one more call to subordinate their interests to those of their white patrons.* There *was* a time when Negroes believed that what was good for labor, or for the country, was good for Negroes; back in 1936, for example, the NAACP magazine, *The Crisis,* urged Negroes to join the CIO because "if they [the Negroes] fight now, side by side with their fellow workers, when the time comes to divide up the benefits they can demand their share." The benefits have long since been divided up—and Negro workers are still demanding their share. They seem to get their share only when the demand is backed up by power; there is no evidence that government, or business, or trade unions, will act on the Negroes' behalf in the absence of pressure from Negro organizations. John F. Kennedy is mourned as a martyr to the cause of civil rights—but Negro activists also recall that the Kennedy Administration did not put its moral and political weight behind the Negro cause until it became clear that the Negroes were moving their fight from the courtroom to the streets. "If the economic conflict in which the Negro is involved is imbued with the hostility of race antagonism," David Danzig has written, "it is not primarily the fault of the Negro." † On the contrary, the "racist" character of the Negro protest movement is due primarily, Danzig argues, to default on the part of corporations, governments, and trade unions. In view of the fact that the Negroes have been denied their rights not as individuals but as mem-

* This concern for the common good—what Professor Edward C. Banfield and James Q. Wilson call the "community-regarding ethos" in their book, *City Politics* (1963)—is, as they point out, found only among "citizens who rank high in income, education, or both." The reason is not that these people are more altruistic, but that their self-interest is more easily advanced by measures labelled "for the common good."

† David Danzig, "The Meaning of Negro Strategy," *Commentary,* February, 1964.

bers of a group, whites can hardly complain when Negroes try to establish their rights and improve their positions on a group basis.

Most of the discussions of Negro demands for preferential treatment and for "reverse quotas" have missed the essential point. The object is not compensation, in the sense of making up to the Negro for past injustices; it is to overcome the tendencies to exclude the Negro which are built into the very marrow of American society. There are, indeed, an incredible number of factors which will operate to prevent any rapid increase in employment of Negroes unless a concerted and special effort is made. A formal policy of non-discrimination, of employing people "regardless of race, color, or creed," however estimable, usually works out in practice to be a policy of employing whites only. Hence Negroes' demand for quotas represents a necessary tactic: an attempt to fix the responsibility for increasing employment of Negroes on those who do the hiring (or in the case of trade unions, on those who control access to the job). As soon as we agree that special measures are necessary to overcome the heritage of past discrimination, the question of numbers—of *how many* Negroes are to be hired in what job categories—inevitably arises. Not to use numbers as a yardstick for measuring performance is, in effect, to revert to "tokenism." The point is not whether there is some "right" number of Negroes to be employed—obviously there is not—but simply that there is no meaningful measure of change other than numbers. For all his opposition to quotas, for example, the late President Kennedy made it clear to the heads of all government agencies that he expected them to increase the number of Negroes in government jobs, especially in jobs at the middle and upper levels of responsibility. Wherever the number of Negro employees did increase, it was because administrative responsibility for hiring more Negroes had been fixed—not because the Kennedy Administration followed a policy of non-discrimination.

Unless responsibility is fixed in this way, policies of hiring more Negroes are likely to result in more talk than action. One reason is corporate bias. In the South, of course, discrimination is conscious and overt; employment of Negroes is limited by the tradition that Negroes not be permitted to work on an equal status with whites, and that they never be placed in a supervisory position over whites. In the North, exclusion of Negroes from the better jobs stems less from conscious corporate decisions to discriminate than from the conscious or unconscious biases of the personnel officers, the foremen, the executives—*i.e.*, all those involved in hiring and promoting. At the heart of this kind of unconscious discrimination is the concept of "place": the notion that certain jobs and certain situations are appropriate, others inappropriate, for Negroes: that is to say, in almost every company, whether through accident or choice, tradition has reserved some jobs almost exclusively for whites ("Negroes wouldn't be happy there"; "I'm not prejudiced, but my customers might object.")

But prejudice is not the only factor tending to hold down Negro employment. "We would hire Negroes," the manager of Du Pont's sales office in Atlanta explained to a *Fortune* correspondent, "but we have no opportunity to do so. On the one occasion that we needed clerical help, we advertised, and our ad stated that we had signed the equal-opportunity agreement. But we had no Negro applicants. They just don't apply."

Of course they don't; the door has been closed too long. As we have seen, their own lives have given most Negroes reason enough to expect discrimination and prejudice, and to try to avoid it whenever they can; until they get positive reassurance to the contrary, Negroes are likely to assume that a firm discriminates, and they are likely to attribute any rejection to their race.* Quite apart from their desire to

* One hopeful sign is that Negroes are beginning to be able to joke about this tendency; witness the story Dick Gregory tells about the Negro who complains to a friend that he was turned down by an

avoid rebuffs, Negroes have no way of knowing when jobs are available. Virtually every study of how people find jobs has indicated that the most common method is recommendation by a relative or friend, usually one working for the same employer; relatively few people find jobs through newspaper advertisements, and even fewer through government or private employment agencies. But painfully few Negroes have relatives or friends working for corporations in anything but menial capacities; the most important means of finding a job in industry thus is not available, since Negroes are outside the web of job gossip.

Industry has to do more than just sit and wait for Negroes to come to their doors; it has to beat the bushes to find them, by recruiting at Negro colleges, at high schools in Negro areas, and at Negro employment agencies, by advertising in Negro newspapers and over Negro radio stations. At least a few corporations seem to be making a real effort to employ more Negroes. IBM now visits seventeen Negro colleges to recruit engineers, mathematicians, scientists, and sales and management trainees. McDonnell Aircraft of St. Louis, which has won praise from Negro militants for its employment policy (Negroes are employed in 127 job classifications) has developed a slide presentation picturing Negroes working alongside whites at every job level, and shows the slides at predominantly Negro high schools in the St. Louis area.

Recruitment is only the beginning. Corporations will have to revise personnel policies which, perhaps unintentionally, discourage Negroes from applying for jobs or from seeking promotions. When the Negro boycotts were under way in Philadelphia in 1962, for example, the president of one ma-

---

employer solely because of his race. "What kind of a job was it?" the friend asks. "A t-t-t-t-elev-v-v-ision announcer," the man replies. In the 1930s and early 1940s, the joke was popular among American Jews; in the earlier version, the stutterer was turned down for a job as a radio announcer because of anti-Semitism.

jor corporation decided to take a look at his company's position in advance of any attack. He discovered that his Negro employees—two hundred out of two thousand—were all at the lowest level, although the company had no overt biases. Upon further examination, it developed that Negroes stayed at the bottom because they never took the written examinations the company used to measure qualifications for promotion; they simply assumed that the tests were designed to give the company an excuse for not promoting them. (Tests are frequently used this way in the South.) Since the tests in any case bore little relation to the job functions involved, the president ordered them replaced with job-performance tests and on-the-job training. As a result, seventy Negroes were upgraded.

If Negro employment is to be increased, firms will also have to find substitutes or shortcuts for the experience they now demand as a prerequisite in certain jobs. A large merchandising chain, for example, recently asked the National Urban League for help in hiring Negroes for a number of jobs, including store managers. But there was an unintentional catch: the firm required ten years of merchandising experience with the chain as a condition for promotion to manager. Since it had never employed Negroes in merchandising jobs before, the requirement obviously made it impossible for them to qualify for at least another ten years. The Urban League suggested that the firm develop methods for testing managerial ability in a shorter time.

It is not enough, moreover, for a firm formally to open jobs to Negroes on a non-discriminatory basis. At Hughes Tool in Houston, for example, the method of filling the skilled jobs that open up is to give existing employees a tryout. A few years ago, the company changed its policy to permit Negroes as well as whites to have a tryout. But since Negroes had been restricted to menial jobs like sweeping the floors, very few were able to qualify for better jobs. As *Fortune*'s Houston correspondent reported, "The past practice of keeping Negroes from running the machines has proved effective in continuing to keep them from running the machines."

All the recruiting in the world, however, and all the changes in personnel policies, would still leave corporations and government agencies short of qualified Negro applicants: Negroes have had neither the incentive nor the opportunity to acquire the qualifications now in demand. It is unrealistic to assume that Negroes *would* be qualified. "White folks seemed always to expect you to know those things which they'd done everything they could think of to prevent you from knowing," Ralph Ellison sardonically remarks in *Invisible Man*. The only solution, therefore, is to hire unqualified Negroes and to train them on the job.

It would be absurd to pretend that such a policy will not create serious difficulties for corporate managers and government officials. Granting more jobs to Negroes may mean fewer jobs for whites, particularly if total unemployment remains high, or at the very least, an end to the monopoly that whites have thus far enjoyed in many job classifications. Negro demands for preferential treatment thus are bound to set up counter-pressures from white workers—or white voters. One result is that businessmen, to their immense surprise, are likely to find that they actually *want* a strong FEPC law forbidding all businesses to discriminate in employment or in customer service; they will need such a law to protect them against employees, trade unions, recalcitrant employers, and hostile elements in their communities.

Efficiency may be lowered by the costs of hiring unqualified Negroes and training them on the job. Even more damage to efficiency may be done by the blow to the morale (and consequently to the productivity) of white employees when firms begin to discriminate in favor of Negroes. To be sure, no corporation is completely consistent in its adherence to the principle of merit; all kinds of subjective and irrational judgments enter into the selection and promotion of employees. But deliberately departing from the merit principle is something else again, and there is no point in pretending the corporations will not pay a heavy price for doing so. The cost of not discriminating in favor of Negroes, however, will be considerably greater, both to business and to the community at large. It will be considerably cheaper for business to subsidize Negro employment for a time than to pay it out in welfare—or in the cost to the community of racial violence.

It will be far easier to do these things, of course, if the present business expansion continues and the economy returns to full employment. During the labor shortages of World War Two, and again during the Korean conflict, business learned that it can put "unqualified" men and women to work by teaching them on the job, or by reorganizing the work where necessary to require less skill.

During World War Two, for example, American optical manufacturers assured naval procurement officers that it was impossible to manufacture more than a few thousand prism binoculars annually; there was a shortage of lens grinders, and it took a number of years to train one. By breaking the lens-grinding operation into several steps, however, the Navy was able to cut training time to a few weeks—and to increase output to a half-million binoculars a year. More recently, industry has had to meet its need for engineers through on-the-job training and upgrading. Between 1954 and 1957, for example, industry increased its employment of engineers by 100,000, or 27 per cent. In the same period only 70,000 engineers were graduated by all American colleges, and not all of them went to work for industry. Clearly, corporations supplied the difference through upgrading, promotion, and transfers from other work.

Some American corporations that operate in the underdeveloped nations have had to be even more ingenious in upgrading unqualified workers, since employing native workers may be the price of staying in the country for any length of time. Aramco, for example, used to import virtually its entire labor force from the United States; it seemed "obvious" that illiterate Saudi peasants could never cope with the complex technology of oil drilling and transportation. Faced with the long-range danger of expropriation, however. Aramco discovered that the Saudis could be taught after all. The company now uses Saudi drilling crews directed by Saudi foremen; roughly one-quarter of the labor time Aramco pays for is spent in education and training of some sort.

Most Negro Americans, needless to say—even those from the rural South—are quite a few notches above the Saudi tribesman in education and training. Given the chance, they can learn as well as whites; the expense of training them represents a cost of broadening the labor pool. There are present or potential shortages in many skilled jobs partly because of rising demands, but in good measure because union training regulations artificially restrict the supply. The pressure to hire more Negroes for skilled jobs may give industry the opportunity to take a fresh look at obsolete training requirements.

There may be a touch of hypocrisy, moreover, in some of the expressions of alarm over what may happen to job standards when more Negroes are employed. No one, after all, has suggested that unskilled Negro laborers be turned into brain surgeons or corporate presidents. What has been suggested is that Negroes be allowed to become plumbers, or electricians, or steam fitters, or carpenters; and, as David Danzig suggested, no one who lives or works in a recently built New York City building is likely to be impressed with the sincerity of the New York building trades unions' concern over maintaining the standards of their craft. Nor is anyone who has had difficulty keeping a new car or a new washing machine in working order likely to be overawed by Detroit's devotion to workmanship.

The way in which business responds to Negro pressures, perhaps more than any other single factor, will determine the character and tone of race relations over the rest of this decade. Businessmen like to think of themselves as conservatives; they have a rare opportunity to conserve American society by repairing what has to be repaired and changing what has to be changed. As we have seen, Negroes have become increasingly cynical about the efficacy of law and the integrity and good faith of white leadership. If they act on their own initiative to create jobs for Negroes, businessmen may be able to convert that distrust and cynicism into some degree of confidence and so, in the phrase of Edmund Burke, "make the Revolution a parent of settlement and not a nursery of future revolutions." If they are to do this, however—if they are to play a truly constructive role—businessmen will have to look beyond the rules and canons of business management. They will need to learn the art of politics in the highest sense of that term, for they will be engaged in what has been called "the politics of repair."

There is a precedent for what businessmen are being called upon to do. In many ways, the current racial conflict resembles the conflict over trade-unionism during the 1930s; businessmen then resented the unionists' demands to share in managerial power, and they were concerned over what would happen to efficiency if extraneous considerations—union membership or seniority, for example—were made a condition of employment or of promotion. The analogy can be pressed too far, of course; there are important differences, the main one being that trade unions could purport to speak for most of a firm's employees, whereas Negro organizations speak only for a minority. The fact remains that the United States averted class warfare in the 1930s because large corporations gradually came to accommodate themselves to trade union power—that is, to negotiate with it. Business has a similar role to play today in averting race warfare.

IX

THE NEGRO AND THE SCHOOL

Shudder, you complacent ones!

—ISAIAH

1

One hundred and twenty years ago, Horace Mann referred to education as "the great equalizer of the conditions of men . . . the balance wheel of the social machinery." The wheel is out of balance. As the one institution with which every Negro comes into intensive and prolonged contact, the public school offers the greatest opportunity to break down the cultural barrier that helps block the Negro's advance into the main stream of American life. But the opportunity is being muffed: no city in the United States has even begun to face up to the problem involved in educating Negro—or for that matter, white—slum youngsters.

To understand the kind of education Negro youngsters need, and the urgency that underlies that need, it is necessary to put the problem of slum schools in the context of the transformation that is affecting *all* public education. And to do that, it may be useful to take a brief look at how the present system evolved. In the early years of the Republic, education was the concern chiefly of the social and economic elite. The content was largely classical, the purpose principally to train clergymen, lawyers, and other community leaders. For the rest of the population, as Abraham Lincoln recalled, "there were some schools, so-called; but no qualification was ever required of a teacher beyond 'readin', writin', and cipherin' ' to the Rule of Three." Sparked by men like Horace Mann, however, the conviction that everyone ought to be educated spread gradually and led to the creation of public schools; but the classical curriculum remained largely unchanged.

Toward the end of the last century the growth of industry was creating the need for a literate working class, and was shifting hordes of illiterate people from the farms to the cities, where there were no chores to keep the children occupied all day. Simultaneously, the large cities were being engulfed by waves of immigration from southern and eastern Europe. The traditional curriculum obviously was suited neither to the capacities nor the needs of children from peasant and frequently alien backgrounds—particularly with the available teachers. Instruction, as a result, degenerated into a singsong concert drill and recitation by rote, and children in droves deserted the schools as irrelevant to the world in which they lived.

It was against this background that the last great change in American education occurred. "Progressive education" and the "life adjustment" curriculum did not spring full-blown from the head of John Dewey. His theories were adopted largely because they met needs strongly felt in American society around the turn of the century. The demands for change came from all sides, as Professor Lawrence A. Cremin has shown in *The Transformation of the School.** Social reformers saw the school as the only public agency able to Americanize the immigrants and lift them out of their squalor. Psychologists and philosophers at Chicago,

* New York: Alfred A. Knopf, Inc., 1961.

Clark, and Columbia universities and elsewhere were developing new theories of behavior and learning that emphasized the interaction between the child and his environment, and that saw learning as a process affecting behavior and social attitudes as well as intellectual skills. And business leaders saw a program of vocational education as the only way in which the United States could keep its place in the international economic race. "You know, as does every manufacturer in this nation know," Frank A. Vanderlip of the National City Bank told a worried business audience in 1906, "that Germany's superiority in international commerce rests almost wholly on Germany's superior school system" —a system, Vanderlip proclaimed, that aimed "to make of each citizen an efficient economic unit." The National Association of Manufacturers had been pushing for a good many years for a broadening of the school's role. "The classical and the general literary studies have their place in all educational systems," President Theodore Search told the NAM convention in 1898, "but it is unfair and unjust to the great material interests of the land to leave out of account the obvious demands of industry and commerce."

And so the schools, tailoring their curriculum to the needs of the time, de-emphasized intellectual discipline and broadened their function to include a concern for health, vocational training, and the quality of community life. For fifty years this system helped the United States to make more smoothly than any other nation the difficult transition from a farming to an industrialized society, at the same time absorbing and "Americanizing" the children of millions of immigrants.

Recently, however, the feeling has been growing that the educational system we have is not "right" for the future needs and responsibilities of American society—not right for white any more than for black students. For a decade or more, critics have been clobbering professional educators for their failure to teach reading, for their excessive interest in children's social adjustment at the expense of intellectual achievement, and for their naïve faith that a simple dose of more money would solve all the schools' ills. (This dissatisfaction, it should be noted, began long before Sputnik; the Soviet achievements in space merely gave added force to criticisms and changes that had been underway for some years before.) Philip H. Coombs, former director of the Ford Foundation's Educational Division, with only slight exaggeration, pronounced the verdict: "Almost everything that the schools and colleges are doing is obsolete and inadequate today. This applies to the curriculum, to the arrangements for teacher training, to textbooks, to organization, to methods of teaching and learning, to school architecture."

The United States is moving away from progressivism not because it is "false" in some absolute sense, but because it badly serves the needs of our time. The growing complexity of organization and the explosive pace of technological and social change are creating an enormous demand that is without historical precedent. Society has always needed a few men with highly developed and disciplined intellects. But no society, until our day, could afford to have more than a few; to be educated meant, almost by definition, to be nonproductive. Indeed, the word "school," and its equivalent in all European languages, comes from a Greek word meaning leisure. (Booker T. Washington reflected this older state of affairs in his denunciations of college education as leaving students unprepared for "fundamental wealth-producing occupations.") Industrial society needed masses of literate but not necessarily intellectual men; hence the school system that developed in the beginning of the century met the needs of American society quite adequately.

It is not meeting the needs of today's society. Today, and even more, tomorrow, requires something the world has never seen—*masses of educated men.* The kind of deadly monotonous assembly line Charlie Chaplin satirized in *Modern Times* no longer reflects the reality of industrial life.

Rather, as Peter F. Drucker has cogently suggested, the prototype of the large productive organization seems increasingly to be the Strategic Air Command base, which must integrate the highly developed skills of thousands of people—pilots, navigators, meteorologists, radio technicians, doctors, mechanics, operations researchers, computer programmers, operators, repairmen, and the like. The result is to reverse the concept of education prevalent throughout recorded history. In this "post-modern age," as Drucker calls it, to be educated is to be productive; indeed, education and knowledge represent the most valuable form of capital. To be uneducated is not only to be unproductive but to be virtually unemployable. Hence the task of the school system is not just to turn out masses of literate men; it is to turn out vast numbers of people educated considerably beyond the level that previous societies demanded only of their ruling elite.

The public schools are just starting to do this for white middle-class children; they are at the beginning of a transformation even more extensive than the one occurring at the beginning of the century. For Negro youngsters, however, the schools have not even begun to begin. It is particularly unfortunate, therefore, that public discussion of the problem of Negro education has been influenced so strongly by James Bryant Conant's *Slums and Suburbs.** The book was useful in arousing public interest in the problem. But it recommended the worst kind of solution—namely, an increase in vocational education.

Conant's emphasis on vocational education bears echoes of Booker T. Washington's discredited approach; it would condemn Negroes to be hewers of wood and drawers of water in a society that needs fewer and fewer such people. Negro youngsters need precisely the same kind of education that white youngsters need. The growing professionalization of the labor force makes knowledge the source of productiv-

* New York: The McGraw-Hill Book Company, 1961.

ity. And the rapidity of technological change means that over the course of his life, the average person may have to change not just his job but his entire occupation—and perhaps not just once but several times. The recent plight of the airplane flight engineers illustrates how rapidly skills can become obsolete. The flight engineering craft, or profession, had a total life span of just fifteen years—from the adoption of the four-engined plane to its replacement by the jet. (The DC-3 was too simple to require an engineer on board; so is the jet.)

Nothing could be more wildly impractical, therefore—and nothing more destructive to the future of an individual or of society—than an education designed to prepare people only for specific vocations or professions or to facilitate their "adjustment" to the world as it is. To be practical now an education must prepare a man for work that does not yet exist and whose nature cannot even be imagined. This can be done only by teaching people how to learn, by giving them the kind of intellectual discipline and the depth of understanding that will enable them to apply man's accumulated wisdom to new conditions as they arise.

There is a place for vocational training, of course; it is sheer snobbishness to insist that *every* student be interested in or able to benefit from an academic program. For youngsters who regard schools as a detention pen, some sort of work-study program may be the best bet. But any useful program of vocational education must start from the premise that *literacy is the most important vocational skill of all.* A committee investigating New York's vocational high schools came upon an incident that dramatizes this fact in an unexpected way. One of the city's newest vocational high schools had graduated a particularly capable auto mechanic and had placed the young man in a large repair shop in the neighborhood. The principal was surprised, therefore, when the young man called a few weeks later to ask his help in finding another job; the principal decided he had better call the first employer to find out what had happened. The employer praised the young man's mechanical ability lavishly, but explained that he had had to discharge him anyway: the lad could not read well enough to read his job assignment each morning on the shop's bulletin board. "Send me someone who can read," he told the high-school principal.

▼

2

No city, to repeat, is doing more than a fraction of what is necessary to give Negro youngsters the kind of education they need—the kind of education to which, in a democracy they are entitled. There is, to be sure, a lot of talk; there are conferences galore about the problems of "the culturally deprived child," or "the gray area schools," or any of the other euphemisms used to avoid mentioning the word Negro, and there are endless (and fruitless) debates over which euphemism is to be preferred. In 1962, for example, the New York City Board of Education urged teachers to adopt an upbeat note in talking about their students. Instead of the terms "low income" or "underprivileged" children, teachers were advised to talk about "children unable to secure much beyond the necessities of today's world because of the modest finances of the family," and the phrase "culturally deprived children" was to be replaced by "children whose experiences, generally speaking, have been limited to their immediate environment."

In all fairness, the large cities have not limited themselves to talk; there is a good deal of experimentation going on, too, and there is no large city without at least one well-publicized "demonstration project" involving "children whose experiences, generally speaking, have been limited to their immediate environment." Indeed, school superintendents collect Ford Foundation grants much the way Indians used to collect scalps in the old frontier warfare days. (When Calvin Gross was appointed Superintendent of Schools in New York City one of the qualifications that seemed to be mentioned most frequently was the amount of Ford Foundation money he had been able to secure while he headed the Pittsburgh schools.) The projects usually succeed admirably; they demonstrate that whatever technique was being used can substantially improve the performance of Negro youngsters.

For the most part, however, nothing much happens as a result; once the "demonstration project" ends, the schools involved slip back into the same old rut. New York's Junior High School 43 provides a classic example. It was there that the famous "Demonstration Guidance Project" was begun in 1956; by showing that with the proper help—very small classes, a great deal of remedial work (especially in reading English, and math) and intensive guidance and counseling—youngsters from the worst sort of slum could complete high school and go on to college, the project stimulated a host of other experiments from coast to coast, and in New York itself led to the well-publicized Higher Horizons program. The Demonstration Guidance Project ended in June of 1962. And in March of 1963, a group of students and teachers walked out of J.H.S. 43 for two hours and, joined by parents, picketed and demonstrated to protest what they called "the destruction of the long-established superior educational standards of the school."

New York City has added a staggering number of special services to schools in slum areas over the last ten to fifteen years; the Early Identification and Prevention program, in which guidance counselors, social workers, and psychologists are assigned to spot and treat symptoms of true emotional and psychological maladjustment; Higher Horizons, which provides cultural and academic enrichment; reading improvement teachers; corrective reading teachers; an All-Day Neighborhood School program, which keeps schools open for group-work programs between three and five o'clock. All told, the city spends some $200 per pupil *more* each year in slum schools than in white middle-class schools. But with it all, third grade pupils in the schools of central Harlem are one year behind grade level in academic performance; by the sixth grade, they have fallen nearly two years behind; and by eighth grade, they are two and a half years retarded. Negro youngsters' IQ scores also decline as they go through school. As United States Commissioner of Education Francis Keppel has said, "education in central Harlem is marked by massive educational deterioration." And New York probably is doing more than any other large city; in most, the picture is even worse.

A few social scientists of conservative bent have pointed to lower Negro scores on IQ and achievement tests as proof of *inherent* Negro inferiority. Dr. Henry E. Garrett, retired chairman of the psychology department at Columbia University, former president of the American Psychological Association, and Visiting Professor of Psychology at the University of Virginia since 1958, has led the attack on what he calls "the equalitarian dogma"—*i.e.*, the notion that all races have the same mental potential. In Garrett's view, "The equalitarian dogma at best represents a sincere if misguided effort to help the Negro by ignoring or even suppressing evidence of his mental and social immaturity. At worst, the equalitarian dogma is the scientific hoax of the century." Garrett's view has been widely popularized in the South by a retired New England businessman, Carleton Putnam, whose book, *Race and Reason,* is a favorite of the White Citizens Council. (October 26, 1961, was officially proclaimed "Race and Reason Day" in Mississippi, and Putnam was honored at a $25-a-plate dinner attended by the governor and some five hundred "patriots.") Garrett himself leans very heavily on the work of a former student, Dr. Audrey M. Shuey, who analyzed some two hundred forty studies of Negro intelligence, covering the period 1913 to 1957.* The Shuey-Garrett analysis indicates that Negro IQs consistently run fifteen to twenty points below white IQs; that the Negro lag is greatest in tests of an abstract nature; that differences between Negro and white youngsters increase with age, the gap becoming largest at the high-school and college levels; and that Negroes score below whites even when socio-economic factors have been equated. These facts, in their view, prove that Negro intelligence is inherently inferior to white intelligence.†

The Anti-Defamation League of B'nai B'rith recently asked four distinguished social scientists—Dr. Henry C. Dyer, Vice-President of Educational Testing Service; Dr. Silvan S. Tomkins, Professor of Psychology at Princeton University; Dr. Ralph H. Turner, chairman of the Department of Sociology at UCLA; and Dr. Sherwood L. Washburn, chairman of the Department of Anthropology at University of California at Berkeley and former president of the American Anthropological Association—to answer a number of questions about the Shuey and Putnam books. The panel reported that the

---

* Dr. Audrey M. Shuey, *Testing of Negro Intelligence*, Lynchburg, Va.: J. P. Bell Co., 1958.

† Some sense of Dr. Garrett's own scientific objectivity may be obtained from this excerpt from his testimony in the 1963 Savannah-Chatham County Case, which the White Citizens Councils tried to use as a means of overturning the Supreme Court's decision in the Brown Case.

> Q. Could you approximate for me the differences between the two groups [*i.e.*, Negroes and whites] so far as your experience goes in these three fields?
>
> *A.* (from Dr. Garrett). Well, I think the great difference comes in the abstract and the verbal side. In social adaptability I don't know of any specific studies but my guess, maybe it's educated, I don't know, could be there isn't any great difference. In the mechanical-motor, I just don't know. I have heard a lot of stories about how Africans fail to put oil in the motors and ruin them and all that kind of thing. . . .

evidence did not justify the conclusion that there are native differences between the intelligence of whites and Negroes. "The nature of intelligence tests is such," the panel argued, "that they are incapable of identifying genetic differences between any two groups." They pointed out that IQ tests "do not measure only innate intelligence; what they measure as well are the effects of opportunity to learn the kinds of items included in the tests, the motivation of the individual taking the test, the meaningfulness of the items for him, and his ability to perform in a test situation. In all these respects, the Negro in our society is disadvantaged in comparison with whites in otherwise similar environments." (The four social scientists would have been even more convincing had they not tried to minimize the evidence. "There is no reason to suppose," they added in a gratuitous aside, "that the relatively small average differences in test scores reflect differences in innate intelligence." But the differences are not relatively small, and the social scientists only weaken their case by pretending that they are.)

What is crucial is the fact, as Dr. Dyer said, that "there are no tests of native intelligence"—that in fact "the concept of 'native intelligence' is essentially meaningless." According to Dr. J. McV. Hunt of the University of Illinois, "the assumption that intelligence is fixed and that its development is predetermined by genes is no longer tenable. Intelligence consists primarily of techniques a child acquires for processing information pouring through his senses." The learning is what counts.* Scientists have discovered, for example, that a good deal of the behavior of animals that had always been regarded as "instinctive" is in fact learned. Experiments have demonstrated, moreover, that monkeys learn how to learn: monkeys who have been trained to take tests are far more skillful in handling new tests that

* *See also* Thomas F. Pettigrew, "Negro American Intelligence; A New Look at an Old Controversy," *Journal of Negro Education,* Winter, 1964.

are given them than monkeys that lack the training. The same is true with rats. But there is no species in which the environment has so great an effect on learning and subsequent performance as man. Differences in Negro and white test scores clearly are related to differences in environment and training. Thus, the IQ scores of Negro youngsters typically *drop* twenty points as they go through school. But when these youngsters participate in projects designed to improve their education, the reverse occurs. In New York's Demonstration Guidance Project, for example, the IQ scores of eight out of ten youngsters improved—and the increases ranged from ten to forty points.

A great deal of the difference between Negro and white scores it is clear, are directly attributable to socio-economic class; lower-class white youngsters have IQs substantially below those of middle-class youngsters, and academic performance is highly correlated with family income. Poverty and the lowered incentives and aspirations that accompany it undoubtedly explain the fact that southern whites, as a group, show IQ test scores as much below the average of Northern whites as Negroes are below the white level. In the intelligence tests administered by the Army during World War One, for example, the median scores for Northern whites was 60.0 compared to only 40.5 for Southern whites—and the same for Northern Negroes.

The fact remains that ordinary measures of socio-economic class do not erase the difference between Negro and white academic achievement; Negro youngsters show twice as much academic lag as lower-class white youngsters. But Dr. Martin Deutsch, Director of the Institute for Developmental Studies of New York Medical College, has indicated that these differences may be due to environmental factors which the ordinary measures of class do not take into account. For one thing, Negro youngsters have a much shorter history of urbanization than whites of the same socio-economic class; more important, a very much higher proportion of Negro youngsters come from broken homes. When Deutsch matched two samples of white and Negro youngsters not only for socio-economic class but also for length of residence in the city and for family structure (that is, he took the same proportion of "whole families" in both samples), the IQ differences washed out completely.

Why, then, do Negro youngsters perform so poorly in school? One answer, suggested by a good many Negroes, is that their youngsters do not learn because they are not taught. They have a point. Teachers are no more free from prejudice than any other group in American society; it seems clear that all too many teachers of Negro children believe in their hearts (even if they do not admit in their minds) that their students are intellectually inferior, that they are incapable of benefiting from a normal curriculum. Even when this attitude is unconscious, the teacher cannot avoid communicating it to the children in some way or other. And the attitude is not always unconscious. Here is Dr. Frank Riessman's description of one of the teachers he encountered in his study:

> As soon as I entered the classroom Mrs. X told me in front of the class that the parents of these children are not professional and therefore they do not have much background or interest in going to college . . . She discussed each child openly in front of the entire class and myself . . . She spoke about each child in a belittling manner . . . She told me in private that "heredity is what really counts," and since they don't have a high culture in Africa and have not yet built one in New York, they are intellectually inferior from birth.*

Every school system has a story, perhaps apocryphal, of a teacher in a Negro slum school who wears gloves so as not to be contaminated by anything. Whether the prejudice is conscious or unconscious, it presents a terrible block to

* Frank Riessman, *The Culturally Deprived Child,* New York: Harper & Row, Publishers, Inc., 1962.

learning. Children, no less than adults, resent being patronized. Equally important, young children tend to fulfill the expectations their elders hold out for them. Hence the teacher who assumes that her children cannot learn very much will discover that she has a class of children who indeed are unable to learn—a prime example of what sociologists call a "self-fulfilling prophecy." "Our greatest enemy," says Jacob Landers, former Coordinator of New York's Higher Horizons Program, now Assistant Superintendent for Integration, "is the phrase 'as well as can be expected.'"

The problem involves prejudices of class as well as color.* For example, teachers who have just moved up into the middle class feel threatened by contact with lower-class children; the youngsters remind them too much of their own origins. Thus, using Negro teachers for Negro children frequently backfires; the Negro teacher—having pulled herself up out of the slum by her own bootstraps—may be more contemptuous of her slum charges than any white. ("If I could do it, why can't they?")

Prejudice aside, the quality of teaching offered Negro youngsters is frequently inferior: schools in Negro areas have a disproportionate number of inexperienced teachers and of "permanent substitutes." To some degree, the inferior teaching is deliberate: Conant found that expenditures per pupil in most big city slum schools ran only half the average in most suburbs. In some cities, expenditures per pupil seem to run less in Negro than in white schools. New York is an exception in this regard—and even with higher per pupil expenditures, schools in Negro areas still tend to be old and overcrowded. (Enrollment of Negro and Puerto Rican students in the city's schools has doubled between the 1957-58

---

* For documentation on the class bias of American public education, *see* Patricia Sexton, *Education and Income,* New York: Viking Press, 1961; and Robert J. Havighurst, "Urban Development and the Educational System," in A. Harry Passow, ed., *Education in Depressed Areas,* New York: Teachers College Bureau of Publications, 1963.

and the 1963-64 school years.) In Chicago (which Dr. Conant, curiously enough, complimented), total appropritions per pupil average 21 per cent less in all-Negro schools than in all-white schools.* A distinguished Chicago minister who lives in an integrated area was horrified to discover that when the Negro registration in his child's school began to climb, the school was shifted in mid-year from one District Superintendent to another, who had an all-Negro district. After this transfer had been made, the school lost its speech therapist, remedial reading teacher, and other special services. The following year, shortages of textbooks began to show up. And then the school began getting an inordinate number of permanent substitutes.

Assignment of inferior teachers is not always deliberate, however. Some school systems are required, by the terms of their contract with a teachers' union, to allow teachers some discretion in choosing where they will teach. Other systems find that, union contract aside, they will lose many good teachers if they do not grant some discretion. And the uncomfortable fact is that only a small minority of dedicated teachers will choose to teach in a slum school. Teachers refuse to teach in a white slum school because of the problem of discipline, because of fear of personal safety, because of experiences of having the tires on their cars slashed or the windows broken, etc., etc. The fact that a school is in a Negro slum merely compounds the problem. Hence, school systems may have little option but to assign newly-hired teachers to the slum schools; and when the newly-hired teachers discover where they have been assigned, they simply decline the position and find a job (for as much or more money) in a safe and placid middle-class suburb.

One way of ameliorating the situation would be to pay higher salaries to teachers who volunteer for slum schools; the proposal was aired in New York City a while back, but

* *Cf.*, U. S. Commission on Civil Rights, *Civil Rights USA: Public Schools North and West, 1962*, Washington, D.C.

was strongly vetoed by the teachers' union. Other methods are being tried. One of the more interesting and hopeful experiments is being conducted by Hunter College in New York with undergraduates preparing for a teaching career. The college has assigned a number of students, all of whom volunteered, to do their student-teaching in Negro slum schools with all the classical problems. The students are given several weeks in which to observe, to become familiar with the school and with the class he or she is to teach, and several more weeks of instruction in how to plan a lesson, how to schedule time, and so on. For the final ten or eleven weeks of the semester, the student teacher takes over the class, but with help, advice and criticism whenever needed (and weekly, whether needed or not) from the co-operating teacher, the school administration, and the Hunter faculty. After classes, the student teacher is brought into contact with the community by visits to housing developments, welfare agencies, local leaders. The program has been quite successful in developing a desire to teach in a slum school; thirty-seven of the fifty-one who volunteered during the first five semesters of the experiment remained after they received their licenses in the school in which they had practiced. But the success is limited; only fifty-one—a small fraction of total enrollment—volunteered! The great majority of students preparing for teaching as a career do not want to teach in "difficult" schools, and they do their best to avoid such schools even for their period of internship—unlike medicine, for example, where most doctors must assume that their training will occur in hospitals and clinics serving the poor and underprivileged.

The teachers cannot really be blamed for their reluctance; the problems encountered in the slum school would be enough to discourage Job himself—and most teachers have considerably less patience than he. Pupil turnover is very rapid, as families move from one rooming house to another. Three elementary schools in New York, for example, had a 100 per cent turnover in student population between the beginning and the end of the 1959-60 school year; in forty-three schools, the turnover ranged between 70 per cent and 99 per cent. Hence the standard quip that a teacher who is absent more than a week may not be able to recognize her class when she returns. A great many children come to school hungry, either because of poverty or because no one has bothered to feed them; as a result, it is not uncommon for children in the lower grades to doze until the mid-morning milk-and-cookie break. A substantial number are rebellious and disorderly, challenging any established authority almost as a matter of principle; the result is that as often as not, maintaining order takes precedence over teaching. In his studies of classroom procedures in Negro slum schools Dr. Deutsch found that even the best teachers frequently had to spend as much as 75 per cent of their time maintaining discipline, leaving only 25 per cent for actual instruction. The discipline problem involves considerably more than maintaining quiet. The pathology of the community outside inevitably spills over into school life, and so teachers must be on guard to prevent violence, to stop some youngsters from extorting money from younger children, etc.; and in junior and senior high schools, the teachers themselves may be physically threatened or actually attacked.

The obstacles to education, in short, are staggering in the Negro slum school—just as they always have been in slum schools. (The preceding recital, in fact, could have been taken out of the literature describing the problem of education at the turn of the century, when immigrants from southern and eastern Europe were inundating the big cities.) There is a tendency, therefore, for educators to place the blame for the schools' failure on the home and on society. "One lesson to be drawn from visiting and contrasting a well-to-do suburb and a slum is all important for understanding American public education," James Bryant Conant wrote in *Slums and Suburbs.* "*The lesson is that to a considerable degree what a school should do and can do is determined by the status and ambition of the families being served.*"

The responsibility for the schools' failure cannot be ducked that easily. The fact is that when Negro mothers take their children to school that first day, they have the same hopes for their children that white mothers have, however uninformed they may be about the way to implement them. The Negro child himself enters with at the very worst a nebulous or neutral attitude toward school and toward learning; most are eager to learn, and teachers describe their first graders as "curious," "cute," "independent," etc. If such children do not learn to read or write, therefore—if by the fourth or fifth grade they see school as an enemy to be hated and fought at every turn, and their teachers see them as "alienated," "angry," "troublemakers" —then the responsibility, and the blame, must be placed on the school. For "it is in the school situation that the highly charged negative attitudes toward learning evolve," as Martin Deutsch has put it. For the school to try to shift the responsibility to the community in which it is located is to deny the basic premise of universal education; if children learn less easily in one community than in another, it is the school's responsibility to do what needs to be done to equalize the situation. This is *not* to argue that the school should become a social work agency; its job is to teach. But in a society that truly believes in universal education, a public school is *not* simply teacher and pupil—Mark Hopkins at one end of a log and a student at the other end; it is Mark Hopkins plus whatever else he needs to make that child learn! "Of all public agencies," the sociologist C. Wilson Record has written, the schools "should be the most energetic and inventive in seeking to break the chain of poor education, poor employment, poor family life, and poor life chances." To argue that the public school should merely sit back and offer its services to those youngsters able and willing to take advantage of them is, in a sense, to deny the premise of universal education. If the school is to educate every citizen, it must, in Record's phrase, "militantly assault the barricade of ignorance and prejudice."

To be passive, indeed, is to surrender in advance, for the school must compete with the far more exciting world of the street; and it must persuade youngsters that education is worthwhile when the evidence of their senses suggests the reverse. "Education is a difficult enough process under any condition," Dr. Carl Hansen, Superintendent of Schools of Washington, D.C., has written, "Because educational effort is primarily an expression of hope on the part of the student . . . an expression of faith . . . that if he delivers a strong effort to improve himself now in school, he will achieve satisfying results in his economic and social life later." This is true for all pupils, argues Dr. Hansen—a leading advocate of "basic education." But the Negro student, paradoxically, must have more hope and faith than the white student. "He is asked to have faith and confidence which at the moment seem unreasonable and unjustifiable." Or as John Fischer, president of Teachers College, has said, every Negro child, on the day he enters school, "carries a burden no white child can ever know, no matter what handicaps or disabilities he may suffer."

It is the responsibility of the school to lift that burden so that the child can learn. No one can really say that the school cannot win its difficult battle with the street; it has never really tried. For all their concern with "the whole child," the blunt fact is that the public schools have never paid much attention to anything but the whole white middle-class child. To a degree that is only now beginning to be seen and understood, the schools have built their curricula on the quite unconscious assumption that children will enter with certain skills and attitudes—skills and attitudes which the middle-class child in America tends to imbibe with the air he breathes, but which the lower-class child, white or black, all too frequently fails to acquire.

▼

3

What must the schools do in order to give Negro youngsters the kind of education they need to compete on equal terms with whites? The root of the problem educationally is that Negro youngsters do not learn to read properly in the first two grades. Their inability to read at grade level becomes more and more of a handicap as they go through school, for the amount of required reading increases at something like a geometric rate. Whether because of this reading disability alone, or because of difficulty in handling abstract concepts that stems from other causes discussed below, Negro children fall farther and farther behind after the fifth grade; the gap accelerates, and their IQs actually decline.

The youngsters' failure to learn to read properly affects much more than their school work; it has the most profound impact on how they regard themselves—and consequently on how they regard school. It takes no genius for a child to know that reading is what school is about in the first few grades. His failure to learn to read, therefore, can only serve to reinforce the negative image he already has of himself because of his color and because of the instability of his background. (On the contrary, the principal way in which people develop a sense of ego, of self-knowledge and self-confidence, is by developing competence in first one area and then in others.) When failure has been repeated frequently enough, it is almost inevitable that the child will begin to hate himself—and to hate school and the teachers which make public the evidence of his failure. And then the vicious circle begins. Because the child cannot read, his attitude suffers; he may simply withdraw from competition, to persuade himself that he really could have passed if only he had tried; or he may become a clown or a rebel. Because his attitude is poor—withdrawn or actively hostile—the teacher reacts in kind. The combination of inadequate reading skill and poor attitude reinforces the failure, which reinforces the attitude. And so it goes.

But why doesn't he learn to read? In American public schools reading is commonly taught in the first grade. The method of instruction takes for granted the fact that the child has completed the "reading readiness" program of the kindergarten year—yet only a relatively small proportion of Negro (or lower-class white) youngsters attend kindergarten. In most school systems, kindergarten attendance is not compulsory; only half the children of kindergarten age actually attend, and they tend to be from the middle class. (One reason is that kindergarten usually lasts for only two hours or so; since a large proportion of Negro mothers work, they may send their children instead to an all-day nursery, where even less is taught than in the conventional kindergarten.) Many school systems make no attempt to encourage children to attend kindergarten, moreover, because they have facilities for only a fraction of the children of kindergarten age, and prefer not to add any more to their burden of school construction. Hence many, if not most Negro children enter the first grade without the reading readiness preparation that the majority of white children have had.

The problem is even more basic than that, however; compulsory kindergarten attendance undoubtedly would improve matters, but it would not solve the problem. The problem, stated as simply as possible, is that the environment in which lower-class Negro children—and lower-class white children as well—grow up does not provide the intellectual and the sensory stimulation they need in order to benefit from the conventional kindergarten and first-grade curricula. For the so-called reading readiness program employed in American kindergartens does *not* teach "reading readiness"—that is, it does not teach the specific skills that a child must have before he can learn to read. To a degree we are just beginning to understand, as the result of research by such men as Martin Deutsch in this country and Moshe Smilansky in Israel, our kindergartens assume, without realizing it, that all children enter school already possessing these skills; the reading readiness program merely teaches children to focus these skills on the art of reading. The schools have been able to make this assumption because middle-class children do, in fact, come already equipped with these skills; they acquire them quite unconsciously from their environment, more or less by osmosis. But the lower-class child, as a rule, has not acquired these skills because of the intellectual and sensory poverty of his environment.

For example, the Negro youngsters (and the lower-class white youngsters, for what we are dealing with here are mainly functions of social class) have much less of a sense of auditory discrimination—less ability to distinguish very subtle differences and nuances in sound—that is essential to reading. For one thing, the noise level in a household in which, say, a half-dozen people, are living in two rooms, tends to be so high that the child is forced to learn how *not* to listen; he develops the ability to wall himself off from his surroundings.* Hence he fails to develop an ability to distinguish between relevant and irrelevant sounds, and to screen out the irrelevant. If, for example, a truck rumbles by

* Dr. Deutsch tells of a youngster in one class he was studying who had the habit of enclosing himself in a closet for fairly lengthy periods of time. The more psychiatrically-oriented members of his staff were ready with the usual Freudian explanations, until Deutsch took the trouble to ask the child why he did it. Seems that this was the only time during the day when the youngster could have any privacy, and could enjoy the feeling of reading in solitude; home was crowded and noisy.

while the teacher is talking, the lower-class youngster hears only one big jumble of sound; the middle-class child has the ability to screen out the irrelevant noise of the truck and listen only to the teacher. More important, the lower-class child has not had the experience of having adults correct his pronunciation; correction of baby speech and of mistakes in syntax or grammar is one crucial way in which the middle-class child learns the ability to distinguish subtle nuances of sound and language—for example, the difference between a "b" and a "p." In the case of the lower-class Negro youngster, particularly in families recently moved from the South, the problem is compounded several times over by the fact that the phonic system of the language he speaks is quite different from the phonic system of the language spoken by the teacher and used in the reading primers.

The lower-class child, moreover, tends to have a poor attention span and to have great difficulty following the teacher's orders. The reason is that he generally comes from a non-verbal household: adults speak in short sentences, if indeed they speak at all, and when they give orders to the child, it is usually in monosyllables—"get this," "bring that." Thus the child has never been obliged to listen to several lengthy sentences spoken consecutively; the speech he hears, moreover, tends to be grammatically and syntactically simple. The result is that the child is unable to follow the middle-class teacher who rambles on for several sentences at a time. Apart from the problem of attention span *per se*, people generally hear only 60 to 80 per cent of any sustained communication; they comprehend without any difficulty because they reconstruct what they have missed—unconsciously—from their knowledge of the syntactical regularities of a language. The Negro child cannot make that reconstruction, for he lacks the knowledge; from the standpoint of syntax and vocabulary, the teacher might just as well be talking another language.

The non-verbal character of the lower-class home means

that youngsters' memory, as well as their attention span, receive less training. Dr. Deutsch has said, "It is adults who link the past and the present by calling to mind prior shared experiences." The fact that language is used less, and that there are fewer shared activities between adults and children, means that the memory function receives much less stimulation. For much the same reason, lower-class children have much less sense of time, and much greater difficulty handling items involving a time judgment, than middle-class youngsters. The non-verbal atmosphere also means that lower-class children have a limited perception of the world about them: they do not know that objects have names (table, wall, book), or that the same object may have several names (an apple is fruit, red, round, delicious); the reason is that the middle-class mother will say, "Johnny, pick up that book from the table and put it back in the shelf," while the lower-class mother may restrict herself to, "Bring *that*; put it *there*," and point, or use other "sign language" to indicate "*what*" and "*where*."

The lack of structure in the lower-class, and particularly the Negro, home also inhibits the child's ability to manipulate the structures involved in learning to read. Boys in particular have never learned to follow through on an assigned task. (Girls have an advantage—partly because of matriarchal tendencies, of course—but partly because they have received the training of setting the table for meals, making beds, etc.) Both boys and girls are poorly motivated, because they have had little experience in receiving approval for success in a task or receiving disapproval for failure; but school is organized on the assumption that children expect approval for success. And since the parents, because of their general non-verbal orientation, do not ask the youngsters about school, the children have no way of knowing that the parents *do* very much want and expect success. For much the same reason, lower-class youngsters do not conceive of an adult as a person of whom you ask questions and from whom you get answers—yet school is based on the assumption that children who do not understand will ask. (Middle-class parents, by contrast, are engaged in almost constant dialogue with their children.)

Given this poverty of experience, it is almost inevitable that the Negro child will fail when he enters school; he simply has not been prepared to produce what the school demands, and by and large the school makes no attempt to adjust its curriculum to the realities of what its children actually know, as opposed to what it is *assumed* they know. The Negro child lacks the skills he needs in order to learn how to read. He also lacks the motivation—the inquisitiveness, the aggressive eagerness to learn, which the schools also assume. Teachers take for granted that children know *what* things are, and assume that their job is to answer *why* they are. But these children do not know what things are, and nothing in their environment has taught them to ask why. Inevitably, therefore, they do not learn to read adequately; and their failure in school confirms and enhances their own sense of lack of worth.

Emphasis, so far, has been placed on Negro youngsters' failure to acquire a specific set of skills—auditory discrimination, sense of time, etc.—which are prerequisites to learning to read. The problem cuts far deeper than that. An impressive body of research in the psychology of cognition and perception as well as in the neurophysiology of the brain, has made it clear that exercise of the mental function early in life is essential to its later development. The human being is born with less than one-third of the adult brain capacity, and there is tremendous growth of the cortex after birth. The way in which the cortex and, indeed, the whole central nervous system develops is directly affected by the environment. Hence, mental alertness and, in particular, the ability to handle abstractions, depends physiologically on a broad diversity of experience in the environment of early childhood. "We know now," says Professor Jerome

Bruner, Director of the Harvard University Center for Cognitive Studies, "that the early challenge of problems to be mastered, of stresses to be overcome, are the preconditions of attaining some measure of our full potentiality as human beings. The child is father to the man in a manner that may be irreversibly one-directional, for to make up for a bland impoverishment of experience early in life may be too great an obstacle for most organisms." Raising a dog, for example, in a highly impoverished environment, one with little variety and no challenge to problem solving, produces an apparently irreversible stupidity in the adult animal. For human beings, even more than for animals, the mind and the senses it mediates must be stimulated if they are not to atrophy. As Bruner puts it, "supply creates its own demand"; in Jean Piaget's words, "the more a child has seen and heard, the more he wants to see and hear."

The lower-class child, therefore, suffers from an overall poverty of environment—visual, verbal, and tactile—that inhabits or prevents learning not just in the first grade, but later on as well. His home is characterized by a general sparsity of objects: there are few toys, few pictures, few books, few magazines, few of anything except people and noise. Fifty per cent of a group studied by Deutsch said they did not have a pencil or pen at home. The youngster's experiences outside the home are equally narrow; in one group Deutsch has studied, 65 per cent of the youngsters had never gone beyond a twenty-five-block radius of their homes. This poverty of environment, as Deutsch observed, "gives the child few opportunities to manipulate and organize the visual properties of his environment." The lower-class child, that is to say, does not have the various shapes and sizes and colors and textures and experiences to manipulate that the middle-class child has. It is not only a question of one home having blocks and another not; the lower-class child also lacks the variety of sizes and shapes of cooking utensils with which the middle-class child almost invariably plays.

Nor is this all, by any means. Living under crowded conditions by itself is hampering to the motor development that is part of a child's intellectual development—a fact made evident in Oscar Lewis' *The Children of Sanchez,** an anthropological study of "the culture of poverty" (in this instance of a poor Mexican family). As a slum infant begins to throw things and to experiment with crawling and walking during the second year of life, he finds himself getting in the way of adults whose tempers are short because of their own discomfort and crowding. "In such an atmosphere," as Professor J. McV. Hunt of the University of Illinois has written, "the activities in which the child must indulge for his own interests and development must almost inevitably be sharply curbed." And when, in his third and fourth years, the child begins asking "what's that?" he is unlikely to get answers, or as Professor Hunt says, "the answers he gets are all too likely to be so punishing that they inhibit such questioning." Because they are preoccupied with the problems associated with their poverty and their crowded living conditions, the parents are only irritated by what they consider the senseless questions of a prattling infant. With few things to play with and little room to play in, the lower-class home, Hunt writes, offers "little opportunity for the kinds of environmental encounters required to keep a two-year old youngster developing at all, and certainly not at an optimal rate."

The problems Negro youngsters have in learning are no different in kind, therefore (and hardly different in degree) from those of any children coming from any other "culture of poverty." Thus, the analysis Deutsch, Hunt, and others have made of the reasons for Negro failure in school are virtually identical with the diagnoses Israeli educators have made of the reasons for the academic failures of the so-called "Oriental Jews"—the children of immigrants from Arabic countries in North Africa (Morocco, Algeria, Egypt) and the Middle East (Iraq, Yemen, Kurdestan). A sizable

* New York: Random House, Inc., 1961.

gap is evident when these youngsters start school: they score, on average, 16 points lower on IQ tests than children coming from a Western European background. And the gap widens as they go through school; by age thirteen, the IQ differential is 22 points. The youngsters do very poorly in school; until remedial measures were taken, very few went on to high school, which is not compulsory, and hardly any to the university. Yet there could be no question about inherent inferiority; for a thousand years, the flowering of Jewish culture and learning was in Arabic countries. Thus, the Talmud was written by Iraqui Jews, and Maimonides spent most of his life in North Africa. Studies by Israeli educators have pointed to the same reasons for these youngsters' poor academic performance as for American Negroes' poor performance: an impoverished environment—a lack of stimulation, particularly of a verbal sort, in the early years—which must be compensated for if it is to be overcome.

The diagnosis clearly indicates the necessary treatment. It is not enough to provide "enrichment" or extra help after the child has entered school—particularly when the extra help does not begin until the third grade, as in New York City's Higher Horizons program. (For some strange reason, the New York City public schools do not provide remedial reading instruction until the third grade. Such a rule is nonsensical; if a child has difficulty learning to read in first grade and again in second grade, the double failure alone may be enough to destroy his capacity to learn.) One of the most unfortunate effects of Dr. Conant's *Slums and Suburbs* has been that it has made the "dropout problem" the center of discussion, and has directed enormous amounts of energy and money into programs designed to keep adolescents in school or to lure them back once they have dropped out. Here again, the effort is being directed at those least likely to benefit, that is, where the chances of success are the smallest. This is not to say that help should not be given to the adolescents; no society can simply abandon a whole group of citizens as beyond redemption. On the contrary, a great deal of experimentation is needed to discover ways of reaching the dropouts and, equally important, of reaching those who remain in school but do not learn. But we will not begin to solve the dropout problem until we recognize that it does not begin in high school, nor even in junior high school. For that matter, neither does it begin in kindergarten or first grade, although this is the point at which the schools, as they now are constituted, must begin to deal with it. It should be clear from the foregoing discussion that the dropout problem begins in the cradle—or, more accurately, at the point at which the child leaves the cradle and begins to crawl around his home, exploring his environment and developing the basis for his future intellectual development.

▼

4

Nothing less than a radical reorganization of American elementary education is necessary, therefore, if the schools are to begin to discharge their obligation to teach Negro youngsters. To reverse the effects of a starved environment—to provide the sensory and verbal and visual stimuli that are necessary for future learning and to teach the specific skills that are prerequisites to learning how to read—the schools must begin admitting children at age three or four, instead of at five or six. The nursery school holds the key to the future—but a very different kind of nursery school from the one with which most Americans are familiar.

There are several reasons for beginning this early. The most important is the need to reverse or counteract the atrophying effects of a starved environment before they have had a chance to take hold. It is between the ages of three and six, in short, that the battle is won or lost. "The two and a half and three year olds are almost universally very curious and friendly," says Dr. Ronald Koegler, a neuro-psychiatrist at UCLA who is experimenting with a Montessori nursery program for "culturally deprived" children, "but by the age of six, the children are already different. The culturally deprived have already been deadened by their environment and are already so far behind the middle-class child that all the best elementary education will not be sufficient for them to catch up." Dr. Koegler may be exaggerating somewhat, but the point he is making is basic; if the schools wait until kindergarten or first grade, they will need to employ many, many more resources to do what they can do with comparative ease at age three or four—if, in fact, they can succeed at all.

By all odds the most important experiment in nursery education for Negro children is a research and demonstration project directed by Dr. Deutsch in ten New York public schools and five day-care centers. Deutsch's ultimate objective is to develop a standardized curriculum and a set of teaching techniques that can be used in similar programs anywhere in the country; some thirty cities are setting up, or talking about setting up, nursery programs more or less modeled on the Deutsch experiment. The curriculum is designed to teach the youngsters the verbal and perceptual skills they need in order to learn to read, and also to bolster their sense of self. There is a great deal of emphasis on teaching labeling—getting across the notion, first, that every object has at least one name, and second, the more sophisticated concept that objects may have a number of different labels, each referring to different attributes. There is a great deal of emphasis, also, on relating verbal and visual signals. For example, a teacher may use puppets or other replicas of people, animals, and objects to illustrate the story she is reading. In addition, a great deal of use is made of toys:

stuffed animals, dolls, color cones (to teach color, shape, size), peg boards, etc. Auditory discrimination is taught through use of a tape recorder, in which background noise is used to mask a relevant sound; the level of the background noise is gradually stepped up, to enhance the child's discrimination. To help develop a sense of self, the rooms always contain mirrors—for many children have never seen themselves in one. One of Deutsch's most successful techniques has been to take a photograph of each child and give a copy to the child and to the parent; 85 per cent of the youngsters had never seen a picture of themselves; the pictures were used, also, to construct a book about the class.

A great deal of attention is paid to the physical arrangements of the classroom, as well as to the curriculum. The emphasis is on order, beauty, and clarity of arrangement—on balancing the use of color, physical objects, and space. This is important, Deutsch feels, because there is so little beauty and so little structure in the childrens' own lives. They need a sense of order and of structure, and they respond amazingly to beauty. (Children will typically comment, "I wish I could live in this classroom," and older brothers or sisters in the same school will express envy at the younger child being in such an attractive room.) Each room is divided into a number of self-contained sections: a reading section with books, as well as tape recorders children can use on their own to play back a favorite story; a music section, with phonograph, records; etc.; a physical activity section with blocks and other toys involving motor skills and coordination. Each section is distinct—clarity is necessary, in Deutsch's view—but the sections are not rigid; they can be rearranged whenever desired. Each child has his own cubby to provide a sense of privacy and a sense of personal possession, both of which are difficult in the slum home. (The rooms are also equipped with one-way observation windows, so that the children can be watched without knowing they are being watched.)

It is not enough just to work with the children; Deutsch tries to work with the parents too—to win their trust, which is essential if the program is to succeed, and to give them some instruction in how to help their children. Once the former is done, the latter is relatively easy: once they have been persuaded that this is a genuine attempt to help their children, not a venture in brainwashing, the parents (or rather, the mothers—55 per cent of the youngsters come from broken homes) are eager to get instruction. Thus, Deutsch and his staff suggest that they encourage their children to talk at the dinner table, especially about school (a completely novel concept to a great many parents), that they give the children toys to play with, praise success—in short, to let the child know that the parent wants him to succeed in school and is interested in what he does. This has enormous impact on the children's verbal ability, for they begin talking about school when they get home, instead of remaining mute; and it has profound effect on increasing motivation.

The youngsters in Deutsch's experimental classes show significant improvements in IQ test scores. The more profound effects may be less measurable, but they are striking to anyone who spends even a few weeks in one of the classrooms observing the children; they change under the observer's eye. Kindergarten teachers who receive youngsters exposed to even as little as six months of Deutsch's experimental program are almost speechless with enthusiasm; in all their years of teaching, they say, they have never had slum youngsters enter as intellectually equipped, as alert, as interested, or as well-behaved.

The proposal to extend public education down to the nursery level is not nearly as radical as it may sound. Israel, with a standard of living only about one-third that of the United States, has already adopted such a policy, and is in process of establishing nurseries for the children of the "Oriental" Jews. And the first demonstration of the value of early childhood education in reversing the effects of poverty occurred nearly sixty years ago, when the Casa dei Bambini was established in a Rome tenement by Dr. Maria Montessori, one of the towering figures in the history of education, and one who is just beginning to be appreciated. Something of a Montessori revival has occurred in the United States in recent years, and several experiments using Montessori methods are in process: one, conducted by Dr. Koegler at UCLA; another, at the New York Foundling Hospital, conducted by Mrs. Nancy McCormick Rambusch, who in good measure sparked the Montessori revival when she founded the Whitby School in Greenwich, Connecticut, a few years ago; another is to be started in September, 1964, in the New Rochelle, New York, public schools.

The Montessori approach may be particularly relevant to our own time, and for all children, for a number of reasons. It emphasizes what psychologists call *intrinsic* motivation, *i.e.*, harnessing the child's innate curiosity and delight in discovery. Each child is free to examine and work with whatever interests him, for as long as it interests him, from the materials that are available. What is available is determined by the Montessori concept of "prepared environment," which places great stress on training the sensory processes: cognition is enhanced by providing appropriate stimuli to *all* the senses: touch, smell, taste, as well as sight and hearing.*

The chief advantage of the Montessori approach, in the opinion of J. McV. Hunt, is that "it gives the individual child an opportunity to find the circumstances which match his own particular stage of development." By solving "the problem of the match," as Hunt calls it, the Montessori ap-

---

* It is now well established that children learn mathematical concepts much more clearly if they are taught arithmetic through their hands as well as through their eyes, *e.g.*, by handling the so-called "Cuisinière rods" or "Stern rods,"—multi-colored wooden blocks of various lengths—which stem from early Montessori equipment.

proach has the corollary advantage of making learning fun, whereas the conventional American approach to kindergarten and elementary school manages to establish remarkably early the notion that learning is unpleasant. ("Let's stop playing with the blocks now, children; it's time to learn our alphabet.") Dr. Montessori's own experience suggests another important advantage: low cost. Her first teacher was a teen-age girl, the daughter of the superintendent of the tenement in which the Casa dei Bambini was opened. (Montessori wanted someone without training, in order to be sure that all her orders were carried out; a trained teacher would "know" that some of Dr. Montessori's instructions would be damaging to the children.) In this one school, this young lady was able to teach between fifty and sixty children ranging in age from three to six; according to the novelist Dorothy Canfield Fisher who spent the winter of 1910-11 there, a substantial proportion of these children learned to read by the time they were five—and learned to read through intrinsic motivation, obviously enjoying themselves in the process. And these, let us not forget, were children from the poorest and most "culturally deprived" homes in Rome.*

Help for Negro students cannot stop with creation of a nursery program, however, though such a program is crucial. The cultural distance between the school and the community, and the disorganization of Negro life, mean that a great many Negro youngsters will need extra help all the way through school, and especially in the early grades. It may be useful, for example, to provide Negro children with texts that provide a better bridge between their own lives and the rich world of Western civilization than, say, the al-

---

* D. C. Fisher, *A Montessori Mother,* New York: Holt, 1912. *See also,* J. McV. Hunt, "The Psychological Basis for Using Preschool Enrichment as an Antidote for Cultural Deprivation," to be published in the *Merrill Palmer Quarterly,* July, 1964, and Nancy McC. Rambusch, *Learning How to Learn,* Baltimore: Helicon Press, 1962.

most universal "Dick, Jane, and Sally" series of reading primers. Unfortunately, the first experiment in creating an "integrated" series of reading primers—*Play With Jimmy, Fun With David,* and *Laugh With Larry,* written by staff members of the Detroit Public Schools, moves in precisely the wrong direction. The books show a well-scrubbed Negro family in the same sort of antiseptic suburban environment that Dick, Jane, and Sally play in, and the level of prose almost makes the "Dick, Jane, and Sally" readers sound like poetry. (The Detroit readers use a much smaller vocabulary; the Detroit experts made tape recordings of Negro children's speech, and discovered that their vocabulary contains only about half as many words as white children's.) There is some reason to assume, however, that what these youngsters need is not the bland pap of the reading primers but some stimulus to the imagination—some evidence that reading is a means of escaping the confines of the slum for something more exciting than a backyard barbecue or a trip to the supermarket.

The United States could learn a good deal about how to help Negro youngsters by studying the Israeli educational system, in which an all-out attempt is being made to use the schools as the means of acculturating its new immigrants in a single generation. Thus, the government has formally adopted a policy of preferential treatment, called "state protection." "Compensatory education begins at the pre-natal level, when amateur social workers visit the pregnant mother and the father, and explain the need to provide verbal and perceptual stimulus; among other things, they teach the parents how to play with the children, and leave a set of toys which the government lends the family for a period of a year or so. The government is rapidly establishing free nursery schools so that the Oriental youngsters can begin school at age three; the curriculum closely resembles the one Martin Deutsch is developing in New York.

Help does not stop at that point, however. The Israeli educators have tried to isolate the critical points in intellectual development. The first is during the nursery school years; the second is in the first and second grade, when the children learn to read. The Israelis are convinced that anyone, even the mentally retarded, can be taught to read; the problem, as Dr. Moshe Smilansky, Pedagogical Adviser to the Minister of Education, says, is simply one of adapting the method of instruction to the state of development in which the child comes to school. Three years of intensive work have convinced Smilansky that 80 to 85 per cent of the Oriental youngsters can be brought up to the expected reading level. The third critical point at which these youngsters need help is the junior-high period (ages twelve to fourteen); they receive up to eleven hours of additional instruction a week, in order to help them adjust to the more complex curriculum they begin to receive, and to help them prepare for high school. In addition to the extra instruction given to all the Oriental youngsters, the government has adopted a separate program for the most academically talented, *i.e.*, the top 25 per cent. The object, quite explicitly, is to provide all the help needed to produce an intellectual elite among these youngsters—to create a group that will go through high school and the university without difficulty, and then move into positions of responsibility in government, in business management, and in the army, thereby demonstrating to the rest of the Oriental community as well as to the Western Jewish community that Orientals *do* have the capacity to move to the top of Israeli society.

One reason for the Israelis' great success is that they have great administrative flexibility; the director of research operates out of the office of the Minister of Education. Thus research results can be translated immediately into administrative policy. The main reason for success, however, is the commitment to the program of "state protection" at all levels of government. The officials in charge of the program (though needless to say, not all the teachers in the field) really believe that there is no inherent difference in intelligence between Oriental and Western youngsters—and that in any case, IQ scores are meaningless as a guide to a child's potential. This conviction is crucial if any program is to succeed in the United States. The traditional American approach has been to see the child as a more or less fixed, static entity that has been determined by genetic environment. Hence the emphasis on IQ: you have to measure what the child is before you can decide what to teach him, and how. The Israeli educators—and people like Deutsch, Bruner, Moore, and Hunt in the United States, and Maria Montessori before them—see the child instead as an "open system." They are interested less in what the child *is* than in what he *can become*, and their aim is to provide whatever materials and techniques are needed to develop the child's intellectual abilities to the fullest. This is a far cry from the so-called "life adjustment" approach so popular in the United States a while ago; indeed, it is its very opposite, since life adjustment assumed irreversibility of a child's nature. The Israelis reject the idea that there is a point at which it is too late to help a child, though they agree that help is far more effective if begun in the nursery years. And they assume that intellectual development is a major source of mental health; children who receive an infusion of competence from the very beginning—who learn "I can" at the start of school—will tend to be stable, well-adjusted individuals.

▼

5

It is impossible to talk about problems of Negro education without some discussion of desegregation and integration. Few judicial decisions in the history of the United States have had the impact of the unanimous verdict rendered by the Supreme Court on May 17, 1954, in *Brown et al v. Board of Education of Topeka et al:*

> . . . In the field of public education the doctrine of "separate but equal" has no place. Separate educational facilities are inherently unequal.

And few decisions have been more violently attacked and maligned—or more completely misunderstood and misrepresented.

The attack on the Court's decision has concentrated on two main points: the Court's reversal of the "separate but equal" doctrine enunciated in *Plessy v. Ferguson,* and its alleged reliance on psychological and sociological evidence in arriving at its finding. Those who attack the Court for reversing a long-standing doctrine ignore the fact, pointed out in the 1954 decision, that *Plessy v. Ferguson* itself represented a reversal of existing law! "In the first cases in this Court construing the Fourteenth Amendment, decided shortly after its adoption," Chief Justice Warren wrote, "the Court interpreted it as proscribing all state-imposed discriminations against the Negro race."

In 1879, for example, the Supreme Court declared that the Fourteenth Amendment "ordains that no State shall deprive any person of life, liberty, or property without due process of law, or deny to any person within its jurisdiction the equal protection of the laws." "What is this," the Court asked, "but declaring that the law in the States shall be the same for the black as for the white; that all persons, whether colored or white, shall stand equal before the laws of the States, and in regard to the colored race, for whose protection the Amendment was primarily designed, that no discrimination shall be made against them by law because of their color?"

Thus, the "separate but equal" doctrine did not make its

appearance until 1896, almost thirty years after the Fourteenth Amendment had been ratified. In enunciating this new doctrine, moreover, the Court majority tried to show that its decision was really consistent with the established interpretation by distinguishing between so-called "political" and "social" rights. The earlier decisions forbidding any discrimination, the Court argued, had applied to political rights, whereas transportation—the subject of *Plessy v. Ferguson*—involved only a social right, which did not matter as much.

One can interpret the 1954 Brown Case decision in one of two ways, therefore. In one sense, it overturned *Plessy v. Ferguson* and returned to the original interpretation of the Fourteenth Amendment—an interpretation made by judges who knew intimately the intentions of Congress in drafting the amendment. But in another sense, the decision was also consistent with *Plessy v. Ferguson;* indeed, the Court was at great pains to demonstrate that whatever it may have been in 1896, education in the United States of the 1950s was very much a political right. At the time the Fourteenth Amendment was ratified or the decision in *Plessy v. Ferguson* handed down, Justice Warren pointed out, "the movement toward free common schools, supported by general taxation, had not yet taken hold. Education of white children was largely in the hands of private groups. Education of Negroes was almost non-existent, and practically all of the race were illiterate. In fact, any education of Negroes was forbidden by law in some states." In reaching its decision in the case at hand, Justice Warren argued, the Court had to consider public education in the light of its present role in American life. "Only in this way can it be determined if segregation in public schools deprives these plaintiffs of the equal protection of the laws." After looking at the present role of public education, the Court concluded that education had become very much a political right. "Today, education is perhaps the most important function of state and local governments," Justice Warren wrote. "Compulsory school attendance laws and the great expenditures for education both demonstrate our recognition of the importance of education to our democratic society. It is required in the performance of our most basic public responsibilities, even service in the armed forces. It is the very foundation of good citizenship . . . In these days," he added, "it is doubtful that any child may reasonably be expected to succeed in life if he is denied the opportunity of an education. Such an opportunity, where the state has undertaken to provide it, is a right which must be made available to all on equal terms."

The only question remaining, therefore, was whether "segregation of children in public schools solely on the basis of race, even though the physical facilities and other "tangible" factors may be equal, deprive[s] the children of the minority group of equal educational opportunities." The answer was simple and direct: "We believe that it does." The guts of the decision, in short, was the Court's finding that segregation is inherently unequal. The Justices undoubtedly were influenced by oral and written testimony of social scientists on the harmful effects of segregation, but this testimony was extraneous; the decision rested on a legal finding that segregation is inherently unequal, not on a sociological or psychological finding that segregation is harmful. As the Court said in its decision, the same day, outlawing segregation in the District of Columbia schools, "Liberty under law extends to the full range of conduct which the individual is free to pursue, and it cannot be restricted except for a proper government objective. Segregation in public education is not reasonably related to any proper governmental objective, and thus it imposes on Negro children . . . a burden that constitutes an arbitrary deprivation of their liberty. . . ." Indeed, whether segregation is harmful or not is quite beside the point: the Constitution guarantees every citizen equal treatment under the law, whether inequality is good for him or bad. In this sense, the Court's citation, in footnote eleven, of psychological and sociological evidence purporting to show that segregation is harmful was an unfortunate irrelevance that diverted attention away from the main thrust of its opinion—an opinion that had been clearly anticipated several years before in *Sweatt v. Painter* and *McLaurin v. Oklahoma State Regents*.

Despite the Court's order "that the defendants make a prompt and reasonable start toward full compliance" and proceed "with all deliberate speed" to admit children to school on a non-discriminatory basis, two of the four public school systems which were defendants in the Brown case—Clarendon County, South Carolina, and Prince Edward County, Virginia—still had not admitted a single Negro to public schools as of February, 1964. (To avoid compliance, Prince Edward County chose to close the public schools.) In Little Rock, Arkansas, where Federal troops had to be rushed in 1957 to control mobs trying to stop nine Negro youngsters from entering a white high school, a mere 123 Negro children, out of a total Negro registration of 6,900, were attending desegregated schools in the 1963-64 school year. In Atlanta, with its reputation for compliance with law, a grand total of 145 Negroes were attending desegregated schools. In the South as a whole, only 30,798 Negro students, or 1.06 per cent of all Negro students, were attending schools with whites—and nearly half of this total was in Texas. In ten other states of the Deep South, fewer than six-tenths of one per cent of all Negro students were in school with whites—ten years after the Supreme Court ruling.

Curiously enough, however, tensions over school desegregation are running higher in the Northern cities than in the South. Negro activists contend that the Supreme Court decision outlawed segregation as such, whether due to intent (as in the South, where state laws require separate school systems) or to accident (as in the North, where pupils are assigned to schools according to where they live, rather than with regard to their color). At the beginning of 1964, NAACP chapters along with other Negro groups had mounted a challenge to de facto school segregation in some eighty-one school systems in eighteen states, and suits to force desegregation were pending in another eighteen cities.

Underlying the tension in the North are two basic factors: Negro dissatisfaction over the quality of education provided in urban slum schools; and Negro frustration over "resegregation"—the rapid increase in the number of schools with predominantly Negro student bodies. In New York City, for example, the number of elementary schools containing 90 per cent or more Negro and/or Puerto Rican students more than doubled between the 1957-58 and 1963-64 school years, and the number of junior high schools in that category increased two and a half times. These increases took place, moreover, despite the fact that the New York City Board of Education had made desegregation a major policy goal in 1955 and had taken a number of positive measures to reduce the amount of de facto segregation.*

The increase in the number of all-Negro schools reflects the basic population trends of the large cities, where Negro population is expanding rapidly and white population is decreasing. (See chapters I and II). The trends are more evident in the schools, in good measure because the Negro population of the cities is younger than the white population. Since proportionately more Negroes than whites are in the child-bearing ages, and since the Negro birth rate exceeds the white, Negroes generally account for a larger proportion of public school population than of the population at large. Negro preponderance in public school enrollment is en-

* These measures have had some effect, despite the increase in the number of all-Negro and Puerto Rican schools. For example, the number of elementary schools with a less than 10 per cent Negro and/or Puerto Rican enrollment declined from 290 to 186; that is to say, the number of integrated schools increased at the same time that the number of all-Negro or Puerto Rican Schools also increased.

hanced by several other factors. In some cities, Philadelphia and Chicago for example, a very large proportion of the whites remaining in the city are Catholics who send their children to parochial schools. Religion aside, many whites are reluctant to send their children to public schools in which the proportion of Negroes is very high, either because of outright prejudice or because they sincerely believe that standards will be lowered or that their children's physical safety will be threatened. The result is that attempts to integrate public schools frequently backfire. In 1949, for example, the New Rochelle school board acted to try to correct racial imbalance in the Lincoln Elementary School, which a decade later became the subject of angry litigation and a major court decision. Since over a hundred white children in the Lincoln school district were attending other New Rochelle public schools as a result of a transfer policy adopted a number of years earlier, and since the Lincoln School at that time had only two hundred Negro students, the Board thought that it could create another integrated school by prohibiting transfer out of the district. Despite the new order, however, the school did not become any more integrated; within a year or two, virtually every one of the white youngsters had either been transferred to parochial school, or had moved out of the Lincoln school district. By 1960, when litigation began, the school population was 94 per cent Negro.

All told, the situation Northern cities face in dealing with de facto segregation brings to mind the observation of an ancient scholar that the presence of a question is no proof of the existence of an answer. To say, as did a recent report of the National Association of Intergroup Relations officials, that what the public schools need "is not techniques, but purpose," is grossly and perhaps dangerously to oversimplify an incredibly complex problem. Purpose is needed, to be sure; without it, Negro anger smolders to the point where communication between black and white becomes extremely difficult. Indeed, one can be certain of only one thing: that failure to do *anything* about de facto segregation will poison the atmosphere of race relations in any community. For Negroes have made school desegregation the touchstone of white sincerity and integrity; what a community does about school integration is generally regarded as the ultimate measure of white sincerity and of white willingness to share power. The reasons are complex: partly historical accident; partly a reaction to Southern defiance of the Supreme Court decision; and partly a reaction to hypocrisy and obfuscation on the part of Northern educators and school boards. With a few notable exceptions, Northern educators and civic leaders have been unwilling to face up to the issues directly or honestly. In some communities, Oakland, California, among others, they have evaded the question through pious insistence on being color blind ("we don't know how many Negro students or teachers we have, because we don't take race into consideration; we deal with students and teachers as individuals") or on being opposed to "social engineering" ("we don't believe in manipulating children in order to achieve some predetermined racial balance"). Other communities—most notably Chicago—have justified a clear pattern of segregation by elevating a technique of school administration, namely, the neighborhood school, into a holy principle.* And a good many—Chicago again is a notable example—have evaded the question by

* "Practically speaking," Professor John E. Coons of Northwestern University School of Law wrote in a report (*op. cit.*) to the United States Civil Rights Commission, "neighborhood schools do not exist in many of the crowded areas of Chicago, unless the requirements of that concept are satisfied by the mere existence of a building called a 'school' which is physically located in something called a 'neighborhood.' If the school is not *adequate* to serve the needs of a neighborhood, it is playing with words to label it a neighborhood school. The most serious charge against the administration seems to be that in many areas it has not been operating a neighborhood school system, but has acted as if it were."

declaiming the evils of "bussing" children all over the city, as if Negroes did not know that white parents who object to having their children transported a mile or two to an integrated school proceed to enroll them in a private day school located five or ten miles away, on the opposite side of town!

The firmest purpose in the world, however, offers painfully little guidance as to what to do to bring about desegregation of the public schools in cities with a large and rapidly growing Negro population. In Washington, D.C., for example, the schools were integrated immediately after the 1954 decision, in the sense that the two separate divisions (one white, one Negro) were abolished. But today, roughly 85 per cent of the children in Washington public schools are Negro. In such a situation, talk of integration is obviously meaningless. Nor is it much more meaningful in New York, except in a few schools on the border between Negro and white neighborhoods. The increase in the number of segregated schools in New York City stems directly from the fact that the number of Negro students increased 53 per cent in just six years (from 1957-58 to 1963-64) while the number of white students declined by 8.3 per cent. (In the same period, the number of Puerto Rican students jumped by 37.6 per cent.) The result was that more than half the first graders in the city as a whole in 1963-64 were Negro or Puerto Rican, indicating that whites would rapidly become a minority of the school system's population. In the Borough of Manhattan, 77 per cent of the elementary school students and 72 per cent of the junior high students were Negro. To talk of integration is naïve, at best; there simply are not enough whites with whom Negroes and Puerto Ricans can integrate.

Yet the fervor of the demands for desegregation is increasing. In June of 1963, June Shagaloff, Special Assistant for Education of the NAACP, admitted that desegregation of the schools of central Harlem and of the major Negro areas of cities like Detroit and Chicago was "obviously" impossible.

("For the schools in central Harlem, of New York City, or of Detroit, or Chicago—any large city—obviously schools cannot be re-zoned. There cannot be a Princeton Plan adopted.* Here we say open enrollment, to permit children to transfer from Negro schools, segregated schools, to white schools; the assignment of children from over-crowded Negro schools to under-utilized white schools; *but for the vast numbers of children who are going to remain,* we also urge that the schools be brought up to standard." [Emphasis added]) Only seven months later, the NAACP—despite Roy Wilkins' evident reservations—joined with other Negro groups in a one-day boycott of the schools to demand rezoning, Princeton Plans, and the like.

The attack on de facto segregation rests partly on the argument that the 1954 Supreme Court decision outlawed school segregation, whether de facto or de jure. But the law regarding de facto segregation is unclear and in a state of flux—in part because no de facto segregation case has yet been considered by the Supreme Court, in part because of the wide variety of circumstances that produce segregation. (The New Rochelle case was appealed to the Supreme Court, but the Court found no grounds for review.) In writing its 1954 decision, the Court quite obviously was thinking only about segregation that is required by law, since the cases before the court involved school districts which maintained separate schools for Negroes and whites, and which forbade Negroes from attending the white schools. "To separate [Negro students] from others of similar age and qualifications *solely* because of their race," the Court argued, "generates a feeling of inferiority . . . Segregation *with the*

---

* The Princeton Plan is a technique whereby a Negro school and a white school are "paired" and, in effect, merged. In the case of a pair of elementary schools, for example, one is used to house the first three grades for the students from both schools, the other to house the fourth through sixth grades. The technique was first adopted in Princeton, New Jersey—hence the name.

sanction of law, therefore, has a tendency to retard the educational and mental development of Negro children. . . ." [Emphasis added] To what degree the decision applies to the de facto segregation of the Northern city, therefore, is moot; judging by the decisions rendered by lower courts, it seems to depend on the particular circumstances. Where segregation is the result of gerrymandered school district lines, for example, segregation is clearly illegal, and the school board has an obligation to correct the racial imbalance, regardless of how long ago the gerrymandering occurred. Thus, in the New Rochelle case, Judge Kaufman ruled that the school board had gerrymandered the Lincoln school district in 1930 so as to withdraw its white students; that between 1930 and 1934, the board had altered the boundaries so as to contain a rapidly growing Negro population in the Lincoln district; and that until 1949, the board had made sure that Lincoln would remain Negro by allowing white students to transfer out of the zone while discouraging transfers by Negroes. After the board's policy banning transfers, adopted in 1949, failed to change the racial balance, it adhered to the status quo. Hence the judge ruled that the board had a duty to remedy the situation.

Where segregation is not due to gerrymandering but is the result simply of racial change in a neighborhood, the courts themselves disagree over whether school boards have any obligation to end the resulting de facto segregation. (The confusion is not likely to be cleared up in the near future; some prominent civil rights lawyers doubt that the Supreme Court will take any of the pending cases on appeal.) For example, the United States Court of Appeals in Chicago, in a November 1, 1963, decision involving the Gary, Indiana, schools, held that "There is no affirmative United States constitutional duty to change innocently arrived at school attendance districts by the mere fact that shifts in population either increase or decrease the percentage of either Negroes or white pupils." And the New York State Supreme

Court, on January 10, 1964, ruled that a school district may not take racial factors into account in attempting to redress racial imbalance. The Federal Constitution, the judge argued, "forbids segregation by law in the public schools. It does not, however, prohibit racial imbalance; nor does it mandate racial change." Indeed, the Court held that a plan drawn up by the New York State Commissioner of Education to end racial imbalance in the Malverne, Long Island, school district violated a provision in the state constitution forbidding schools from taking race, creed, or national origin into account in admitting children to public school. Since the Commissioner's plan reassigned children to different schools according to their race in order to reduce the number of Negro children in an 85 per cent Negro elementary school, the Court held that he "in effect . . . ordered a gerrymandering of the attendance area zones." The fact that children had been assigned to schools outside their normal attendance zones, in the Court's opinion, denied these children admission to the school in their normal zones because of their race.

Only fourteen days later, however, the United States District Court in Brooklyn ordered the Manhasset, Long Island, school board to end de facto segregation in its Valley Elementary School. The school had been all-white when built, and school district lines had never been altered; racial change in the neighborhood served by the school, however, had made the school virtually all-Negro. In granting an injunction sought by the NAACP to restrain the school district from continuing its school zoning policies, Chief Judge Joseph C. Zavatt held that "the separation of the Negro elementary school children is . . . segregation by law—the law of the school board. In the light of the existing facts, the continuance of the defendant board's impenetrable attendance line amounts to nothing less than state-imposed segregation. In a publicly supported, mandatory state educational system," he held, "the plaintiffs have the civil right not to be segregated, not to be compelled to attend a school in which all of the Negro children are educated separate and apart from over 99 per cent of their white contemporaries." Since the school board fixes the attendance lines, Judge Zavatt argued, the board "must determine when, if ever, these policies should be modified." In this instance, he added, by failing to change attendance lines which permitted the creation of an all-Negro school, "the defendant board has transgressed the prohibitions of the equal-protection clause of the Fourteenth Amendment."

But the case against de facto segregation rests on more than just legal grounds. A great many argue that Negro children cannot receive an equal education in an all-Negro environment—that a segregated school, is inherently unequal *whatever* the reasons underlying the segregation. A number of white educators and civic leaders have expressed agreement. For example, Dr. James E. Allen, Jr., New York State Commissioner of Education, announced in June of 1963 his department's conviction "that the racial imbalance existing in a school in which the enrollment is wholly or predominantly Negro interferes with the achievement of equality of educational opportunity and must therefore be eliminated from the schools of New York State." (This statement underlay the order redressing racial imbalance in Malverne which was overruled by the State Supreme Court.) Dr. Allen's statement of guiding principles went on to argue that "modern psychological and sociological knowledge seems to indicate that in schools in which the enrollment is largely from a minority group of homogeneous ethnic origin, the personality of these minority group children may be damaged. There is a decrease in motivation and thus an impairment of ability to learn. Public education in such a situation is socially unrealistic. . . ." And the Commissioner's Advisory Committee on Human Relations and Community Tensions stated a number of principles which it felt should guide local school boards, among them the conviction that "The presence in a single school of children from varied racial, cultural, socio-economic and religious backgrounds is an important element in the preparation of young people for active participation in the social and political affairs of our democracy." The Committee therefore proposed that "In establishing school attendance areas one of the objectives should be to create in each school a student body that will represent as nearly as possible a cross-section of the population of the entire school district. . . ."

There is very little evidence, however, that putting lower-class Negro and middle-class white children together in the same classroom is anything more than an act of democratic faith. To take a child who comes from a poverty-stricken and intellectually-deprived background, who has received an inferior and inadequate education, and who therefore is performing several years below grade level, and to thrust him into a class with whites performing above grade level without first removing or compensating for his disabilities, may be much more damaging to his ego than keeping him in a segregated classroom. In New Rochelle, for example, where the first and most important de facto school segregation case was tried and won, the initial results seem to have been unfortunate. Negro children from the Lincoln School, in a poverty-stricken neighborhood, were transferred to the Roosevelt School, in an upper-class white neighborhood where the average annual income was $25,000 and where in most homes both parents were college graduates. The disparity in ability was more than either the white or the Negro students could cope with. "Some of the transferees," Professor John Kaplan of Northwestern University Law School wrote in a staff report for the United States Commission on Civil Rights, "instead of being stimulated by the educational aspirations of the Roosevelt children, seemed to give up trying at all." (In a number of classes, no white child's performance was as poor as the best of the Negro children.)

Nor does contact with Negroes necessarily produce empathy on the part of white school children. On the contrary, the contact may have the reverse effect when the difference in color is accompanied by a wide difference in class, and therefore in academic performance and behavior. "The most unfortunate aspect" of the transfer of Negro students to the upper-class white school in New Rochelle, in Professor Kaplan's opinion,

> has been its creation of racial stereotypes in the minds of the Roosevelt children . . . White children from a liberal background who had had no contact with Negroes before but whose home and school life taught ideals of brotherhood and the equality of man were thrown together with children of a far lower socio-economic and cultural level who happened to be Negroes. One teacher said, "Some of the Roosevelt children actually understand that this is a cultural and not a racial difference, but all they see is that the Negro children are not as bright, clean, honest, or well behaved as they."

As a result of this and similar experiences, a good many Negro community leaders are having second thoughts about the wisdom of current techniques of ending de facto segregation. "It would be unhealthy to take our children out of our own community to attend school in another," the Reverend Dr. William M. James of Harlem's Metropolitan Community Methodist Church has said. "We, in the so-called under-privileged communities, cannot look to those outside of our communities for total cure of our ills. This will not work." A good many ministers are dubious about the "open enrollment" plans which, until fairly recently, were regarded as the best solution. "Open enrollment" has a number of defects, not the least of them being the fact that painfully few Negroes take advantage of the plan. Those who do tend to be the most upwardly-mobile families in the area; the result, all too often, is that removing the brighter, more highly motivated youngsters from an all-Negro school leaves that school still all-Negro, but in worse condition than it was in before. At the same time, the youngsters who have transferred to a "white" school discover that the new school lacks a good many of the special services—reading teachers, speech teachers, guidance counselors, etc.—that they were used to or depended upon in the all-Negro school. There are real questions, too, as to whether the loss of contact with children from their own neighborhood outweighs the advantages of integration.

Large-scale transfers of Negro children to schools in white neighborhoods also raise questions whose answers are by no means obvious. Should the Negro children be put in heterogeneous classes in the new school, in which case they tend to perform at the bottom of the class if the school draws from middle-class and upper-class families? Or should they be put in homogeneous classes, *i.e.*, classes grouped according to academic ability—in which case they are again segregated in the new school? The latter seems pointless: nothing is gained by transporting youngsters several miles in order to keep them segregated. Yet dumping youngsters who are reading several years below grade level into a class with children reading several years above grade level, as the New Rochelle experience suggests, is not likely to enhance the former group's ego nor lead to meaningful encounters between the two races.

Large-scale transfers of white students to schools in Negro neighborhoods, which a number of militant integrationists now advocate, is equally unrealistic, as Dr. Kenneth B. Clark of City College, has pointed out. Such suggestions in Dr. Clark's view, "are unrealistic, irrelevant, emotional and diversionary." If the city were to try to send middle-class children into Harlem schools, he argues, it would be done "only under conditions of intense and prolonged protest" that would "clearly lead to a disruption of the educational process, and [would] not affect positively the education of any child." Some rabid integrationists are clearly prepared to pay the price; as already mentioned, Rev. Milton Galamison, chairman of the committee coordinating the integration demands of New York Negro groups, has stated bluntly that he would rather see the city school system destroyed than continue on a de facto segregated basis. It is hard to imagine any position more irresponsible to the real needs and interests of Negro children, who need the public schools even more than white middle-class children. Nor can Reverend Galamison's statement be dismissed as mere harmless rhetoric. The fact is that the public school system is in real danger. The great development of the public schools in the first half of this century, as Professor Cremin demonstrated in *The Transformation of the School,* was due to a remarkable coalition of trade unions, businessmen, and ethnic groups, each of which saw public education as the solution to its particular problem. That coalition has been breaking down in recent years, and it has not been replaced by any other; there are today relatively few powerful interest groups committed to the public schools. If Negroes join the attack on public education, the result could be its disintegration and replacement by a system of subsidies for private schools.

Some integration leaders, to be sure, see the demand for integration merely as a device to force "the white power structure" to improve the education offered Negro children. "Having a white child sit next to my Negro child is no guarantee that mine will learn," Isaiah Robinson, chairman of the Harlem Parents Committee has said, "but it is a guarantee that he will be taught." Some activists, moreover, do not even care whether white children sit next to Negro children; they see the demand for integration simply as a lever to pry more money and services out of the school board. (The only way to get the whites to lay out the funds needed to reconstruct the schools of Harlem, in this view, is to frighten them with demands that white children be transported into

Harlem's schools.) All too many Negro leaders, however—and all too many white liberals—have become prisoners of their own rhetoric, denouncing as inadequate any measure that falls short of full desegregation and attacking any proposals for compensatory education as a reversion to the old doctrine of "separate but equal."

However sincere such proponents of integration may be, there is an element of irresponsibility in their rigidity. It cannot be denied that school systems could do more than they are doing to speed desegregation, although many measures proposed might be self-defeating by leading to further reductions in the number of white students.* But neither can it be denied that only a small minority of Negro students would be affected even if the large cities were to take every conceivable measure to desegregate their schools; the majority of Negro youngsters would continue to attend segregated schools.

If this be so, then the thesis that Negro students cannot receive an adequate education in an all-Negro school needs to be carefully examined. It has not been; on the contrary, the thesis has been advanced without any real substantiation. To the extent that there is any evidence—and there is amazingly little—it suggests the reverse. The pioneering research by Kenneth and Mamie Clark, for example, suggested that Negro children attending Northern integrated schools had more self-hatred (or fewer positive images of themselves) than children attending segregated Southern schools.† The lesson of black nationalism (and of The Wood-

---

* Some integrationists respond by saying, in anger, "Let the whites leave; then we'll take over the city." Their anger is understandable—but it raises a serious question as to whether their objective is integration, as they claim, or power for its own sake.

† *See* Kenneth B. Clark and Mamie Phipps Clark, "The Emergence of Racial Identification and Preference in Negro Children," reprinted in E. E. Maccoby, T. M. Newcomb, & E. L. Hartley, *Readings in Social Psychology*, Third Edition, New York: Henry Holt & Co., 1958. The Clarks showed Negro children white dolls and colored dolls, and

lawn Organization, discussed in the next chapter) suggests that Negroes must first learn pride in self and in their heritage before they can learn to relate easily to people of a different color. Indeed, the fervor with which some integrationists insist that equal education is impossible in an all-Negro school sounds suspiciously like self-hatred on their part. Their arguments, moreover, carry a serious danger of becoming self-fulfilling prophecies: if you shout loudly enough and long enough that Negro youngsters cannot learn in an all-Negro school, the children almost certainly will not learn.

Let there be no misunderstanding, however: none of this discussion is intended to derogate in any way the importance of school integration. Integration is vitally important not so much for Negroes as for whites, who must learn to live in a world in which they are indeed the minority. Education, moreover, should do more than develop the powers of the intellect; it should, in addition infuse youngsters with a commitment to the brotherhood of man, with a vision of the beauty and nobility of which man is capable—and a realization of the depths of depravity to which he can sink. We have seen, in our own generation, how that greatest of all educational institutions, the German university, became the instrument of utter depravity because it had no commitment except to the intellect. Its lack of commitment was itself a commitment to amorality. There is no educational system which does not have a value system implicit within it; the value system is expressed in the way in which the system is organized and structured, even more than in the subject matter taught. There is no point in teaching about the brotherhood of man, therefore, unless the school system

---

asked them, among other questions, which doll they preferred to play with. A majority of the children in both the Southern and the Northern schools preferred to play with the white dolls—but a larger proportion of the Northern children expressed the preference, which the Clarks used as an indication of self-hatred.

is organized to treat all men as brothers; a segregated school system is not likely to impart any strong convictions about racial equality.

Thus, integration is a moral imperative—the greatest moral imperative of our time. But integration should not be confused with the mere mixing of Negroes and whites in the same classroom, or in the same school, or in the same neighborhood. To throw white and black youngsters into a classroom in the name of integration, without regard to what one may reasonably expect to happen, is to violate the Commandment which prohibits the worship of false gods; it is to sacrifice the children for the sake of an abstract principle. Given the realities of population change in the large cities—more important, given the harsh and painful truth of what three hundred fifty years of exclusion have done to the personality and mentality of Negro youngsters—the public schools need techniques for meaningful integration every bit as much as they need purpose.

How, then, are we to achieve meaningful integration—integration which leads to genuine contact, to real communication with and understanding by each group of the other? The only honest answer is that genuine integration will not be possible until the schools in Negro neighborhoods—and the schools in white slum areas as well—are brought up to the level of the very best schools in each city; until the schools do their job so well that children's educational performance no longer reflects their income or their social status or their ethnic group or their color. To say this is not to suggest indefinite postponement, but to demand that the public schools stop dithering with projects and demonstrations and turn immediately to their most pressing task; neither the large cities nor the nation as a whole can afford a public school system which fails to educate between 50 and 80 per cent of its Negro students.

To say this, of course, is to contradict the current dogma, which condemns any program of compensatory education, no matter how massive, as a return to "separate but equal," hence as an expression of prejudice. Because of this tendency to label, and the accompanying competition for militancy, a good many Negro leaders who really share this view are afraid to express it, for fear of having the "Uncle Tom" or "handkerchief head" label pinned on them. They may very well be exaggerating the danger of speaking the truth, however. There is very little evidence that the mass of Negroes care very much about sending their children to school with whites, or about having whites sent to school with their children. But there is a great mass of evidence, (from opinion surveys, sociological studies, and the like) suggesting that Negro parents *are* deeply concerned about the inadequate education their children are receiving, and that they desparately want better education.*

One group of Negro leaders, headed by Kenneth Clark and Rev. Eugene Callender, has already had the courage to face up to the realities of the education problem in central Harlem. Their views are expressed in a report issued by Harlem Youth Opportunities Unlimited, Inc. (HARYOU), a group set up with funds from the President's Committee on Juvenile Delinquency and Youth Crime. (Professor Clark serves as Chief Project Consultant; Dr. Callender, who is minister of the Church of the Master in Harlem, Moderator of the Presbytery of New York, and chairman of the board of directors of the Harlem Neighborhoods Association, serves on the HARYOU board.) The HARYOU Report (*Youth in the Ghetto: A Study of Powerlessness*) is quite uneven, but its chapters on education rank as perhaps the best analysis yet published of Harlem's educational problem

---

* *See*, for example, *Youth in the Ghetto: A Study of the Consequences of Powerlessness*, a report published by Harlem Youth Opportunities Unlimited, Inc. (HARYOU). *See also*, Inge Lederer Gibel, "How *Not* to Integrate the Schools," *Harper's*, November, 1963; and various news reports in the *New York Times* summarizing the researches of Joseph Lyford for The Fund for the Republic.

and of the measures needed to solve it. The authors mince no words about their belief in public school integration and their distrust of many of the measures taken so far to achieve it. But they also make it clear that the children of Harlem must not be sacrificed either to the dogmas or the personal ambitions of civil rights leaders.

HARYOU's main proposition is "that this vicious cycle of educational inefficiency and social pathology can be broken only by instituting an educational program of excellence in the schools of deprived communities," and their most important recommendation is a proposal to establish compensatory nursery programs for all Harlem children. In the long run, they argue, excellence requires an end to segregation. But in the short run—"during that period required to obtain more adaptive, democratic, non-segregated schools for all children"—compensatory education is necessary, for 50 per cent of the elementary school and 80 per cent of the junior high school students, need massive remedial work if they are to be brought up to grade level. "A program for the attainment of educational excellence for the children in Harlem's schools," they argue, "cannot be delayed or obscured by ideological controversies such as 'separate but equal.' These are important and difficult issues, but they cannot be given precedence over the fact that the present generation of Negro children have only one life within which they can be prepared to take their places in the mainstream of American society . . .

> These children cannot be sacrificed on the altar of ideological and semantic rigidities. The struggle of the civil rights groups for a better life for these children is made more difficult, if not impossible, if the methods of the struggle become dominated by inflexible emotional postures. Heroics and dramatic words and gestures, over-simplified either-or thinking, and devil hunting might provide a platform for temporary crowd pleasing, ego satisfactions or

> would-be "leaders," but they cannot solve the fundamental problems of obtaining high quality education in our public schools and the related problem of realistic and serious desegregation in these schools. *Meaningful desegregation of the public schools in New York City can occur only if all of the schools in the system are raised to the highest standards, and when the quality of education in these schools is uniformly high—and does not vary according to income or the social status of the neighborhood. The up-grading of quality of education in predominantly Negro and Puerto Rican schools to a level of educational excellence is an unavoidable first step in any realistic program for the desegregation of these schools.* [Emphasis added]

Or as Abraham Lincoln put it in his first Inaugural Address, "The dogmas of the quiet past are inadequate to the stormy present . . . Let us disenthrall ourselves."

X

THE REVOLT AGAINST "WELFARE COLONIALISM"

> So long as we read about revolutions in books, they all look very nice—like those landscapes which, as artistic engravings on white vellum, look so pure and friendly: dung heaps engraved on copper do not smell, and the eye can easily wade through an engraved morass.
>
> —HEINE

> One should never wear one's best trousers to go out and battle for freedom and truth.
>
> —IBSEN

1

Even if the schools were to be transformed into institutions of perfection overnight, it would take another generation before the impact was felt; the "payoff" would not begin until the youngsters now of nursery school age reached their majority. The United States cannot wait that long; we cannot simply write off the present generation of Negroes—the men and women who have dropped out of school or who are past school age, and who need help so desperately. Hence a growing number of liberals of both colors, reflecting the wistful American notion that if only we had enough money to spend, we could solve all problems, have urged the creation of a Federal "crash program" to remove the disabilities that bar Negroes from full participation in American life. Whitney Young of the Urban League, for example, has proposed a "domestic Marshall Plan" on behalf of the Negro, the cost of which might be from a few billion to ten billion dollars a year.

But look what the first few billions have bought! The rate of expenditure for public assistance has been rising rapidly in every large city, without making a dent in any of the problems they are supposed to solve. Indeed, a good many of these expenditures seem to have been a waste of money at best, and at worst a positive disservice to the people they are supposed to help. Relatively few disinterested students would agree with the social worker-turned-novelist Julius Horwitz, that the whole welfare system is an "ugly, diseased social growth [that] must be removed from American life." But few can argue with the studied judgment of Professor S. M. Miller of Syracuse University: "Welfare assistance in its present form tends to encourage dependence, withdrawal, diffused hostility, indifference, ennui."

A growing number of social scientists and government officials, in fact, have acquired a growing sense of disenchantment with the entire welfare-social worker-settlement house approach. These are not reactionaries anxious to cut taxes by forcing relief clients to move somewhere else, but men genuinely concerned with solving the day-to-day problems of the poor. And they are troubled by the evidence that the present welfare system is self-perpetuating—that far from relieving dependency, it *encourages* dependency. Thus, a study of public assistance in New York State, made by the management consulting firm of Greenleigh Associates for the Moreland Commission, reported that existing policies and procedures lead to *increased* dependency. And a national study of the Federal Aid to Dependent Children Program, made by M. Elaine Burgess and Daniel O. Price of the University of North Carolina for the American Public Welfare Association, called for major changes to reduce long-term dependency and prevent the continued development of second-generation dependents.

Nor does the answer lie in expanding the number of social workers, settlement houses, mental health clinics, and the like. In New York City, for example, the *Directory of Social and Health Agencies* contains 721 pages; social work is one of the city's major industries. In the Harlem-Upper Manhattan area alone, according to a study by the Protestant Council of the City of New York, there are some 156 separate agencies serving an estimated 240,000 people—roughly 40 per cent of the total population of the area. Without question, there are gaps here and there in the services offered, and many existing services are grossly inadequate. But it seems clear that the solution to Harlem's problems does not lie in any expansion of social agencies.

There is no dearth of agencies and programs elsewhere in the city, either. Municipal expenditures for youth services, for example, have approximately tripled since the beginning of the postwar period, to some $800 million a year, exclusive of expenditures by private agencies. As a recent survey, made at the city's request by the Institute of Public Administration, reported, "this enormous effort has not abated the major social problems affecting children and youth." On the contrary, the Institute argued, many programs "tend to perpetuate the conditions they are intended to alleviate." For example, the Aid for Dependent Children (ADC) Program "tends to produce female-centered households, with increased rates of illegitimacy and other undesirable results." Other programs, by concentrating on symptoms rather than causes, may simply substitute a new set of symptoms for the old. For example, herculean efforts by the city's Youth Board, the police, the courts, and a host of voluntary agencies, succeeded in taming the fighting gangs that had erupted in the early 1950s. But if ever there was a Phyrric victory, this was it; "bopping" has now been replaced by alcoholism and drug addiction, which are much harder to combat, and far more crippling in their long-run effects. And so it goes.

New York City probably is exceptional in the number and variety of its welfare programs, but the fact remains that virtually every large city has increased its welfare budget at least in proportion to, and more often than not faster than, the growth in the number of people being served. No honest man can suggest that the accomplishments have been remotely commensurate with the effort. On the contrary, one sometimes has the feeling that welfare agencies almost welcome failure, for failure if repeated frequently enough only demonstrates the need to expand their services still more. In appealing for governmental or private support, these agencies remind one of J. Edgar Hoover's requests for more financial aid to fight communism: his agency is the only "bulwark against the communist threat"; but that threat seems somehow to grow rather than diminish, in spite of all the work of his agency. So with the social agencies in the fight against delinquency, family disorganization, drug addiction, and so on.

What has gone wrong? Why the failure? These questions must be answered before we can propose an alternative course of action.

What has gone wrong, primarily, is that social agencies and social workers have concentrated far too much on symptoms rather than on causes—and on symptoms seen and treated individually rather than in connection with other symptoms. This concern with symptoms has been a reflection, in good measure, of the preoccupation of the social work profession with case work and the study and treatment of individual maladjustment. The goal, that is to say, has been to teach maladjusted individuals how to adapt themselves to society as it is, rather than to change those aspects of society that make the individuals what they are.

Unlike the early sociologists who were reformers, contemporary sociologists and social workers, as Professor Lewis Coser has commented, have focused attention "predominantly upon problems of adjustment rather than upon conflict; upon social statics rather than dynamics"; they have been concerned largely with "the maintenance of existing structures and the ways and means of insuring their smooth functioning." Social workers, in particular, have made Freud their God when they should have been worshipping at the shrine of the sociologist Emile Durkheim. For the problems of the slum stem far less from individual neuroses (though certainly there are plenty of those) than from an objective lack of opportunity, from a social system that denies the individual dignity and status.*

The result, as *West Side Story* suggested with some wit, is that slum youngsters regard social workers with a good deal of scorn; more to the point, they see them as "con men" sent to hypnotize them into accepting a society they loathe—a society which denies them (or seems to deny them, which amounts to the same thing) the means to achieve the goals to which they are exhorted to aspire. To a degree, at least, the gang members, the delinquents, the dropouts, the ordinary slum dwellers are justified in their cynicism: Americans have used welfare programs and social work agencies the way the Romans used bread and circuses—to keep the poor happy and non-threatening.

The obsession with "case work" and individual pathology has had another extremely unfortunate effect: the great bulk of resources, financial and professional, have been concentrated on a very small proportion of slum dwellers, the

* *See*, for example, Richard A. Cloward and Lloyd Ohlin, *Delinquency and Opportunity*, Glencoe, Ill.: The Free Press, 1960.

so-called "multi-problem families." There is a growing mass of evidence that those receiving the greatest assistance are the ones least likely to benefit from it. Dr. Thomas Gladwin, for example, has suggested that there may be considerable merit in reviving the old distinction between "the deserving poor" and "the undeserving poor." The great majority of slum dwellers, that is to say, work hard for very little material reward; they try their best to raise themselves, and their children, out of the morass in which they find themselves. Their problem is not any lack of good intent, but simply that their best is not good enough. These are the "deserving poor." The "undeserving poor"—those who, for whatever reasons of individual or social pathology, are truly anti-social in their behavior, destroy other peoples' lives or property, trade in narcotics, pimping, or whoring—in fact represent a small proportion of slum society. The fact that the deserving and the undeserving poor live in the same neighborhood and in much the same way reflects a common state rather than a common interest, and limited social welfare resources might be far more effective if directed at the deserving rather than at the undeserving poor.

In the last analysis, however, the failure of the enormous American social welfare effort stems from the same factor that has produced the political strain between Negroes and white liberals: the social workers' preoccupation with doing *for* people instead of doing *with* them—a preoccupation that destroys the dignity and arouses the hostility of the people who are supposed to be helped. All too often, social services are motivated by a sense of superiority, a patronizing "white man's burden" attitude that would offend the most thick-skinned slum dweller. One of the most precise (and most revealing) statements of this policy of "welfare colonialism," as some critics call it, is contained in a report made public in the fall of 1962 by Raymond M. Hilliard, Director of the Cook County (Chicago) Department of Public Aid. "Other members of society," the report declares, "the teachers, the legal authorities, the social workers find themselves faced with a growing gap of communication, a steadily increasing 'no-man's land' between themselves and those they wish to help . . . This group [the welfare recipients] understands less and less of what is expected of it and how it can go about fulfilling its duties and responsibilities, just as those who wish to help them find it more and more difficult to communicate with them and to know how to go about helping them. But at such a point, society can no longer accept the passive role of mere support; it must begin to lead and direct the individual." Hence the report urges an extension of the concept of "social uplift through social discipline" which Hilliard had enunciated a year before: relief recipients are to be forced to go to school, on penalty of losing their welfare benefits, for "Society stands in the same relation to them as that of parent to child . . . *Just as the child is expected to attend classes, so also the 'child-adult' must be expected to meet his responsibility to the community.* In short, 'social uplifting'—even if begun on the adult level—cannot expect to meet with success unless it is combined with a certain amount of 'social disciplining'—just as it is on the pre-adult level." [Emphasis added]

It is not surprising that the "child-adults" who inhabit the slums hate the colonial administrators who come to "uplift" them through "social discipline," or that they try to sabotage the disciplinarians' program. "They're all around the neighborhood," an East Harlem adolescent interviewed by Richard Hammer of the *New York Times Magazine* says of social workers, "and most of them are rat fink types. They act like they think we're not human. They think they've got all there is, and all they've got to do is convert us to think and do what they think and do. Then everything will be just great. But, man, these jerks pop up in the morning with their little briefcases, and they cut out for their homes a hell of a way away around five or six at night, and that's it. If you ever are nuts enough to go to one of them," he adds, "they hand you the old crap, 'Now, son, you shouldn't feel that way.'" But as often as not, the boys *should* feel that way.

And so the social workers and civil servants remain alien in a world they never understand and frequently do not even see. There is a large "youth center" in Harlem, for example, whose administrators draw great satisfaction from the fact that the center's professional staff provides counseling to some five thousand youngsters a year. But the staff did not know that the center also served as a major contact point for the sale of narcotics, or that the heads of the local narcotic ring met every Sunday morning in the center's swimming pool—facts discovered quite easily when the staff of HARYOU began interviewing Harlem youth.

There is a more or less perpetual state of war, moreover, that is waged between municipal welfare departments and their clientele. The system of welfare developed during the 1930s, when the United States was in the depths of the Great Depression; its architects were economists (or social workers influenced by economists) whose main objective was to get more money into circulation, thereby stimulating consumer expenditures and "priming the pump" of prosperity. Hence, welfare departments did not make any attempt to increase the employment possibilities of their clientele. The result was to increase the sense of dependency. In the postwar period, welfare departments have taken on a police function as well as a relief function: the United States has never quite lost its Puritanic suspicion that those who receive relief are thereby touched by immorality, and to that suspicion has been added the fear that people might be receiving relief who are not eligible for it. In New York City, which has had perhaps the most enlightened and sympathetic relief administration, welfare workers are called "investigators," which is what they are. In almost every city in fact, the administration of welfare has become a police function. The result, as Professor S. M. Miller puts it, is that "the poor, thought of as being ignorant, illiterate, and unimaginative, have developed a variety of ways of coping with the welfare worker; evasion is frequent as recipients become 'welfare-wise.' And so we have a typical situation of a great deal of police and control efforts on one side and a considerable amount of matching efforts at evasion on the other. The stalemate that is reached is one where frequently there is repugnance on the part of authorities and lack of respect on the part of recipients."

To be sure, many social workers—perhaps the majority—do not see themselves as "social disciplinarians"; they are motivated by the best of intentions, by a genuine desire to be of service. But whatever the motive, the results tend to be the same: to destroy the individual's sense of dignity, or to increase his sense of dependency, or to arouse his hostility. For as we argued in chapter VII, the politics of human life do not permit of equality or freedom when one person is constantly in the position of magnanimous donor and the other in the position of perennial recipient. "We act as though taking help is about as comfortable, and at least as much of a good, as giving it," Elizabeth H. Ross of the District of Columbia Department of Public Welfare has said. "We have more or less convinced ourselves that accepting help is not necessarily a submission, nor an effort." But it *is* a submission—one that erodes the dignity and destroys the spirit.

In the case of the Negro, moreover, this error is compounded by an apparent inability to understand the most basic fact about behavior in the Negro slum. As we have seen in chapter III, the Negroes' failure to "acculturate" is due only partly to ignorance or indifference; they do not acculturate because they regard doing the things implied by that term as treason to their race—as "going along with Mr. Charlie's program." To compound matters, government officials, civic leaders, and foundation executives who should know better have developed a habit in recent years of announcing great new programs of social uplift without taking the trouble to talk first to the people who are going to be uplifted. The result is that the do-gooders, to their amazement and consternation, find themselves attacked instead of welcomed. When, a few years ago, Mayor Robert F. Wagner of New York City proudly announced a bold new program of mental health for Harlem, he was greeted by an explosion of anger; Harlem leaders forgot their own bickering long enough to unite in an attack on "welfare colonialism" and a demand that any new programs be developed by the community itself. In city after city, in fact, supposedly supine Negroes have been turning on their benefactors with such slogans as "we refuse to be planned for as though we were children," "we're tired of being guinea pigs in sociological experiments," and the like.

▼

2

What all this means is that Negroes, like every other group, can really be helped in only one way: by giving them the means with which to help themselves. "Our healing gift to the weak," as Eric Hoffer has wisely written, "is the capacity for self help. We must learn how to impart to them the technical, social and political skills which would enable them to get bread, human dignity, freedom and strength by their own efforts." For in the last analysis their rejection of the conventional offers of help—the resentment they show—springs less from the injustice per se than from their sense of inadequacy and impotence. Thus, Mary Burch, a distinguished educator and civic leader in Newark, New Jersey, who founded The Leaguers Inc., one of the few Negro-operated social agencies in the East, insists that every adolescent in her program give at least one hour of service a week to some community agency. "They've always been on the receiving end," Mrs. Burch says; "they have to learn how to give if they're to develop into responsible adults." For the same reason, Mrs. Burch refuses to dole out alms to any of her youngsters. If a child needs eyeglasses, for example, The Leaguers will finance the purchase—but the youngster is required to take on some job that will enable him to earn enough to repay the advance. The program has been remarkably successful in preparing Negro youngsters for college and in finding scholarship money for them. Another reason for The Leaguers' success—important in this day of multi-million-dollar projects—is that its aims are modest and its program unpretentious, it is truly an indigenous operation.

In the last analysis, however, Negro children will be able to climb out of their slums en masse only if they see their parents doing the same—only if the adults of the community are involved in action on their own behalf. For it is the disorganization of the community at large—the evidence on all sides that their parents are unable to control their own behavior, unable to impose sanctions on people who threaten the community's well-being—that persuades the young that the cards are stacked against them, that the omnipresent "they" will not permit them to "make it" in any legitimate form, and so leads them into apathy, withdrawal, or rebellion.

But can this be done; can the adults be mobilized? The answer, quite simply, is that it *has* been done—in Chicago, where The Woodlawn Organization, created in late 1960, has become a major factor in that city's life and politics. Indeed, TWO is the most important and the most impressive experiment affecting Negroes anywhere in the United States. It is a living demonstration that Negroes, even those living in the worst sort of slum, can be mobilized to help themselves, and that when they are, neither the Negro community nor the city as a whole can ever be quite the same again.

Formation of TWO represents the first instance in which a large, broadly representative organization has come into existence in any Negro district in any large American city. The Woodlawn Organization is set up as a federation of other representative groups: some eighty-five or ninety in all, including thirteen churches (virtually all the churches of any influence in the community), three businessmen's associations, and an assortment of block clubs, neighborhood associations, and social groups of one sort or another. All told, the organizations represented in TWO have a membership of about thirty thousand people; some twelve hundred of them attended the organization's second annual convention in May of 1963.

Existence of any sort of large organization in Woodlawn would seem to be almost a contradiction in terms; an oblong slum running south of the University of Chicago campus and containing between eighty and a hundred fifty thousand people, depending on how the area is defined, Woodlawn is almost a prototype of the disorganized anomic neighborhoods into which Negroes have been moving. In the 1920s, Woodlawn was part of the University community—a highly desirable residential area with broad tree-lined streets, excellent transportation facilities, and a nice admixture of private homes and apartment houses. The neighborhood began to deteriorate during the Depression, when big apartments were cut up into smaller units in an effort to rent them; and the process continued during World War Two. Even so, a report issued by the City Plan Commission in 1946 declared that "Woodlawn always has been a good community" and called for a program of neighborhood conservation to keep it that way.

The conservation program never was put into effect, however, and Woodlawn resumed its decline as the postwar rush to the suburbs got under way. Thus around about 1950, Negroes began moving in; the trickle rapidly turned into a torrent as Woodlawn became the "port-of-entry" for Negroes moving to Chicago from the South. (The Illinois Central Railroad's Sixty-third Street Station—the next-to-last stop on the line that runs northward from Mississippi, Louisiana, Tennessee and Kentucky—is in the Woodlawn area. There are some weeks when fully half the passengers traveling to Chicago from those states disembark in Woodlawn.) By 1960, Woodlawn had become a virtually all-Negro slum.* Although nearly 25 per cent of the area's residents receive some form of welfare, they pay an average of $84 a month in rent—more than $10 *above* the city average—for which they occupy an average housing unit of 2.2 rooms. A birth rate 25 per cent above the city's average has put pressure on the capacity of the local public schools. There is a flourishing traffic in gambling, narcotics, and prostitution, especially in one stretch under the elevated subway tracks; the commercial business district is active but declining, with large numbers of stores vacant. In short, Woodlawn is precisely the sort of obsolecscent, decaying, crowded neighborhood which social workers and city planners assume can never help itself—the sort of neighborhood in which even such advocates of social action as S. M. Miller assume that "directed, concerted action toward political or any other kind of goals is extremely unlikely."

But Woodlawn *is* helping itself; it is taking concerted action toward a wide variety of goals. The impetus for TWO came from three Protestant ministers and a Catholic priest who had come together through their concern with the spiraling decline of their neighborhood and the indifference of both the city and the University of Chicago, located just to the north of Woodlawn. The clergymen had "worn out the

* The change in the color of Woodlawn's residents seems to have changed the area's history as well; thus, a 1962 city report on "Key Social Characteristics of the Woodlawn Community" suggests, in contradiction to the 1946 report, that as a result of "almost planless growth since the 1893 Columbia Exposition," the community had been deteriorating for more than a half-century.

seats of several good pairs of trousers attending an uncountable number of meetings held to 'do something about Woodlawn' "—meetings which seemed only to lead to still more meetings. "We were watching a community dying for lack of leaders, a community that had lost hope in the decency of things and people," one of the founders, Dr. Ulysses B. Blakeley, co-pastor of the First Presbyterian Church and Moderator of the Chicago Presbytery, explains. "Outsiders consider a place like this a kind of zoo or jungle; they may mean well, but they choke us. It seemed to us that any effort would be futile unless our own people could direct it, choose their own goals, and work for them, grow in the process, and have a sense again of the rightness of things."

After investigating various approaches to community organization, therefore, the clergymen "took the plunge," as Dr. Blakeley and his co-pastor, Dr. Charles T. Leber, Jr., described it in *Presbyterian Life:* they called on Saul D. Alinsky, executive director of the Industrial Areas Foundation, and invited him to help organize the Woodlawn community. A sociologist and criminologist by training, Alinsky is a specialist in creating mass organizations on a democratic basis "in order that the so-called 'little man' can gather into his hands the power he needs to make and shape his life." His organizing career began in the late 1930s, when he was one of the principal architects of Chicago's much admired Back of the Yards Neighborhood Council, which turned the stockyards area—the locale for Upton Sinclair's *The Jungle*—into one of the most desirable working-class neighborhoods in Chicago.* When his success in organizing the Back of the Yards

* Critics of Alinsky now point to Back of the Yards and suggest that *anyone* could have organized the area, since the residents are virtually all Catholics. But when Alinsky began his organizing work, the stockyards area quite literally was a jungle. The residents were Catholic, all right—but they belonged to an incredible number of churches, each representing a different nationality or ethnic group at war with all the others. Animosity between them was so great that Catholic priests ministering to one ethnic group literally were not on speaking

evoked requests to do the same in other cities, Alinsky organized the Industrial Areas Foundation, a non-profit institution which has organized some forty-four groups across the country. The most notable of these, until the formation of The Woodlawn Organization, were in California, where the IAF organized some thirty communities of Mexican-Americans and welded them together in the Community Service Organization. The Industrial Areas Foundation's President is Dr. George N. Shuster, retired president of Hunter College and now assistant to the president of Notre Dame University; the board of directors includes, among others, Mrs. Valentine E. Macy, whose husband is a power in New York Republican politics; Ralph Helstein, president of the Packinghouse Workers Union; Cecil North, former president of Metropolitan Life Insurance Company; Rev. Ralph Abernathy, second-in-command under Rev. Martin Luther King; and Meryl Ruoss, chairman of the Institute of Strategic Studies of the Board of National Missions of the Presbyterian Church.

"Took the plunge" is an apt way of describing what the Woodlawn ministers did in approaching Alinsky, however—for he is nothing if not controversial. Indeed, he delights in controversy; one of his basic premises, he likes to say, is that *all* important issues are controversial. Alinsky's opponents (few of whom have bothered to read *The Prince*) see him as Machiavelli reincarnated; Alinsky has been attacked, at various times, as a communist, a fascist, a dupe of the Catholic Church, the mastermind of a Catholic conspiracy (Alinsky is Jewish), a racist, a segregationist, and an integrationist seeking to mongrelize Chicago. His supporters are equally

---

terms with priests from other ethnic backgrounds. Alinsky managed to unite all the Catholics—and then to forge a working alliance between the local Churches, the Chicago Archdiocese, and the Packinghouse Workers Union—at the time (though no longer) under communist domination. Paradoxically, the Back of the Yards organization has become very conservative in recent years: *e.g.*, it has been quite effective in keeping Negroes out of the neighborhood.

immoderate in their praise; as Drs. Blakeley and Leber wrote, "No one in the city is as detested or as loved, as cursed or as blessed, as feared or as respected." Certainly no one in recent memory has had as great an impact on the city of Chicago; and none in the United States has proposed a course of action or a philosophy better calculated to rescue Negro or white slum dwellers from their poverty or their degradation. For Alinsky is that rarity of American life: a superlative organizer, strategist, and tactician who is also a philosopher (or a superlative philosopher who is also an organizer, strategist and tactician).

The essential difference between Alinsky and his enemies is that Alinsky really believes in democracy: he really believes that the helpless, the poor, the badly-educated can solve their own problems if given the chance and the means; he really believes that the poor and uneducated, no less than the rich and educated, have the right to decide how their lives should be run and what services should be offered to them, instead of being ministered to like children. "I do not believe that democracy can survive, except as a formality," he has written, "if the ordinary citizen's part is limited to voting—if he is incapable of initiative and unable to influence the political, social and economic structures surrounding him."

The individual can influence these structures only if he has power, for power means nothing more or less than the capacity to make one's interests felt in the decisions that affect him. There are two sources of power, in Alinsky's view: money and people. Since the residents of Woodlawn and of areas like it obviously have no money, their only source of power is themselves—which is to say the creation of an effective organization. Alinsky's frankness about power is upsetting to a good many people who regard open discussion of power as somehow lacking in taste—the equivalent, almost, of discussing one's marital life in public. For power, as John Kenneth Galbraith has written, plays a curious role in American life. "The privilege of controlling the actions or of affecting the income and property of others is something that no one of us can profess to seek or admit to possessing. No American ever runs for office because of an avowed desire to govern. He seeks to serve . . . The same scrupulous avoidance of the terminology of power," Galbraith adds, "characterizes American business. The head of the company is no longer the boss—the term survives only as an amiable form of address—but the leader of the team. No union leader ever presents himself as anything but a spokesman for the boys." *

Alinsky takes delight in violating this etiquette. "The only reason people have ever banded together," he baldly states, "and the only reason they ever will, is the fact that organization gives them the power to satisfy their desires or to realize their needs. There never has been any other reason." In his view, people join a trade union to develop enough power to force a change in their working conditions; they join a political party in order to have a power instrument that can win an election and carry out their political objectives; they organize a church as a power instrument to convert others to their religious belief. "Even when we talk of a community lifting itself by its bootstraps," Alinsky says, "we are talking of power. It takes a great deal of power to lift oneself by one's own bootstraps."

To create such a power structure in an area like Woodlawn, however, requires enormous skill and effort, and a break with convention. The reason most efforts at organizing slum neighborhoods fail, Alinsky argues, is not the nature of the community but the objectives of the organizers and of the methods they use. Most approaches to community organization, as Professor Dan W. Dodson has written, involve "more of an emphasis on how to get the different vested interests together to slice up areas of 'service' than . . . a

* John Kenneth Galbraith, *American Capitalism*, Boston: Houghton Mifflin Company, 1956.

consideration of how to get people genuinely organized in fighting for the things which would bring them dignity and respect." The conventional appeal to homeowners' interests in conserving property values is useless in a community in which the majority of people rent, and in which the homeowners would have to sell if forced to comply with the building code. A call for civic pride falls flat in a community which hates its neighbors and which is convinced it is going to be bulldozed out of existence sooner or later; neighborhoods like Woodlawn are too drab and dismal to cause anyone to rally around them. Even civil rights is too much of an abstraction. "The daily lives of Woodlawn people," an early Alinsky memo on Woodlawn suggested, "leave them with little energy or enthusiasm for realizing principles from which they themselves will derive little practical benefit. They know that with their educational and economic handicaps they will be exceptions indeed if they can struggle into a middle-class neighborhood or a white-collar job. "Instead of these appeals of the conventional neighborhood organizer and group worker, Alinsky uses the classical approach of trade union organization: he appeals to the self-interest of the local residents and to their resentment and distrust of the outside world, and he seeks out and develops a local, indigenous leadership.

While indigenous leadership is crucial if the organization is to mean anything in the lives of its members, the initial impetus must come from the outside, and the mean and difficult job of building the organization must be handled by full-time organizers who know how to conquer the apathy of the slum and how to weld its disparate fragments into a unified whole. For the indigenous leaders of the slum area are not in touch with each other; without training, they lack the skills needed to keep a large organization running; and in most cases it has never occurred to any of them to lead a mass organization. (If any one thing is known in the Negro slum—or the white slum, for that matter—it is that you can't fight

City Hall.) Just as no factory would ever be organized without stimulus and guidance from the outside, so no slum can be organized without a good deal of help.

But the Industrial Areas Foundation insists that help be used to make the local community self-sufficient, not to keep it dependent. Alinsky will not enter a community unless he is invited by something like a cross-section of the population, and he usually insists, as a condition of entering, that the community itself, no matter how poor, take over the full responsibility for financing the new organization within a period of three years.* Alinsky has a standard way of dramatizing the importance of financial independence at the convention at which a new group formally approves its constitution. The audience is usually full of enthusiasm and terribly proud of the constitution, which local citizens have hammered out over a long period of time. Alinsky takes a copy of the document, looks at it briefly, and then tosses it to the floor, announcing to the startled audience: "This constitution doesn't mean a damned thing. As long as the IAF organizers are on my payroll they'll do what I damn well tell them to do and not what it says on any paper like that." After a shocked silence, someone in the audience invariably calls out, "I don't understand. I thought you were on our side!" "I am," Alinsky answers back. "But think of the number of people who've come down here telling you the same thing, and how many turned out to be two-timing, double-crossing S.O.B.s. Why should you trust me? The only way you can be sure that the aims in that constitution are carried out is to get the organizers off my payroll and onto your payroll. Then *you* can tell them what to do, and if they don't do it, you can fire them and get someone who will."

---

* Because of the poverty of Woodlawn, and even more because of the long tradition of Negro dependence, Alinsky has found it necessary to stretch that period by a year or two. TWO is on its way to financial independence, however; as of January, 1964, it had $10,000 in its treasury.

Once the Industrial Areas Foundation enters a community, the process of building an organization follows a fairly standard pattern:

- Organizers from the Industrial Areas Foundation filter through the neighborhood, asking questions and, more important, listening in bars, at street corners, in stores, in peoples' homes—in short, wherever people are talking—to discover the residents' specific grievances;
- At the same time, the organizers try to spot the individuals and the groups on which people seem to lean for advice or to which they go for help: a barber, a minister, a mailman, a restaurant owner, etc.—the "indigenous" leaders;
- The organizers get these leaders together, discuss the irritations, frustrations, and problems animating the neighborhood, and suggest the ways in which power might be used to ameliorate or solve them;
- A demonstration or series of demonstrations are put on to show how power can be used. These may take a variety of forms: a rent strike against slum landlords, a cleanup campaign against a notorious trouble spot, etc. What is crucial is that meetings and talk, the bedrock on which middle-class organizations founder, are avoided; the emphasis is on action, and on action that can lead to visible results.

In this way, the new organization begins to take form as a supergroup comprising many existing member groups—churches, block clubs, businessmen's associations—and of new groups that are formed purely as a means of joining the larger organization. As the organization begins to move under its own steam, the IAF men gradually phase themselves out and local leaders take over. This does not mean that volunteers take over the whole work load, however. One of the cardinal principles of the IAF is that a full-time paid staff is necessary if a community organization is to continue to function; volunteers, especially in a slum neighborhood, simply do not have the time. But the local leaders take on the responsibility for making decisions and for meeting the budget; sometimes they hire one of the IAF organizers as a permanent staff head, sometimes they come up with their own organizers.

So much for general principles and procedures. The actual work of creating The Woodlawn Organization was begun in the spring and summer of 1960, eighteen months after the four ministers had called on Alinsky for help. (He had told them he would not come in to Woodlawn until a representative committee had extended the invitation.) By this time, the invitation was being extended by the Greater Woodlawn Pastors Alliance with support from most other organized groups in the community. The organizing effort was made possible by grants from the Catholic Archdiocese of Chicago, the Presbyterian Church of Chicago, and the Schwarzhaupt Foundation, a private philanthropy which has supported Industrial Areas Foundation projects elsewhere in the United States.

How do you begin to organize an area like Woodlawn? As Nicholas von Hoffman, then chief organizer for the IAF (now a reporter for a Chicago daily) put it with studied casualness, "I found myself at the corner of Sixty-third and Kimbark and I looked around." It did not take much looking or listening to discover, as might be expected in a Negro slum, that one of the things that "bugged" residents the most was cheating and exploitation by some of the businessmen of the area. In most low-income areas, credit-purchasing is a trap; naïve and semi-literate customers are high-pressured into signing instalment contracts without reading the fine print or having it explained. According to Dr. Leber, there were instances of customers being charged effective interest rates as high as 200 per cent; second-hand merchandise was represented as new; and prices bordered on outright piracy: a $6 diamond chip in a gaudy ring setting would be sold for $250, with a "Certificate of Guarantee" that it was a real diamond. (It *was* a real diamond—but one worth only $6.) Credit-purchasing aside, many merchants took unfair advantage of their customers' ignorance; food stores, for example, gave short weight, overcharged, and in a few cases actually rigged their cash registers to give false totals.

Hence, when the IAF organizers started fanning through the community, complaints began to pile up. Here was an issue, moreover, on which the legitimate businessmen in the area could unite with the consumers, for the crooked merchants hurt business for everyone else. As a result, TWO—bringing together the leaders of the Businessman's Association, some of the ministers, and some of the indigenous leaders who were being turned up—worked out a Code of Business Ethics covering credit practices, pricing, and advertising. To implement the Code, TWO set up a Board of Arbitration consisting of four representatives from the Businessman's Association, four from consumer groups, with an impartial chairman from outside the community elected by the eight Board members.

If this had been all, however, TWO would have been stillborn. To publicize the Code, and to publicize the new organization, a big parade was staged in which nearly a thousand people marched through the business section carrying signs, singing, and creating enough of a stir to make the front pages of most Chicago newspapers. The next Saturday, a registered scale was set up at a nearby Catholic church, along with an adding machine; people who shopped at the markets suspected of giving false weights and improper totals brought their packages directly to the church, where they were weighed, and cash register slips checked and the false weights and false totals publicized. Most of the offending merchants quickly agreed to comply with the "Square Deal" agreement. To bring recalcitrant merchants to terms, leaflets were distributed through the community accusing them of cheating and urging residents to stay away.

The Square Deal campaign served its purpose. It eliminated a considerable amount of exploitation and chicanery on the part of Woodlawn merchants. More important, it made the residents of Woodlawn aware of the existence of the new organization and drove home the fact that through organization they *could* improve some of the circumstances of their lives. Two years later, a TWO vice-president recalled that it was the Square Deal campaign that brought him into the organization, and that really put TWO on a solid footing. "We showed people that they don't have to accept everything, that they can do something about it," he said—"but that they have to be organized to do it."

To capitalize on the enthusiasm this campaign created, the IAF staff men moved next to organize rent strikes in a number of Woodlawn buildings. Wherever a substantial majority of the tenants could be persuaded to act together, a tenants' group was formed which demanded that the landlord, within some stated period of time, clear up physical violations that made occupancy hazardous or uncomfortable—broken windows, plumbing that did not work, missing steps from staircases, inadequate heat, etc. When the landlords ignored the ultimatum, TWO organized a rent strike: rents were withheld from the landlord and deposited in escrow in a special bank account. To dramatize the strike on one block where several adjoining buildings were involved, residents spelled out "This Is A Slum" in huge letters on the outside of the building. If the landlord remained recalcitrant, groups of pickets were dispatched to march up and down in front of the landlord's own home, carrying placards that read "Your Neighbor Is A Slumlord." The picketing provided a useful outlet for the anger the tenants felt, and gave them an opportunity, for the first time in their lives, to use their color in an affirmative way. For as soon as the Negro pickets appeared in a white suburban block, the landlord was deluged with phonecalls from angry neighbors demanding that he do something to call the pickets off. Within a matter of hours landlords who were picketed were on the phone with TWO, agreeing to make repairs.

Landlords were not the only ones who were picketed;

over-crowded and segregated schools became a target, too. When William G. Caples, president of the Board of Education, refused to meet with TWO to discuss their complaints —he denounced the organization as "the lunatic fringe"—a delegation of eighteen Protestant and Catholic pastors staged a sit-in at the executive offices of Inland Steel, where Caples was public relations vice-president; at the same time, TWO rank-and-filers circled the building on the outside, carrying placards denouncing Caples as a segregationist. (Caples resigned the following month "because of the pressure of company business.") And when Superintendent of Schools Benjamin Willis denied that overcrowding could be relieved by transferring Negro students to all-white schools, TWO sent "truth squads" of mothers into neighboring white schools to photograph empty and half-empty classrooms. (In one elementary school, which was 81.5 per cent Negro, classes averaged 48.4 students per room; a school nine blocks away, but 99 per cent white, had an average of 28.4 pupils per room.) TWO members also staged a "death watch" at Board of Education meetings: a large group would attend each meeting wearing long black capes, to symbolize the "mourning" of Negro parents over the plight of their children.

It is precisely this sort of tactic that leads some of Alinsky's critics to denounce him as an agitator who deals in hate and who incites to conflict, a troublemaker whose stated goal is to "rub raw the sores of discontent," as an early TWO memorandum put it. "The fact that a community may be stirred and organized by 'sharpening dormant hostilities' and 'rubbing raw the sores of discontent' is not new," says Julian Levi, executive director of the South East Chicago Commission and mastermind and director of the University of Chicago's urban renewal activities. "The technique has been proved in practice in the assembling of lynch mobs." (Levi and the University have been trying alternately to discredit Alinsky and to ignore him since he began organizing Woodlawn.) As an example of the methods to which he objects,

Levi cites a TWO leaflet naming a local food store and warning people to "watch out" for short weights, spoiled food, and short-changing. "If this is what this merchant is really doing," Levi says, "he should be punished by the court—but with all the safeguards the law provides. This is not the way people should be taught to protect themselves," he argues; they should be taught to register complaints with the Department of Health (about spoiled food), and Department of Weight and Measures (about short weights), and the Police Department (about short change). Levi similarly deplores the use of rent strikes. If landlords were violating the building code, he argues, TWO should have brought action through the Building Department, the way the South East Chicago Commission does, instead of taking the law into its own hands.

But slum dwellers, as Levi surely knows, have been complaining to the Building Department and to other city agencies for years, to no avail. The reason the South East Chicago Commission is able to get rapid action on complaints it registers with the Building Department or any other city agency is that it has what politicians call "clout": the Commission is the urban renewal arm of the University of Chicago, whose board of trustees includes some of the most influential businessmen and politicians in the city. As Professors Peter H. Rossi and Robert A. Dentler said in their study of the University's urban renewal program in the Hyde Park-Kenwood area, Levi "could in effect represent the most powerful community interests in demanding protection from the Chicago Department of Buildings and the Mayor's Housing and Redevelopment Coordinator. Pressure on real estate speculators was also channeled through the University's strong connections with the business community. Banks and insurance companies were warned that their funds were in jeopardy when invested as mortgages on illegally converted property in the area. Insurance companies were persuaded to suspend policies written on badly maintained properties.

Publicity about the ownership of notorious slum properties was given to the press, which published unflattering accounts of the abuse of housing decency." * TWO had none of these gentlemanly weapons at its disposal—hence its need to use cruder tactics.

For all their self-righteous indignation over Alinsky's tactics, moreover, the University of Chicago and its South East Chicago Commission, have never shrunk from the blunt and naked use of power when their interests seemed to require it. Consider this account by Rossi and Dentler:

> When a real estate speculator purchased a six-family apartment house and promptly moved in nine Negro families, the local block group of the Hyde Park-Kenwood Community Conference spotted the move . . . The day after the nine families moved in, Julian Levi visited the speculator, threatened him with legal action for violating the housing code, and confronted him with evidence of overcrowding; at the same time a generous offer to buy was made by the University real estate office. The speculator sold the apartment dwelling to the University on the next day and one day later the nine Negro families were moved out by the University's real estate managers. *Had this purchase and eviction not been possible, legal action through municipal channels would at best have achieved the levying of fines against the speculator—months and possibly even years after the conversion occurred. Thus, it is one matter to threaten prosecution via the courts and another to be able to buy up properties which are in violation of the law.* [Emphasis added]

In any case, Levi's criticisms miss the point—that the tactics he deplores are designed to serve more than one end. In the case of the fledgling Woodlawn Organization, the most urgent need was to persuade the local population that it could solve some of its problems through organization. It is

* Peter H. Rossi & Robert A. Dentler, *The Politics of Urban Renewal,* Glencoe, Ill.: The Free Press, 1961.

impossible to understand Alinsky's tactics, in fact, without understanding the basic dilemma inherent in organizing any slum area, and particularly a Negro slum. The basic characteristic of the slum—its "life style" so to speak—is apathy; no organization can be created unless this apathy can be overcome. But slum residents will not stir unless they see a reasonable chance of winning, unless there is some evidence that they *can* change things for the better. This reluctance to act is perfectly understandable; it is not true that the very poor have nothing to lose. Quite the contrary. In some respects, they have more to lose than the middle class; they face the danger of having their relief checks cut off, of losing an unskilled patronage job, of having a son on probation remanded to jail—of suffering any one of a host of reprisals a politically-oriented bureaucracy can impose. (One of the differences between the lower-class Negro communities and middle-class white communities is that the latter clamor for more protection *by* the police, while the former frequently demand—and need—protection *from* the police. Certainly the traffic in narcotics, gambling, and illicit sex that is omnipresent in every Negro slum could not go on without the active cooperation of the local police.)

Quite frequently, therefore, the apathy that characterizes the slum represents what in many ways is a realistic response to a hostile environment. But realistic or not, the adjustment that is reached is one of surrender to the existing conditions and abdication of any hope of change. The result is a community seething with inarticulate resentments and dormant hostilities repressed for safety's sake, but which break out every now and then in some explosion of deviant or irrational behavior. The slum dwellers are incapable of acting, or even of joining, until these suppressed resentments and hostilities are brought to the surface where they can be seen as problems—*i.e.*, as a condition you can do something about.

And so Alinsky pleads guilty to the charge of being an agitator, of arousing dormant hostilities or rubbing raw the sores of discontent: that is precisely the point of what he is doing! "The community organizer," he writes, "digs into a morass of resignation, hopelessness, and despair and works with the local people in articulating (or 'rubbing raw') their resentments." In telling them over and over again, " 'You don't have to take this, and you can do something about it,' he becomes a catalytic agent transmuting hidden resentments and hostilities into open problems." His job is to persuade the people to move—to be active, to participate, in short to develop and harness the power necessary to change the prevailing patterns. "When those prominent in the status quo turn and label you an agitator, they are completely correct, for that is, in one word, your function—to agitate to the point of conflict."

But agitation by itself is not enough; the inhabitants of a slum like Woodlawn must be convinced not only that a solution is possible but also that it is probable; they must see some tangible evidence that banding together will give them the capacity to alter the circumstances of their lives. To use the language of war (for that is what it is), the only way to build an army is by winning a few victories. But how do you gain a victory before you have an army? The only method ever devised is guerilla warfare: to avoid a fixed battle where the forces are arrayed and where the new army's weakness would become visible, and to concentrate instead on hit-and-run tactics designed to gain small but measurable victories. Hence the emphasis on such dramatic actions as parades and rent strikes whose main objective is to create a sense of solidarity and of community.

Once this guerilla warfare begins, the best organizing help of all frequently comes from "the enemy"—the established institutions who feel themselves threatened by the new organization. What really welded the Woodlawn community together, for example, was the University of Chicago's announcement, on July 19, 1960, that it planned to extend its "South Campus" into Woodlawn by annexing an adjacent strip a block wide and a mile long. Woodlawn residents had no particular attachment to the area in question, which was filled with an amalgam of warehouses, rooming houses, empty lots, and old hotels that served mainly as centers of prostitution. But they suspected that annexation of this strip was simply the prelude to bulldozing a large part of Woodlawn itself for middle- and upper-income apartment and town houses. There was ample basis for their fears; urban renewal projects had been going on for some time under University sponsorship in the Hyde Park-Kenwood district north of the University, designed in good measure to clear Negroes out.* Unless they acted quickly to establish the principle that no plan be adopted for Woodlawn without active participation by Woodlawn residents in the planning process itself, the community might be faced with a *fait accompli.* ("The characteristic mode of action of the University and of the South East Chicago Commission," Rossi and Dentler wrote, "was to develop plans quickly, announce proposals in general terms, and then obtain quick approval through political leverage downtown.") And so TWO immediately and loudly demanded that the city defer approval until University and city planning officials sat down with TWO and negotiated a long-term plan for Woodlawn. Otherwise, the organization warned, Woodlawnites would lie down in front of the bulldozers and wrecking equipment to prevent them from moving in. Some three hundred TWO members crowded into a City Plan Commission hearing and succeeded in blocking the quick approval the University had expected.

---

* There is ample documentation of this fact in Rossi and Dentler's *The Politics of Urban Renewal.* For example, "Asked by our interviewer why the University did not consider expansion to the east (which in many ways seemed more plausible than expansion in Hyde Park), a respondent high in the University administration replied that the area to the east contained 'our people' . . . Whether one liked it or not, neighborhood conservation and renewal meant the preservation of Hyde Park-Kenwood as a primarily *white* middle-class residential neighborhood."

The Negro tenants and homeowners were not the only ones alarmed by the University's announcement. Having seen the small businessmen of the Hyde Park-Kenwood area destroyed by the University's urban renewal program, the Woodlawn merchants became concerned over the way in which the University's plans might affect them. Conversations with University and city officials only served to increase their apprehension. For example, Julian Levi appeared at a meeting of the Woodlawn Businessman's Association; according to George Kyros, a local restaurant proprietor, Levi "said we could either accept the plan and help it or sit back and watch it go through." Phil Doyle, head of the Land Clearance Commission, was even less reassuring. "He said the biggest investment he would advise us to make in our business was one coat of paint," Kyros recalls. "I've never seen people feel so bad." The upshot was that the businessmen voted unanimously to join TWO in fighting the University's program.

And so the University of Chicago obligingly supplied the whipping boy—itself—that was needed to unite tenants, homeowners, and businessmen in a common cause. Even before the South Campus proposal, the University was generally hated in Woodlawn—in part because it was white, in part because of its "Negro removal" tactics in the Hyde Park-Kenwood area, and in part because of a barbed-wire fence the University had put up to protect its campus against the Woodlawn community.

Woodlawn's dislike for the University was returned in kind. "Woodlawn is a terrible neighborhood," a University spokesman exclaimed, "and if these people want to preserve it, I don't know what's become of American values." Not every University official saw the dispute in quite such simple terms, but few, if any, seemed to have any doubt that right was on their side. "The University of Chicago is one of the few really first-rate things in the city of Chicago," Julian Levi told this writer in the spring of 1963, when the dispute was coming to a head, "and it needs more land if it's going to continue to be first rate." Levi's job, as he defined it, was to get the land the University needed, and if possible, to create a compatible community as well. But getting the land came first. A certain degree of conflict seemed inevitable—for the University, as Levi explained it, would be there thirty, fifty, a hundred years from now, whereas the people in the surrounding community would long since have departed. It was understandable that the local residents might want to put their short-run interests first; but the University had to keep its eyes fixed on the long run.

The University may have kept its eye fixed firmly on the long run, but its knee was in its opponent's groin. In February of 1961, for example, Carl Larsen, the University's Public Relations Director, together with Julian Levi and another P.R. man, called on several Chicago dailies to warn them against "the evil forces" of Alinsky, the Industrial Areas Foundation, the Catholic Church, and TWO. They brought with them a dossier on Alinsky and his foundation containing a number of items; the main one was a copy of the Industrial Areas Foundation's income tax return showing various Catholic groups as its principal source of financial support in the year in question. (How the University happened to have a copy of the Foundation's tax return has never been explained.) The same income tax return was included in a dossier which the University sent to this writer in the fall of 1961, via a friendly reporter, in the hopes of dissuading me from including a section on TWO in an article I was preparing for *Fortune* Magazine. When I asked the reporter what the income tax return was supposed to demonstrate, other than support of the IAF by the Catholic Church, he replied that that *was* the point. In his opinion, which reflected that of the University's spokesmen, Catholic support was itself enough to discredit the IAF and TWO.*

* Among the other items in the dossier was a photostat of a *New York Times* article of January 24, 1960, reporting the split-up of the Chel-

When the Chicago dailies balked at running the proposed article, Larsen, Levi, and company persuaded the editor of the University's weekly student paper, the Chicago *Maroon*, to take up the cudgels. They also arranged for the Law School to check the article; as a result, it was copyrighted under the name of the writer—a rarely used procedure which guaranteed the University immunity against any possible suit for libel. The article, which attracted a great deal of attention—University P.R. men were still distributing copies nine months later—ran in the March 3, 1961, issue under a banner headline reading CHURCH SUPPORTS "HATE GROUP." It continued as follows:

> An organization now working in Woodlawn and dedicated to "sharpening dormant hostilities" received over $56,000 last year from the Chicago Catholic Bishop and the National Conference of Catholic Charities.
>
> The *Maroon* has learned that the controversial Industrial Areas Foundation (IAF), which is now helping the Temporary Woodlawn Organization to "organize" the south side community, also received approximately $43,000 from the two Catholic groups in 1958.
>
> In recent months, the TWO has attempted to organize residents of Woodlawn in opposition to the University of

---

sea Community Council, which Alinsky had helped organize on a part-time basis. The Hudson Guild, a settlement house whose director had served as the community's spokesman until the broader-based organization was formed, led a number of groups in withdrawing from the organization when its will was thwarted. The *Times* suggested that trouble in the Council arose from two fundamental questions: "Should an indigent section of the community be allowed to block desirable development just because it can muster a majority vote?" "Has a community house, or any other small group, the right to impose its will on the majority of the area's population even if it is for the good of the community?" (The "good of the community," in this instance, was an urban renewal plan designed to tear down the low-income housing in the area and replace it with middle-income co-operatives). The groups pulling out of the Council, the *Times* reporter indicated, answered "yes" to the second question. So, presumably, did the University of Chicago administration.

> Chicago's plans for building a "South Campus" between 60th and 61st, Cottage Grove to Stony Island.

The article went on to quote Rev. Walter Kloetzli, a Lutheran minister who has been carrying on a vendetta against Alinsky for some years, to the effect that the Catholic-IAF-TWO conspiracy was designed to keep Negroes locked into Woodlawn in order to preserve the all-white parishes in the areas southwest and southeast of Woodlawn. "These people are trying desperately to maintain the White-Negro status quo in areas south of Woodlawn," Reverend Kloetzli argued, "and they anticipate that redevelopment in Woodlawn will cause an influx of Negroes into areas southwest and southeast of Woodlawn."

The fact of the matter was that Kloetzli's charges had been aired two years previously, and found to be unsubstantiated, at a meeting of some thirty Presbyterian, Lutheran, and Catholic representatives called to discuss the IAF's intervention in Woodlawn. Alinsky had answered the charges to the satisfaction of virtually everyone present, and afterwards had submitted to them a twenty-four-page memorandum replying to fourteen questions raised by the churchmen. In a letter to the editor of the *Maroon*, the distinguished Lutheran theologian Joseph Sittler, a member of the faculty of the University of Chicago's Divinity School, called the March 3 article "irresponsible" and formally protested its publication. "The Roman Church," Dr. Sittler added, "has, indeed, enumerated through an extended statement of Cardinal Archbishop Meyer, a wise and charitable policy" regarding integration.

The Archdiocese in fact has been one of the most outspoken advocates of integration in the city of Chicago. Indeed, it was the Archdiocese's position on race relations and housing that brought it into conflict with the University. University officials apparently have regarded the Church as an enemy ever since 1958, when Monsignor John Egan, Executive Director of the Cardinal's Committee on Community Organization and Urban Renewal, criticized the then-pending Hyde Park-Kenwood urban renewal program. Monsignor Egan saw the program, quite rightly, as a venture in Negro removal; he pointed out that plans called for demolition of a great deal of adequate housing occupied largely by Negroes, and that few of these residents would be able to afford the new apartments and houses that were to be erected. Monsignor Egan also criticized what he considered inadequate provisions for relocation and insufficient safeguards for property owners whose homes were not torn down in the first wave of bulldozing; the plans permitted acquisition of homes later on for such reasons as "obsolete layout" of a building.

In any event, the Woodlawn Organization certainly was not the product of any Papist conspiracy. On the contrary, the organization represents one of the most meaningful examples of Protestant-Catholic co-operation to be found anywhere in the United States. (Dr. Sittler described the meeting at which Alinsky answered the Kloetzli charges as one of the most hopeful instances of Protestant-Catholic amity to have occurred in four centuries.) As we have seen, the organization was created as a result of close collaboration between Father Martin Farrell, paster of Woodlawn's largest Catholic church, and the Reverend Drs. Blakeley and Leber, co-pastors of Chicago's oldest Protestant congregation, the First Presbyterian Church of Chicago; financial support came from both Presbyterian and Catholic sources. This collaboration extended down to the church members; when Father Farrell's church gave him a testimonial dinner on the occasion of his twenty-fifth anniversary as pastor, tickets to the event were sold in a number of Protestant churches in Woodlawn, and almost as many Protestants as Catholics attended. Equally important, this ecumenical spirit affected Chicago's Protestant and Catholic church leaders, too. Cardinal Meyer, for example, is a staunch proponent of inter-church co-operation on social problems, believing that joint social action rather than dialogue provides the soundest basis for an ecumenical movement. The result has been collaboration of the Archdiocese, the Chicago Presbytery, and the Church Federation of Chicago. The involvement of church leaders of all denominations in social action to improve the Negro's lot is TWO's most enduring contribution. The example is spreading to other cities. In Kansas City, Missouri, for example, Presbyterians, Catholics, and Methodists are collaborating in an attempt to develop a TWO-type program, while Catholics, Presbyterians, and Lutherans are working together in Gary, Indiana.

The controversy over the South Campus plan has been revealing in another respect. There has been a great deal of talk, in recent years, about ways of increasing "citizen participation" in city planning, especially urban renewal planning; federal legislation now requires local citizen participation in the formulation of renewal plans as a condition of federal aid. The Woodlawn experience indicates that "participation" means something very different to planners and to the academic researchers on whom they lean, than it does to the people being planned for. To the former, "citizen participation" means that the local residents are given a chance to air their views *after* the plans have been drawn, not before; planning, in this view, is a matter for experts, and "participation" is really thought of as "acquiescence." Thus Rossi and Dentler hail the Hyde Park-Kenwood Community Conference as the outstanding example of citizen participation in urban renewal planning—but they also point out that the organization did not play a significant role in influencing the specific details of the plan. Its achievement was to create popular acceptance for a plan which, at least in part, was inconsistent with the organization's stated objectives. Hence the two scholars conclude that "the maximum role to be played by a citizen-participation movement in urban renewal is primarily a passive one." Professor James Q. Wilson is even more blunt: "If one's goal is urban renewal on any really large scale in our cities," he writes, planners would be well-advised to eschew any real citizen participation. For "the higher the level of indigenous organization in a lower-class neighborhood, the poorer the prospects for renewal in that area . . . Perhaps this explains," Professor Wilson adds, "why most local urban renewal directors made no effort to encourage citizen participation except on a city-wide basis—with little or no representation from the affected neighborhood." *

Certainly the Chicago city planners showed no eagerness to engage the Woodlawn residents in any active role. Indeed, the planners' response to Woodlawn's demand that it be given responsibility and allowed to exercise initiative in planning for its own future was a proposal to inundate the area with paternalism. Thus, the City Plan Commission, in March of 1962, presented a comprehensive plan for Woodlawn which included a huge program of urban renewal clearance, conservation, and rehabilitation; a massive investigation of illiteracy, ill-health, crime and unemployment; and a pilot attack on these problems to be financed by large government and foundation grants. In response to a question as to whether the planning committee had been guided by opinions from the community, the committee's Coordinating Consultant replied, "There is nobody to speak for the community. A community does not exist in Woodlawn." And Professor Philip Hauser, another consultant, volunteered his view that "The people there have only one common bond, opposition to the University of Chicago," and added gratuitously, "This is a community that reads nothing."

The two consultants were quickly disabused of their view. TWO responded with rhetoric ("We don't want to be

* *Cf.*, James Q. Wilson, "Planning and Politics: Citizen Participation in Urban Renewal," *Journal of the American Institute of Planners*, November, 1963.

planned for like children"; "We're tired of being pawns in sociological experiments"). But it did something unique in the annals of urban renewal: in conjunction with the Businessman's Association, it hired a firm of city planners to make a detailed critique of the city's proposal and to come up with alternate proposals. The critique pointed out a number of glaring contradictions between the City Plan Department's evaluation of Woodlawn in 1946, when it was all-white, and in 1962, when it was virtually all-Negro; for example, the 1946 report found that "land coverage in the community is not excessively high," while the 1962 report complained of dangerous overcrowding of both land and buildings, although no new construction had taken place in the interim. The critique also pointed out that the city's program would demolish a substantial number of attractive, well-kept homes in an area of relatively high owner-occupancy, but left untouched the bulk of the area classified as the most blighted.

To the discomfiture of the planners, TWO attacked the city's "social planning" as vigorously as it attacked the urban renewal planning. "Self-determination applies in the field of social welfare," the organization resolved at its 1962 convention. "Therefore the best programs are the ones that we develop, pay for and direct ourselves . . . Our aim is to lessen burdens in practical ways, but in ways that also guarantee we will keep our personal and community independence. We go on record as unqualifiedly opposing all notions of 'social planning' by either government or private groups. We will not be planned for as though we were children." Far from pleasing them, Woodlawn's desire for independence seemed only to anger the planners, whose "Papa knows best" attitude was being attacked on all sides. "Some of their resolutions against welfare are singularly unfortunate," Professor Hauser observed. "What would they do without welfare?" Others called the resolutions "revolutionary" and even "subversive." The Woodlawnites were puzzled. "They've been calling us 'welfare chiselers' and 'dependent' and everything else in the book," said one TWO Negro. "Now they distrust us for trying things for ourselves." "Do you think it's possible," a TWO organizer asked Georgie Ann Geyer, a reporter for the *Chicago Daily News*, "that someone other than the Negro has a vested interest in welfare?"

The distinguished University of Chicago sociologists and the professional planners may not have gotten the message (they have scrupulously ignored TWO's existence), but the politicians did. Concerned for his political life, Mayor Richard Daley forced the reluctant Chancellor of the University of Chicago to meet with TWO representatives in the Mayor's office; the negotiators agreed on a compromise which called for construction of low-income housing on vacant land *before* any existing buildings were torn down. For the first time in the history of urban renewal in the United States, people displaced by demolition will have new homes waiting for them in the same neighborhood. Instead of the usual wholesale replacement of lower-class housing by "middle-income" units, Woodlawn will be renewed in steps. Only houses beyond salvage will be torn down; units to be rehabilitated will be repaired without evicting tenants. And city officials agreed to give TWO majority representation on the citizens planning committee that will draw up further plans and supervise their execution; Mayor Daley personally called Dr. Blakeley to ask him to serve as chairman.

Forcing the University of Chicago and the city planners to take account of the desires of the community is not the only victory The Woodlawn Organization has won. Before TWO was formed, every school in Woodlawn save one was on either double shift or overlapping session, and Board of Education members had announced that they saw no possibility of eliminating the double shift in their lifetime. By the spring of 1963, the double shift had been dropped and overcrowding substantially reduced. TWO has persuaded a number of Chicago firms to open up jobs for Negroes; it has stimulated a number of local block organizations to clean up and maintain their neighborhoods, and has forced landlords to repair their property. TWO's attacks on "the silent six" Negro aldermen of the Dawson machine has forced an unaccustomed militancy on them, and thereby changed the whole complexion of Chicago politics. In the process, TWO's president, Rev. Arthur M. Brazier, has become the principal spokesman on civil rights for Chicago Negroes; before TWO was organized, Reverend Brazier had been an obscure minister of a Pentacostal church concerned almost exclusively with the next life. The leadership and organization strength TWO has provided is the only thing that has kept Chicago's civil rights coalition together, and Brazier has the eloquence and ability to go on to become a major figure in the national civil rights movement.

What makes The Woodlawn Organization significant, however, is not so much what it is doing for its members as what it is doing *to* them. "The most important thing to me about the forty-six busloads of people who went to City Hall to register," Alinsky commented at the time, "was their own reaction. Many were weeping; others were saying, 'They're paying attention to us'; 'They're recognizing that we're people.' " Eighteen months later, an active member observed, "City Hall used to be a forbidden place, but we've made so many trips there and seen so many people that it's beginning to feel like a neighborhood store." Other members expressed themselves in much the same way: "We've lost our fear of standing up and expressing ourselves"; "We don't have to go hat in hand, begging, anymore. It's a wonderful feeling." What is crucial, in short, is not what the Woodlawn residents win, but that *they* are winning it; and this makes them see themselves in a new light—as men and women of substance and worth.

Besides giving its members a sense of dignity and worth, the Woodlawn Organization has given a good many people a sense of direction and purpose and an inner discipline that has enabled them to overcome the "floundering phenomenon." "This has been the most satisfying and rewarding period of my life," one TWO officer remarked in the spring of 1963. 'The organization has given me a real sense of accomplishing something—the only time in my life I've had that feeling." Indeed, activity in TWO has completely reshaped this man's life; he remembers the date and even the hour of the first TWO meeting he attended; he dates events from that time, the way a happily married couple dates events from their wedding day. But TWO has done more than just give purpose and meaning to his life, important as that is. Like so many other Woodlawnites, he had been accustomed to waste enormous amounts of time and energy through sheer inefficiency, *i.e.*, personal disorganization. This made the initial organizing work more difficult than anything the organizers had ever encountered in white slums; at first, every little venture seemed to fail because of the personal disorganization. Even such an apparently simple matter as rounding up a half-dozen people to hand out leaflets at a particular time loomed as a major task: the six selected would turn up at different times, the leaflets would be lost or misplaced, the volunteers would get bored before they had finished distributing the leaflets, etc., etc., etc. Bit by bit, however, the members learned how to accept orders, how to carry out a simple task and follow through on it; then they began to learn how to give orders, how to organize a rent strike or a rally, how to handle a meeting, how to talk on their feet and debate an issue, how to handle opposition. The result, for those who have been actively involved in the organization, has been to transform their existence, for the discipline of the organization gradually imposes itself on their own lives. And as the individual learns to organize his own life, he learns how to relate to others. "We've learned to live together and act as a community," another TWO activist says. "Now I know people all over

Woodlawn, and I've been in all the churches. Two years ago I didn't know a soul."

It would be inane to pretend that Woodlawn has become a model community; it remains a poverty-stricken, crime-ridden slum, though a slum with hope—a slum that is developing the means of raising itself by its own bootstraps. Most of the problems that make Woodlawn what it is—high unemployment, lack of education, family disorganization, poor health, bad housing—cannot be solved by a community organization alone. Help is needed; enormous resources must be poured into Woodlawn in the form of compensatory education, job retraining, advice on child-rearing, preventive medicine, etc. But experience in every city in the nation demonstrates that any paternalistic program imposed from above will be resisted and resented as "welfare colonialism." *TWO's greatest contribution, therefore, is its most subtle: it gives Woodlawn residents the sense of dignity that makes it possible for them to accept help.* For help now comes (or seems to come, which amounts to the same thing) not as the result of charity but as the result of their own power; they have decided what services they need and what services they would like to have. Hence programs which the community, in the past, would have avoided with contempt as one more instance of "Mr. Charlie's brainwashing," are now eagerly sought after. Thus, negotiations between TWO and the University of Chicago have led to development of a nursery school program designed to reverse the effects of cultural deprivation. Negotiations between TWO and a team of psychiatrists enabled the latter to set up some promising experiments in group therapy; the psychiatrists and social workers work through TWO's network of block clubs to bring people into the program. When a program enters Woodlawn with TWO's endorsement and recommendation, it carries a cachet that greatly multiplies its chances of success.

▼

3

The Woodlawn experience deserves—indeed, requires—the most careful study by anyone, black or white, interested in solving "the Negro problem." Unfortunately, it is not getting that attention—at least not from academic researchers and foundation executives, who seem to be repelled by the controversy in which TWO basks. Not a single social scientist from the University of Chicago, for example (as of February, 1964, at any rate) has shown the slightest interest in TWO; with the most important social laboratory in the country across the street, they have turned steadfastly the other way. The large foundations have shown much the same lack of interest.

Yet The Woodlawn Organization is invaluable not only as a demonstration that a Negro slum community can be mobilized to help itself, but because it shows that co-operation is possible between whites and Negroes of the most militant stripe. The Woodlawn experience demonstrates that white help is valuable in a number of ways. Negroes have been so conditioned to accepting their plight as inevitable that it sometimes (though less and less frequently) takes whites to convince them that the status quo can be changed. White help is invaluable, secondly, in supplying the organizational know-how, and in overcoming or compensating for "the floundering phenomenon"; white advice can be useful also in advising the indigenous Negro leaders on how to approach the whites with whom they must deal. (Many of these leaders have had no contact with whites except in an employer-employee relationship; for such a man, the first trip to City Hall or to the Board of Education can be a terrifying experience.) Because of the poverty of the Negro community and the absence of any tradition of giving, white financial support is also essential if the organization is to get off the ground.

If Woodlawn demonstrates the need for white help, it also shows that help can be given in ways that build rather than destroy the Negroes' self-reliance and dignity and pride. Unquestionably, a good many TWO members must have been suspicious of their white allies during the early months or even years. But the whites proved their credentials by yielding the reins as rapidly as possible. In the first year, white ministers supplied most of the direction and served as spokesmen. But they moved more and more into the background as indigenous leadership began to develop. By 1963, for example, some of the most active members of the Education Committee were ADC mothers.

Where will the necessary support come from? Not from the government, in all likelihood; no government, no matter how liberal, is going to stimulate creation of a power organization that is sure to make its life uncomfortable. The much-heralded "Mobilization for Youth" project on New York City's Lower East Side, for example, which has received some $14 million from the Federal, state, and local governments and from the Ford Foundation, is based upon a sociological theory very similar to Alinsky's. "The long-range target in a service program," the Mobilization prospectus argues, "should not be the individual delinquent or even the conflict gang but, rather, the community itself . . . In the long run, the young will be far more responsive to an adult community which exhibits the capacity to organize itself, to manage its own problems, to impose informal sanctions, and to mobilize indigenous resources for young people, than they will be to a community which must have these functions performed by external agents." But the fact that the agency's funds come largely from government, together with the fact that the board of directors is dominated by representatives of the old-line settlement houses and social work agencies, makes it difficult for the Mobilization staff to act according to its stated principles. The Prospectus itself reveals the compromises that had to be made to develop a program inside "The Establishment." "An important assumption of Organizing the Unaffiliated," the document states, "is that the successful involvement of lower-class persons requires that *they be allowed greater freedom than is usually permitted low-income participants in community-wide activities.*" [Emphasis added] The Prospectus goes on to state quite candidly that "There is, of course, a contradiction inherent in the proposal to establish 'independent' lower-class community organizations under Mobilization sponsorship. Mobilization is responsible to a wide variety of groups. Issues with which lower-class organizations deal may threaten some of these groups, which may exert pressure to control the fledgling." The pressure was not long in coming. On January 30, 1964, a group of twenty-six public school principals in the area denounced the agency for turning community organizers into "full-time paid agitators and organizers for extremist groups" and encouraging the organizers to "war against individual schools and their leaders." The principals demanded the removal of George Brager, Mobilization for Youth's Program Director, and called for an investigation by the Superintendent of Schools and by Mobilization's sponsors. Spreading dissension among parents and teachers, the principals complained, "constitutes an abuse of the noble purpose for which great sums of Federal and municipal money were originally appropriated.

Support is no more likely to come from the large foundations. They are too frightened of controversy and too deeply committed to paternalism to be able to offer Negro slum dwellers "the healing gift" of self-help. The Ford Foundation, for example, which is sponsoring large-scale "gray area" programs in five cities (Boston, New Haven, Oakland,

Philadelphia, and Washington) plus a state wide project in North Carolina, has bet millions on a grandiose fusion of paternalism and bureaucracy. As Mitchell Sviridoff, executive director of Community Progress, Inc., the Ford Foundation's arm in New Haven, Connecticut, has suggested, the nature of the urban problem

> calls for a unique effort—an effort that treats social problems as being so tightly inter-related in their causative characteristics that anything short of a comprehensive preventive attack on the totality of the city's social problems and their causes is unrealistic and ameliorative in its effect at best. And so we must work in the fields of education, housing, employment, retraining, recreation, neighborhood organization, equal rights, and social services within a framework in which specific programs in these various critical areas are not isolated efforts but instead integral parts of a carefully developed total social plan.

A "total social plan": the concept is a little frightening, but one has to make allowances for foundation executives who get carried away by flights of rhetoric. Certainly no one could take exception to the argument that social problems are so tightly interrelated that they require a co-ordinated attack. The crucial question raised by Sviridoff's oratory is, who is to do the planning for whom? The answer is all too plain. "The composition of the Board of Directors" [of his non-profit corporation], he told a Maryland Social Welfare Conference, "is a reflection of the basic community-wide consensus which has been achieved. Represented on the Board is the Community Council, the United Fund, the Board of Education, the Redevelopment Agency, the Citizens Action Committee, Yale University, the New Haven Foundation, and the Mayor's Office." Everybody, in short, except the people being planned for.

In Philadelphia, the people being planned for in a $1.7 million Ford Foundation project are hardly even mentioned, let alone represented. The prospectus for the Philadelphia Council for Community Advancement, set up by the Ford grant to direct and co-ordinate "a total social plan" for North Philadelphia, that city's Harlem, is a sixty-page document; the first mention of the word "Negro" comes on page 40. (The term is not used again until page 49, in the penetrating observation, "gray areas are inhabited by whites and Negroes alike.") According to the preface, the sponsors "mean planning to consist of collaborative examination of problems and aspirations, shared criticism of existing programs, and the evolution of a comprehensive program of action and research, based on the consensus of the participants." But the document itself makes it clear that the North Philadelphians' collaboration is to consist largely of participation in the programs laid down by the PCCA. Thus, the prospectus suggests that the North Philadelphia office maintained by the Health and Welfare Council be expanded, so that "If the citizenry should want to 'Go Fight City Hall,' *they would have an effective mechanism to speak for them at a local level.*" [Emphasis added] The notion that the citizens conceivably might want to speak for themselves obviously never occurred to the academicians, government officials, and "civic leaders" who drew up the document. On the contrary, the prospectus goes on to raise the question: "How might the challenges and problems facing a community be better communicated to the citizenry so that the citizenry can be better informed and motivated to participate in the community decision-making process?"—as if the residents of the Negro slum needed to be told what their problems are! Small wonder that when the program was announced, Cecil Moore, the newly-elected and rabidly militant president of the Philadelphia NAACP, called on Negroes to boycott the program, and to boycott the Ford Motor Company as well. Ford Foundation officials, to be sure, had discussed their program with some of the city's "responsible" leaders, but they had ignored the "irresponsible" ones who more closely reflected mass

Negro opinion. (A good many middle-class Negroes who regarded Moore as a dangerous rabble-rouser, felt constrained in this instance to support him out of resentment at this example of white welfare colonialism.)

The Ford programs, therefore, are well-intentioned but self-defeating. Besides paternalism, they reflect a naïve search for "community-wide consensus"—a search which leads the Foundation to eschew "goals which emphasize the self-interests of some at the expense of others," as Dr. Paul N. Ylvisaker, director of the Foundation's Public Affairs Division, says. Unlike the nation as a whole, Ylvisaker complains, "The American metropolis . . . has no preamble of noble objectives" comparable to the Preamble to the United States Constitution. "Without these soaring objectives," he argues, "we become in the metropolis but a collection of warring self-interests concerned with the means rather than the ends of human existence . . . 'We the people' become 'Some of us people' and 'Some of you people.' "

The result is that the Ford Foundation all too often flees the really hard and controversial issues that lie at the heart of the Negro problem—issues that involve the most fundamental conflict of interests between Negroes who want jobs and white trade unionists reluctant to surrender their job monopolies; between Negro tenants and white landlords; between Negro homeowners and white universities seeking land for expansion, and so on. The Preamble to the Constitution defines a set of "soaring objectives," to be sure—but the framers of the Constitution were realists well aware of the role of self-interest in human affairs. "Rich and poor alike," Madison wrote in The Federalist papers, "are prone to act upon impulse rather than pure reason, and to narrow conceptions of self-interest."

The rigid dichotomy which Ylvisaker draws between means and ends, moreover, has little relevance to the hurly-burly of life as it is actually lived; as we have argued repeatedly, it is in the act (or the means) of working for freedom or equality that one gains freedom or equality. Even Rev. Martin Luther King, who yields to no one in his ability to define soaring objectives, has come to see that the kind of distinction Ylvisaker draws between means and ends is the liberal's form of obfuscation and delay. "I must confess that over the last few years I have been gravely disappointed with the white moderate," Dr. King wrote in his famous reply to the Birmingham clergymen who had urged him to end his demonstrations. "I have almost reached the regrettable conclusion that the Negroes' greatest stumbling block in the stride toward freedom is not the White Citizens Councilor or the Ku Klux Klanner, but the white moderate who is more devoted to 'order' than to justice; who prefers a negative peace which is the absence of tension to a positive peace which is the presence of justice; who constantly says 'I agree with you on the goal you seek, but I can't agree with your methods of direct action.' . . . Shallow understanding from people of good will," Dr. King added, "is more frustrating than absolute misunderstanding from people of ill will. Lukewarm acceptance is much more bewildering than outright rejection."

The Preamble to the Constitution, moreover, with the objectives Ylvisaker admires so greatly, was the result of a controversial revolution fought with whatever means were at hand. Men like Sam Adams, who destroyed the private property of others in the Boston Tea Party, General Francis Marion, the Swamp Fox, whom the British denounced as a criminal (he did not engage in warfare "like a gentleman or a Christian"), and Thomas Jefferson, who indulged in considerable exaggeration, distortion, and omission in drafting the bill of particulars against the British in the Declaration of Independence, would not have understood Dr. Ylvisaker's careful distinction between means and ends. But then, as Saul Alinsky suggests sarcastically, none of the Founding Fathers would have merited a grant from the Ford Foundation.

AFTERWORD

> The time is short, the hour is late, the matter is urgent. It is not incumbent upon us to complete the task; but neither are we free to desist from doing all we possibly can.
>
> —*The Ethics of the Fathers*

It would be naïve, of course, to suggest that there is only one way—Alinsky's way—to solve the Negro problem. Apart from anything else, there is only one Alinsky, whereas there are Negroes in almost every large city of the North; thus, a great many approaches have to be tried. And Alinsky's methods unquestionably carry a fairly high degree of risk. Militancy can become an end of its own, and power can be misused and abused; as Professor S. N. Miller has written, those who are enduring poverty are not the exclusive repository of wisdom about how to overcome it. Alinsky freely admits the dangers. Anything that is worthwhile, he argues, carries a calculated risk; and we can be sure that any time we solve one problem we will create new ones in the process. The only assurance he can give, he tells groups interested in his approach, is the assurance that comes from a faith in the democratic process: "The faith that people, when organized and given a *bona fide* opportunity to participate in the molding of their own destiny, will in the long run do the right thing." Dan Dodson of NYU, who has studied Alinsky's work more closely than any other academician, delivers a more pungent verdict: "There is an old proverb that 'You can't beat a horse with no horse'—and Alinsky has the only horse."

We need to find or develop many more horses, for the Negro demand for equality and justice will not be stilled, except perhaps for an occasional respite. Nor will racial tensions be relieved in the foreseeable future. As Rev. Martin Luther King wrote from his Birmingham jail cell:

> We who engage in non-violent direct action are not the creators of tension. We merely bring to the surface the hidden tension that is already alive. We bring it out in the open where it can be seen and dealt with. Like a boil that can never be cured as long as it is covered up but must be opened with all its pus-flowing ugliness to the natural medicines of air and light, injustice must likewise be exposed, with all of the tension its exposing creates, to the light of human conscience and the air of national opinion before it can be cured.

And so the years ahead will be harsh and painful, but a necessary prelude to the peace that, hopefully, will follow. It would be absurd to pretend that any set of policies adopted by government or private groups can bring racial peace within the next few years. For one thing, the Negroes' impatience, bitterness, and anger, as we have argued before, are likely to increase the closer they come to full equality. This is not a quirk of Negro character but a characteristic of all disadvantaged groups: the closer they are to their goals, the harder it is to understand or justify the disparities that remain. Indeed, it is a commonplace of history that revolution (and the Negro protest movement resembles a revolution in many ways) stem from hope, not despair; from progress, not stalemate. And the nearer to triumph the revolutionaries get, the tougher they usually become.

And the tougher their opponents become. For all the talk

of the dangers of Negro protests erupting into violence, the most serious outbreaks of violence in 1963 came from whites determined to block the Negro advance with any means: the murder of four Negro children in the bombing of a Birmingham church, the assassination of Medgar Evers, the murder of William Moore. Nor has the violence been limited to the South. There is an ugly streak of violence in the American character that erupts when racial change occurs; we can expect this ugliness to come to the surface more and more.

To solve the Negro problem, therefore, will require difficult and occasionally heroic decisions on the part of businessmen, educators, and civil and political leaders, and changes in the behavior of Americans in every walk of life: teachers and students, employers and employees, trade union officers and members, parents and children. Those who hesitate to act because of the magnitude of the problem or the character of the opposition should ponder the stricture of Edmund Burke: "The only thing necessary for the triumph of evil is for good men to do nothing." Nor can there be any question about the moral issue involved, unless we are to discard the Judaeo-Christian tradition altogether. "Unlike any other social problem religion has ever had to come to grips with," Rev. Will D. Campbell of the National Council of Churches has written, "here is one on which there is no room for argument . . . It was settled for the Jews in the wilderness when they were admonished to accept the Ger, the sojourner, the stranger within their gates . . . and it was settled for Christendom at Pentecost when members of every race and nation and tongue were 'altogether in one place hearing the mighty words of God.'" The question, therefore, is no longer what to do, but whether there is still time in which to do it.

INDEX

About the Author

CHARLES E. SILBERMAN was born in Des Moines, Iowa, in 1925; he was educated in the New York City public schools and at Columbia College (A.B., 1946) and the Graduate Faculty of Political Science, Columbia University. He was on active duty in the U.S. Naval Reserve from 1943 to 1946.

Currently a member of the Board of Editors of *Fortune* Magazine, Mr. Silberman served as an Associate Editor from June, 1953, to January, 1961, at which time he was elected to his present position. His writings on race and related matters include "The Remaking of American Education" (*Fortune,* April, 1961), "The City and the Negro" (*Fortune,* March, 1962), and "The Businessman and the Negro" (*Fortune,* September, 1963). Mr. Silberman was a contributor to *Markets of the Sixties,* by the Editors of *Fortune,* and to a number of volumes of articles collected from *Fortune.*

Before joining *Fortune,* Mr. Silberman was a member of the Economics Department of the Columbia University School of General Studies, and a lecturer at the College of the City of New York and the Training Institute of the International Ladies Garment Workers Union. At present, he is a Lecturer in Economics at Columbia. He is listed in *Who's Who in America* and *Who's Who in World Jewry.*